SIX CHARACTERS IN SEARCH OF A REPUBLIC

CLINTON ROSSITER *is John L. Senior Professor of American Institutions at Cornell University, and has also been Pitt Professor of American History at Cambridge University. His books include* The Supreme Court and the Commander in Chief, Constitutional Dictatorship, The American Presidency, Parties and Politics in America, Marxism: The View from America, Conservatism in America, Alexander Hamilton and the Constitution, *and* Seedtime of the Republic, *for which he received the Bancroft Prize, the Woodrow Wilson Foundation Award, and the prize of the Institute of Early American History and Culture.* Six Characters in Search of a Republic *is a revised version of part two of* Seedtime of the Republic.

Mr. Rossiter has been a consultant to the Ford and Rockefeller Foundations, is general editor of the series of books on "Communism in American Life" sponsored by the Fund for the Republic, and was a contributor to Goals for Americans, *the Report of the President's Commission on National Goals* (1960).

Clinton Rossiter

SIX CHARACTERS IN SEARCH OF A REPUBLIC

Studies in the Political Thought of
the American Colonies

A HARVEST BOOK

Harcourt, Brace & World, Inc., New York

THIS BOOK IS A REVISED VERSION OF PART II OF *Seedtime of the Republic*

PRINTED IN THE UNITED STATES OF AMERICA

Let us recollect and impress upon our souls the views and ends of our own more immediate forefathers, in exchanging their native country for a dreary, inhospitable wilderness. Let us examine into the nature of that power, and the cruelty of that oppression, which drove them from their homes. Recollect their amazing fortitude, their bitter sufferings,—the hunger, the nakedness, the cold, which they patiently endured,—the severe labors of clearing their grounds, building their houses, raising their provisions, amidst dangers from wild beasts and savage men, before they had time or money or materials for commerce. Recollect the civil and religious principles and hopes and expectations which constantly supported and carried them through all hardships with patience and resignation. Let us recollect it was liberty, the hope of liberty for themselves and us and ours, which conquered all discouragements, dangers, and trials.

—JOHN ADAMS, 1765

PREFACE

THIS little book, a revised version of Part II of *Seedtime of the Republic*, presents the lives and thoughts of the six most notable and representative political thinkers of a "libertarian" cast of mind in the colonial period of American history: Thomas Hooker of Connecticut, Roger Williams of Rhode Island, John Wise and Jonathan Mayhew of Massachusetts, Richard Bland of Virginia, and Benjamin Franklin, citizen of Philadelphia, Boston, London, and Paris.

Hooker and Williams were men of the seventeenth century, transplanted Englishmen whom we call Americans only by courtesy—and in response to feelings of grateful piety. Wise, Mayhew, and Bland were men of the eighteenth century, native-born Americans who were still just as English as American in temper, loyalty, and outlook. Franklin, too, was a man of the eighteenth century who, thanks to a fate that was unkind to Bland and cruel to Mayhew, lived long enough to become a full-blooded American. Yet even he, throughout most of his life, was a colonist, an "Englishman in the wilderness," and thus a man engaged, as were the other five, in a "search" that had no end he could recognize clearly.

The search, of course, was for the free, self-governing, proud, and united Republic of the United States, and if in the end it proved one of the most successful in all history upon which men of colonial status have embarked, this fact, surely, can be ascribed in part to the rise well before 1765 of a political faith dedicated to the kind of ethical, ordered liberty that lies at the core of our traditions. That is why I have thought it important to tell and retell the story of these remarkable men, for among them they expressed, while America was still not America but simply a loose collection of colonies, every principle in the philosophy of liberty that was announced to all mankind in 1776, and that then became the intellectual foundation of the great experiment of 1787. This book is, as it were, an impressionistic rendering of the political thought of colonial America; the vehicles (or would it be media?) of my attempt at historical impressionism are the minds and achievements of six men who should satisfy all but the most insatiable longings for heroic symbols of a long-dead age.

The selection of these representative thinkers was, all things considered, not too difficult an undertaking. Williams, Wise, and Franklin were automatic choices, the first two because of the libertarian fervor of their writings, the third because he was at once the greatest man and greatest democrat to live in colonial America. Hooker and Mayhew, too, were relatively easy selections. The former was the most notable popularist within the authentic Puritan tradition; the latter was the most eloquent representative of American Whiggery. Bland was brought in only after a long and otherwise frustrating search for an articulate

Southerner, but once included he seemed entirely worthy to stand with the others.

At least fifty other prominent colonists who lived or spoke in the cause of liberty were examined with rigor and rejected with reluctance. Some of them—Dr. Robert Child of Massachusetts (1613-1653), Nathaniel Bacon of Virginia (1647-1676), Jacob Leisler of New York (1640-1691), Dr. John Clarke of Rhode Island (1609-1676), David Lloyd of Pennsylvania (1656?-1731), Josias Fendall of Maryland (1620?-1687), James Alexander of New York (1691-1756), and Andrew Hamilton of Pennsylvania (?-1741)—were men of action rather than of speculation. No one of these attractive and important figures left a large enough body of ideas in writing to be judged a serious political or social thinker. Others—John Woolman of New Jersey (1720-1772), Anthony Benezet of Pennsylvania (1713-1784), Christopher Sower (Sauer) of Pennsylvania (1693-1758), Francis Daniel Pastorius of Pennsylvania (1651-1720), and Samuel Davies of Virginia and New Jersey (1723-1761)—were simply not political enough in their approach to the problems they declaimed upon so nobly. Still others—George Mason, Patrick Henry, Thomas Jefferson, the Lees, Stephen Hopkins, James Otis, James Wilson, Samuel Adams, John Adams, Joseph Hawley, James Iredell, William Henry Drayton, John Dickinson, Charles Carroll—were only beginning their intellectual and political careers in the 1760's. They must be classed as Revolutionary rather than colonial thinkers.

Another description of men who did not have the necessary qualifications, principally because they served as purveyors of other men's ideas, was the liberty-minded journalists: Thomas Fleet of the *Boston Evening-Post*, James Franklin of the *New-England Courant* and *Rhode-Island Gazette*, Gamaliel Rogers and Daniel Fowle of the Boston

Independent Advertiser, John Peter Zenger of the *New-York Weekly Journal,* Andrew Bradford of the *American Weekly Mercury,* William Bradford of the *Pennsylvania Journal,* and the patriotic team of Benjamin Edes and John Gill of the *Boston Gazette.* William Penn, too, was studied at length. He was finally and reluctantly discarded as an Englishman who, like Dean Berkeley, spent too little time in America to be considered a colonist. The popular New England preachers of the eighteenth century, at least a half dozen of whom could have been given a full and loving presentation, are adequately represented by Wise and Mayhew.

Had considerations of space and art made it necessary or possible to include a seventh man, he would have been William Livingston of New York (1723-1790). Although he did not hit his full ·stride as a public figure until after his removal to New Jersey in 1772, this bold son of New York's most distinguished family had been in enough rousing political battles before 1765 to satisfy any five ordinary men. In the course of such incidents as the struggle over the founding of King's College, Livingston gave literary vent to a well-rounded political faith. In the end, three considerations blocked his inclusion: the difficulty in distinguishing his writings from those of his comrades-in-arms in the "New York Triumvirate," John Morin Scott and William Smith, jr.; the large proportion of his writings published after 1765, a fact that classes him with Otis and Samuel Adams rather than with Bland and Mayhew; and the clinching point that his principal ideas were expressed in the letters and pamphlets of Mayhew, Franklin, and Bland.

One other and more regrettable omission must be noted: the absence of any man who spoke for the advancing frontier. Although one or the other of the chosen six expounded every important doctrine in colonial political thought, it would have been useful and fitting to have heard some of these ideas from an authentic frontiersman. But a minute examination of the public and private literature of the colonial frontier led me to the ineluctable conclusions that the political voice of the early West never did speak clearly through any one outstanding man, and that when it did speak—through petitions, declarations, and letters to the newspapers—it adopted a tone of loyal deference that either belied the true sentiments of the men of the frontier or proved them far less radical than is commonly supposed. The nearest thing to a frontier political thinker was Hermon Husband of North Carolina (1724-1795), the penman of the Regulator movement. His literary remains are too sketchy to support his claim—not that he ever made one—to be considered a political thinker. His writings were entirely characteristic of the frontier: straightforward recitals of grievances, tearful descriptions of the horrid excesses of "arbitrary power," and deferential pleas for lower fees, more equitable laws, and friendlier officials.

The men of the frontier, like most men of the tidewater, believed in an uncritical way in higher law, natural rights, the covenant, and constitutional government, but these beliefs were never once carefully expounded by any man or group. While we must regret the absence of one clear voice out of the old West, we can be satisfied that Williams, Wise, and Franklin expressed all the ideas that are properly identified with frontier democracy.

In conclusion, I would make two points that I have made before in presenting the political thought of an earlier America. First, I have done my best to let each of these men speak for himself. I hope it will be understood that the apparently inordinate length of some of the excerpts from sermons, letters, pamphlets, and documents in these pages is a product of design and not of dereliction. Second, in every one of these chapters, with the possible exception of the one on John Wise, I have had to make a special effort to bring a reasonable amount of order to a political philosophy marked by charming disorder. The result, I hope, is a book that should leave no doubt in the mind of anyone who reads it carefully that America was dedicated to liberty long before it became free and independent. The political ideas of the American Revolution were the magnificent product of long generations of colonial experience, not an exotic doctrine hastily imported to justify resistance to an overweening King and Parliament.

CLINTON ROSSITER

Ithaca, New York
March, 1964

CONTENTS

For an extensive bibliographical and documentary annotation of these chapters, see pages 499-518 of Seedtime of the Republic.

CONTENTS

1

THOMAS HOOKER

"The Light of the Western Churches"

ONCE upon a time, in Hartford, Connecticut, there lived
a wonderful man named Thomas Hooker. The undisputed
facts of his life are so few that many accounts of him
seem almost like fairy-tales. No one knows what he looked
like, yet two splendid statues of him gaze out sternly over
the bustling of the insurance peddlers. No one knows where
he rests in dust, yet a gravestone proclaims his triumphs
and talents.

Historians agree upon the crowning act of his life,
that he was "the chief instrument" in the founding of
Connecticut, and upon the quality of his character, that
he was, as Cotton Mather wrote, "a person who while doing
his master's work, would put a king in his pocket." They
do not agree, however, on the thoughts he entertained or
the nature of the government he helped establish. One
line pictures Hooker as the first American democrat, Con-

necticut as the first American democracy, and the Fundamental Orders of 1639 as "the first written constitution of modern democracy." John Fiske and the loyal sons and daughters of Connecticut have been the most devoted of this school, but such respectable scholars as Parrington, J. T. Adams, and J. M. Jacobson are also charter members. Let Professor Johnston of Princeton speak for this group:

> It is on the banks of the Connecticut, under the mighty preaching of Thomas Hooker and in the constitution to which he gave life, if not form, that we draw the first breath of that atmosphere which is now so familiar to us. The birthplace of American democracy is Hartford.

Other historians, less eloquent and more critical, have challenged these high-flown claims. The most outspoken has been Perry Miller, who insisted that the representation of Hooker as democrat "rests upon a misreading of two or three of his utterances," and asserted that Hooker's "religious and political opinions were thoroughly orthodox." As for Connecticut, C. M. Andrews pictured it as "a Puritan state, of the same flesh and blood as Massachusetts, and in her beginnings [representing] even better than her neighbor the Puritan ideal of a Heavenly City of God."

The truth lies somewhere between these extremes, neither of which does full justice to Hooker and Connecticut nor expresses their significance for the rise of liberty in colonial America. Hooker was certainly no democrat in our sense of the word, nor can we look upon Connecticut as a genuine democracy. On the other hand, he was not quite so orthodox as Professor Miller wanted us to believe, and it is exactly here that his life and philosophy thrust themselves upon the student of American thought. If he stood fast in orthodoxy, he faced toward freedom and even took several steps into the democratic future. For this reason—that he represents the forces of liberty inherent in Puritanism more vividly than any other colonist of the seventeenth century—Hooker's life affords "a pattern well worthy of perpetual consideration." Let us once again summon "the famous servant of Christ, grave godly and judicious Hooker," that he may testify to the virtues of New England Puritanism.

I

Thomas Hooker, noblest of the New England Puritans, was born in 1586 in the hamlet of Marfield, Leicestershire, England. The few faint facts we know of his parentage point convincingly to an origin in yeoman stock. Although Mather tells us that Hooker's mother and father "were neither unable, nor unwilling to bestow upon him a liberal education," their chief service was to stand out of the way of a gifted child intent upon rising, at least intellectually, above his ancestral surroundings. Hooker achieved his education through scholarships and self-help, first at the grammar school in Market Bosworth where Samuel Johnson was later to serve as an unhappy usher, then at Cambridge where he made his way by waiting on fellow students at table. His college was Emmanuel, that "mere nursery of Puritans," where John Cotton and Nathaniel Ward also learned of new and sterner religious doctrine.

Having taken his B.A. in 1608 and M.A. in 1611, Hooker lingered on at Cambridge for a number of years as catechist and lecturer. This was the critical period of his life. He underwent a religious experience of soul-shattering intensity and body-racking duration, and he began a regimen of meditation and rhetoric which was to earn him a reputation as one of the most learned and powerful preachers of old and New England. We have the testimony of the illustrious William Ames "that though he had been acquainted with many scholars of divers nations, yet he never met with Mr. Hooker's equal, either for preaching or for disputing." It is worth noting in this regard that most of Hooker's twenty-seven extant works were actually transcriptions from his sermons, in several instances the work of persons who "wrote after him in short-hand." Whatever their other merits as literary works, they are pre-eminent in Puritan literature for shrewdness of imagery.

The record of Hooker's English ministry was one of huge popular and scant ecclesiastical success. He was first, from about 1620 to 1625, minister of a tiny country parish in Esher, Surrey. Already a preacher of marked nonconformist sympathies, he was able to occupy this position only because its living was "donative," that is, dependent upon a patron and therefore not requiring presentation to a bishop and induction by his order. Some time during his stay at Esher he married the "waiting-woman" to his patron's wife—Susanna Garbrand, companion of all his years and mother of his several children, a woman about whom we know nothing more.

In 1625 Hooker removed to Chelmsford in Essex, where he served four years as lecturer in St. Mary's Church. His learning and eloquence, his talent for the kind of preaching that silences hecklers and torments doubters, made him one of the most conspicuous nonconformists in all England. By the time that William Laud removed to the See of London in July 1628, Hooker was marked for early suppression. The lecturers, "the people's creatures," who "blew the bellows of their sedition," were now to be brought to orthodox heel. The most famous of the lecturers in Laud's own diocese was one of the first to feel the heavy hand of that truculent bishop who, in his own perverse and unwitting way, had so much to do with the settling of America. A letter from Samuel Collins, Vicar of Braintree, to Chancellor Duck, Laud's zealous accessory in uprooting dissent, tells why Hooker could not be left to pursue his nonconformist labors in peace:

Since my return from London I have spoken with Mr. Hooker, but I have small hope of prevailing with him. . . . All would be here very calme and quiet if he might depart. . . . If he be suspended its the resolution of his friend and himself to settle his abode in Essex, and maintenance is promised him in plentifull manner for the fruition of his private conference, which hath already more impeached the peace of our church than his publique ministry. His genius will still haunte all the pulpits in ye country, where any of his scholers may be admitted to preach. . . . There be divers young ministers about us . . . that spend their time in conference with him; and return home and preach what he hath brewed. . . . Our people's pallats grow so out of tast, yt noe food contents them but of Mr. Hooker's dressing. I have lived in Essex to see many changes, and have seene the people idolizing many new ministers and lecturers, but this man surpasses them all for learning and some other considerable partes and . . . gains more and far greater followers than all before him. . . . If my Lord tender his owne future peace . . . let him connive at Mr. Hooker's departure.

Late in 1629 Hooker was forced to retire from his position at Chelmsford, and a few months later, having unsuccessfully sought refuge from Laud as a schoolmaster at Little Baddow, he fled to Holland and the fellowship of many other dissenting exiles. His attention had already been called to America. We have proof, in letters to John Winthrop, that Hooker was wanted badly for the Massachusetts experiment and was being importuned as early as 1628 to go over with the first emigrants. In 1632 a band of people left Essex for America and settled near Boston under the expectant label of "Mr. Hooker's company." Finally, in July 1633, having returned to England and narrowly escaped capture by the King's officers, Hooker sailed for America on the *Griffin,* in company with John Cotton, John Haynes, and Samuel Stone, his own *fidus Achates.* Stone was to serve at Hooker's side until the master's death and then succeed him in the pastorate of the church at Hartford. Hooker and Cotton were fugitives from religious persecution in the most obvious sense, for "they gat out of England," as John Winthrop put it, "with much difficulty." Unlike some of their less fortunate brothers-in-dissent, they "gat out" with uncropped ears and unslit nostrils.

In Winthrop's *Journal* there is this entry for October 11, 1633: "A fast at Newtown, where Mr. Hooker was chosen pastor, and Mr. Stone teacher, in such a manner as before at Boston." Thus was solemnly founded what is today the First Church of Christ in Hartford, and thus did "noble Hooker" mount to the pulpit in which he at last, through his fourteen remaining years, found the peace and opportunity for service he had always sought in vain.

The ordinations of Hooker and Cotton ("before at Boston") were an event of great moment for the course of ecclesiastical and political history in the American colonies. Neither of these famous Puritans had been a separatist in England, yet each, when he finally took up the leadership of his American congregation, was ordained in a manner that was separatist, primitive, and essentially democratic. What the humble folk of the Scrooby-Leyden-Plymouth congregation had done out of conviction in 1620, the proud elders of Boston and Newtown (now Cambridge), and of the eight or nine other churches in the Bay colony, did out of necessity between 1629 and 1633: They built their new churches on the Congregational principle of the competence of each body of believers to form its own church-estate and to choose and ordain its own officers. This had been done at Salem in 1629, to the dismay of many Puritans still in England, and it was done repeatedly in the founding of the other wilderness churches. In the very act of crossing the Atlantic, these nonseparatist Puritans became separatist Congregationalists. However vigorous their protests against the brand of "Brownism," we can read in Winthrop's own words what took place "before at Boston": an act of pure, though yet unacknowledged Congregationalism. At the outset of his ministry in America Hooker found himself the pastor of a covenanted church, one that was separate from the Church of England, and indeed from all other churches in the world, in everything but the inconsistent theories of a few of its members.

II

In May 1634 there resounded through the tiny colony the first noticeable rumble of collective discontent. The point of origin was Newtown on the Charles, where Hooker had been installed only seven months before. The method of expression was a petition of the inhabitants complaining of "straitness for want of land" and asking "leave of the court to look out for enlargement or removal." After a scouting party had explored the Agawam and Merrimac regions with the General Court's permission and had failed to discover what the Newtown congregation was seeking, another party explored Connecticut without permission and discovered it in abundance: rich meadow-lands at a comfortable distance from Massachusetts. The next step in the founding of Connecticut is most honestly related in Winthrop's spare and hardy style:

September 4 (1634). The general court began at Newtown, and continued a week, and then was adjourned fourteen days. Many things were there agitated and concluded. . . . But the main business, which spent the most time, and caused the adjourning of the court, was about the removal of Newtown. They had leave, the last general court, to look out some place for enlargement or removal . . . and now they moved, that they might have leave to remove to Connecticut. This matter was debated divers days, and many reasons alleged pro and con. The principal reasons for their removal were, 1. Their want of accomodation for their cattle, so as they were not able to maintain their ministers, nor could receive any more of their friends to help them; and here it was alleged by Mr. Hooker, as a fundamental error, that towns were set so near each to other.

2. The fruitfulness and commodiousness of Connecticut, and the danger of having it possessed by others, Dutch or English.

3. The strong bent of their spirits to remove thither.

Against these it was said, 1. That, in point of conscience, they ought not to depart from us, being knit to us in one body, and bound by oath to seek the welfare of this commonwealth.

2. That, in point of state and civil policy, we ought not to give them leave to depart. 1. Being we were now weak and in danger to be assailed. 2. The departure of Mr. Hooker would not only draw many from us, but also divert other friends that would come to us. . . .

Upon these and other arguments the court being divided, it was put to vote; and, of the deputies, fifteen were for their departure, and ten against it. The governor and two assistants were for it, and the deputy and all the rest of the assistants were against it, (except the secretary, who gave no vote;) whereupon no record was entered, because there were not six assistants in the vote, as the patent requires. Upon this grew a great difference between the governor and assistants, and the deputies. They would not yield the assistants a negative voice, and the others (considering how dangerous it might be to the commonwealth, if they should not keep that strength to balance the greater number of the deputies) thought it safe to stand upon it. So, when they could proceed no farther, the whole court agreed to keep a day of humiliation to seek the Lord, which accordingly was done, in all the congregations, the 18th day of this month; and the 24th the court met again. Before they began, Mr. Cotton preached, (being desired by all the court, upon Mr. Hooker's instant excuse of his unfitness for that occasion). . . . And it pleased the Lord so to assist him, and to bless his own ordinance, that the affairs of the court went on cheerfully; and although all were not satisfied about the negative voice to be left to the magistrates, yet no man moved aught about it, and the congregation of Newtown came and accepted of such enlargement as had formerly been offered them by Boston and Watertown; and so the fear of their removal to Connecticut was removed.

This memorable passage from the most priceless original narrative of American history tells us a great deal about the standing of Hooker among his contemporaries. Certainly the only man who could have challenged his superiority in the gifts by which the world judges its preachers was John Cotton, and not until well after Hooker's departure did the Boston teacher make secure his ascendancy in the Bay area. Until then it was Hooker before all other ministers who was sought out for advice and support, especially in the squabbles that seem to have made up at least half the early history of the colony. Even after his removal he was several times importuned, not always successfully, to return to Massachusetts to provide guidance for those less resolute. He was the common property of the New England churches. The roster of preachers upon whom Hooker had a decided, often decisive influence is an honor roll of New England Puritanism: John Cotton, John Davenport, Thomas Shepard (his son-in-law), John Norton, Samuel Stone, John Eliot (his assistant in Little Baddow), Nathaniel Rogers, John and Francis Higginson, Richard Mather, and many others.

We can only speculate about the reasons for the removal of the Newtown congregation to Connecticut. The first two arguments put forward by the petitioners seem substantial enough. The promise of plentiful and fertile land was to beckon Americans westward from security for generations to come. But this does nothing to explain why these particular congregations should have been the first to move out, since they were certainly no more straitened "for want of land" than several others in the Bay. The evidence, which has been examined and re-examined by generations of historians, sifts down in the final winnowing to two main conjectures: that there were personal rivalries between Haynes and Winthrop, and between Hooker and Cotton, carried on in a more or less polite character but steadily building up to a major civil feud; and that the people of these restless congregations, paced in this as in other affairs by their beloved Hooker, were becoming increasingly dissatisfied with the oligarchic tendencies of the ruling element in the Bay colony. We have the testimony of William Hubbard that "after Mr. Hooker's coming over, it was observed that many of the freemen grew to be very jealous of their liberties."

In either case—whether emphasis be placed on the simple economic motive of land hunger or the more complex human motives of personal jealousies and of impatience with an oppressive religious and political order—the founding of Connecticut was an event of profound historical import, both as fact and symbol. Factually, a new colony established itself one farther step removed from English oversight, a colony in which the fermenting process of self-government could take place with the least possible interference from the home country. Symbolically, the removal of "Mr. Hooker's company" was the first overt indication of the popular urges beneath the apparently integral autocracy of New England Puritanism, as well as the first of the westward migrations within America itself. For those who interpret the rise of American democracy in terms of never-ceasing pressure on the frontier, the bold exodus of these few families is an epic of American history. "Westward the course of empire takes its way."

The westward course of these first pioneers was not exactly imperial in sweep. Temporarily restrained by the cajoling of the General Court and the grant of additional lands, the men of Newtown—and soon of Dorchester, Watertown, and Roxbury as well—would not be still. Through the summer of 1635 little bands of impatient inhabitants of these towns, some with permission from the Court and some without, moved westward to the Connecticut. And finally, in late May 1636, with the Court's permission, and indeed under its commission,

> Mr. Hooker, pastor of the church of Newtown, and the most of his congregation, went to Connecticut. His wife was carried in a horse litter; and they drove one hundred and sixty cattle, and fed of their milk by the way.

Thus were founded the river towns of Hartford, Windsor, and Wethersfield, and with them the colony of Connecticut. Within a year almost eight hundred people were settled in the new Zion.

III

Granted that Hooker was no democrat, Connecticut no democracy, and the Fundamental Orders no constitution in the modern sense of these words, the fact remains that the Connecticut experiment was dissimilar enough from the Massachusetts oligarchy to constitute an evident step in the direction of free society and popular government. Before investigating Hooker's political ideas, we must examine the government to which he gave his support and blessing.

The first government of Connecticut, which preceded the arrival of the main body under Hooker, was simply

the rudimentary pattern of "government by the acknowledged elders" that was to guide hundreds of other frontier
bands and settlements. The extent of formal government
was a single constable appointed and sworn by the General
Court of Massachusetts for the protection of the settlers.
On March 3, 1636, the Court issued a commission bestowing broad powers of government for one year on eight
selected members of the emigrating congregations. This
commission included a provision for convening the "inhabitants of the towns" into a general assembly "to procede
in executing the power and authority" granted to the
commissioners. Regular government may be said to have
begun in April 1636, two months before Hooker's coming,
with the gathering of five of the commissioners in Connecticut to swear in constables and pass a few orders. The first
General Court met at Hartford in 1637 and resolved almost
quixotically "that there shalbe an offensive warr agt the
Pequoitt." Finally, in 1638, with "the Pequoitt" thoroughly
butchered and their threat to the colony erased, the settlers
turned to the business of erecting their own government.

The Fundamental Orders of Connecticut were adopted
by the General Court on January 14, 1639. The architects
of this celebrated document were probably John Haynes,
the leading member of Hooker's congregation, Roger Ludlow, the keenest legal mind in all New England, and Hooker
himself, whose sermons and wise counsel pointed out the
path for the others to travel. We can only guess at the
mechanics of formation and adoption, for there is a complete gap in the public records of the colony from April 5,
1638, to April 11, 1639. The weight of evidence points to
the establishment of a small committee by the General
Court, then a series of informal consultations to which
Hooker was called, and finally the writing of a draft by
Roger Ludlow. The form of government thus set in motion

was simply an extension of the informal government of the first two years of the colony. In most, but not all, important respects the Fundamental Orders were a faithful model of the charter government that had been left behind in Massachusetts Bay.

The preamble is in essence a civil compact in which "we the Inhabitants and Residents" of the three towns did "assotiate and conioyne our selues to be as one Publike State or Commonwelth." The purposes of the government were two: "to mayntayne and presearue the liberty and purity of the gospell of our Lord Jesus"; and "to order and dispose of the affayres of the people," for which "an orderly and decent Gouerment" was declared to be necessary.

Eleven short articles then describe in barest detail the manner of government these good Englishmen found orderly and decent. The central organ was the General Court, which met twice a year: in April primarily for elections, in September for legislation and general business. The Court consisted of the governor (as moderator, with a tie-breaking vote), six assistants (or "Magestrats"), and four deputies from each town. The governor, who had to be a church member and former magistrate, was elected yearly by the "admitted freemen" of the colony. He could not succeed himself. The magistrates were also elected yearly by the freemen. The deputies, who had to be freemen themselves, were the choice of the "admitted Inhabitants in the seuerall Townes."

In the General Court was lodged "the supreme power of the Commonwelth"—executive, legislative, judicial, military, electoral, consultative, and constituent. It could make and repeal laws (including the provisions in the Fundamental Orders), levy rates, dispose of lands, appoint and remove the "publike Officers" necessary to execute the laws, and in general "deale in any other matter that concerns the

good of this commonwelth." Neither the governor nor the
magistrates had a "negative voice," nor could the Court be
adjourned, prorogued, or dissolved except by its own vote.
Specific provision was made for the Court to convene itself
in the event the governor and magistrates should neglect or
refuse to call it. Finally, the Court decided which inhabitants were to be admitted as freeman and thus made first-
class citizens.

It should be clear that the primitive form of government
ordained in the Fundamental Orders of 1639 was in no
sense a democracy, constitutional or otherwise. The generations of patriotic historians and provincial orators who have
insisted that Hooker and his companions did establish the
first American democracy have distorted the minds and
purposes of these excellent men. More than that, they have
robbed them of their proper position in the long process
through which American democracy came finally to fruition. The cardinal point about democracy in the colonies,
which bears endless repeating every time a historical society
meets to hallow the great men of old, is this: Democracy
was never *established* in colonial America, except perhaps
in the Rhode Island of Roger Williams; democracy, wherever and to whatever extent it existed before 1765, *evolved*.
Here is the true significance of the Connecticut adventure
of Hooker, Haynes, Stone, and Ludlow: the fact, less
spectacular but more meaningful than the fancies of Fiske
and Johnston, that they built a plainly marked way-station
on the road from seventeenth-century England to nineteenth-century America.

In short, the Fundamental Orders are to be remembered
and studied, not because they were democratic, but because
they were half-aristocratic and half-popular—a curious and
thoroughly English amalgam of Puritan authoritarianism,
Congregational liberalism, corporate flexibility, incipient

Whiggery, and Connecticut experimental popularism. In most particulars, the government of Connecticut was like that of Massachusetts, but at least four arrangements were clearly and designedly more liberal than those which had been imposed on the Bay colony. First, no religious qualification for the suffrage was fixed upon freemen or inhabitants. Second, definite restrictions were placed upon the authority of the magistracy—for example, the provision for convening the General Court with or without gubernatorial and magisterial approval, and that permitting the deputies to meet before the regular court "to aduise and consult of all such things as may concerne the good of the publike" and to judge the validity of their own elections. Third, the "inhabitants," if not possessed of full political rights, were nevertheless empowered to elect deputies to the Court. Fourth, the governor was limited in power and forbidden to seek immediate re-election. Finally, not even a passing reference to any outside authority is found in the Fundamental Orders. Massachusetts was ignored; so, too, was Charles I. The origin of government in Connecticut was a clear-cut instance of free political association.

In practice as in fundamental law the early government of Connecticut was more popular than that of Massachusetts. The absence of a religious test for the right to participate in political affairs, the moderate conduct of the magistrates, the clear reluctance of the clergy to push too far into the civil domain—these were signs of a more tolerant, less controversial manner of conducting public business than the ways of the oligarchy in Massachusetts. The steps forward—such as an order of October 1639 setting up a committee to codify and publish the laws, and one of April 1646 requesting Ludlow to draw up a complete "body of Lawes"—and the steps to the rear—such as an order of February 1644 giving the magistrates a "negative voate" over the legislative activities of the General Court—were taken with a minimum of civil commotion. The people of Connecticut were more homogeneous, to be sure, and thus more easily governed than the troublemakers of Massachusetts. Yet the beginnings of Connecticut's legendary "steady habits" date from a period when the stewardship of the Puritan elite was moderately and conscientiously discharged and the plain people given more voice than they had ever enjoyed in Massachusetts or England.

After Hooker's death there were several instances of reversion to more aristocratic government, instances that call our attention more explicitly to the popular character of the original Fundamental Orders. In 1657, as climax to an upsurge of aristocratic displeasure over the laxity of the towns in admitting inhabitants to the franchise, a property qualification was fixed in the laws. In 1660 the prohibition against an incumbent governor's seeking re-election was abandoned. Finally, in 1660, the authority of the restored monarchy was recognized, as of course it had to be. The scheme of government set out in the royal charter secured by John Winthrop, jr., in 1662 was simply an extension of what had developed under the Fundamental Orders. The charter was to serve until 1818.

Here, then, is evidence that Connecticut under Hooker, if not a full-blown democracy, was a distinctly less autocratic civil society than Massachusetts. The spirit of political liberalism was lighted in America during the first years of the wilderness settlements, in but one or two places more brightly than in early Connecticut. And in a very real sense this early experience was a reflection of the popular leanings of the great New England Puritan, Thomas Hooker.

IV

We turn now from the primitive self-government of the first western settlement to the political ideas of the preacher who contributed abundantly to its success. In approaching "incomparable Hooker," we must again take note that here was no hot rebel against the New England Way, no Roger Williams or Anne Hutchinson or Robert Child or Thomas Morton. Rather, he was a man of commanding influence within the Puritan system, a man of whom Cotton Mather could write, "I shall now invite my reader to behold at once the *wonders of New England,* and it is [in] one *Thomas Hooker* that he shall behold them." Hooker was the matchless representative of the virtues of early New England—a man whose life refutes the easy assumption that John Endicott and John Norton were the authentic Puritans and proves that within Puritanism itself were seeds of political liberty.

The attempt to revive Hooker as a seventeenth-century Jefferson has led to confusion about his ecclesiastical views. Just as J. T. Adams strained the facts to set him up as the political antithesis of Winthrop, so Parrington ignored them to set him up as the ecclesiastical antithesis of John Davenport and John Cotton. Nothing could be further from the truth. Hooker was orthodox to the marrow of his rugged old bones. The timeworn diaries and histories that defended the New England Way, and the tracts from old England that assaulted it, are choked with references to Thomas Hooker. They make plain the conviction of friend and foe that here indeed was the great man of the western churches. None but an orthodox minister would have been called on to lead the face-to-face scrimmage with Williams and "Mistris Hutchison," to preside over the early synods, and to compose New England's Reproof Valiant to the "many books coming out of England . . . against the congregational way." Hooker was at least as proper a Puritan as Cotton and Winthrop.

That Hooker was a Puritan of the Puritans is simply another way of saying that we must stretch the point to the limit to speak of him as a political thinker. His references to matters political and social were few and scattered. A feeling of piety flooded his heart and mind so completely that he rarely contemplated man or society except as instruments of God's great plan. His prime, almost exclusive, intellectual concern was with ecclesiastical organization and religious doctrine. The observations he registered about the type of political institution best suited to man's earthly needs were projections of his thoughts about the structure of the true church. The few unblended political ideas that we can quarry from the massive pit of Hooker's religious writings are little more than offhand references to "that resemblance" which church polity "hath with all other bodies politick." The few political ideas that appear in the handful of his extant letters and sketchily reported sermons on civil affairs were efforts to deal with political organization in the same terms in which he had dealt with church organization.

It is therefore imperative to note that Hooker, though he stood like the Charter Oak itself on the same stern ecclesiastical ground as Cotton and Davenport, faced in a somewhat different direction. The discrepancy between Hooker's orthodoxy and Cotton's was primarily one of emphasis. Hooker's *Summe of Church-Discipline* and Cotton's *Way of the Congregational Churches Cleared* appeared as peas in the Puritan pod to detractors and defenders of the New England churches. But in these differences of emphasis the popular tendencies in New England

Puritanism received their first impetus. Hooker's differences
with Cotton were differences*of degree, but in time these
often become differences of kind.

In placing a little more emphasis on the covenant of
man to man than on that of man to God, on the congregation than on the elders, on the "right hand of fellowship"
than on the discipline of the synod, on the reason in man
than on his sinfulness, on practice than on doctrine, on
evangelism than on speculation, on the New Testament
than on the Old, Hooker pried open a door that later generations of New England churchgoers swung wide for
liberty. Professor Miller admitted that Hooker had "perhaps a greater feeling for the inner meaning of the Congregational tradition." The "perhaps" is gratuitous, for he
was clearly the better Congregationalist. He would have
no truck, even in his orthodoxy, with the open Presbyterianism of Rutherford or the unavowed presbyterianism
of Cotton.

The sum of Hooker's political ideas is found in four
dissimilar sources: (1) the Fundamental Orders of 1639,
which Ludlow drafted but Hooker inspired, and which
contained nothing contrary to his political tastes; (2) *A
Survey of the Summe of Church-Discipline*, which was
famous for generations in Massachusetts and Connecticut
as a defense of New England Congregationalism; (3) a
letter to John Winthrop, written probably in November
1638, in which Hooker's political disagreements with the
Massachusetts leaders are most positively asserted; and (4)
the sermon of May 31, 1638, to the Connecticut General
Court, preserved in the form of a listener's notes.

Hooker wrote *The Summe of Church-Discipline* much
against his will and only at the urgent request of his fellow
ministers. It was in substance a reply to that excellent
Scottish churchman, Samuel Rutherford, whose *Due Right*

of Presbyteries (1644) had been the most bone-rattling salvo fired by the Presbyterians in their barrage against the New England churches. Hooker's manuscript, along with another by Davenport, was dispatched to England in early 1646 on a ship that disappeared into the Atlantic wastes never to be seen again—except by certain sack-consuming citizens of New Haven on a thundery June evening several years later. When Hooker had become convinced of the loss of his manuscript, he turned even more reluctantly to producing a substitute. *The Summe* was unfinished at his death and was seen to the London printer by other hands. Even in this form it was a brilliant exposition of Congregationalism. Although Hooker deals specifically with ecclesiastical organization, he several times makes clear that his ideas of the nature of the covenant, the power of the elders, and the role of the people are equally applicable to civil society. Here and there in the thorny thickets of *The Summe* are observations on "law, nature, and reason" which reveal the political ideas of a more popular Puritanism. The search is wearying but altogether rewarding.

The immediate occasion of the letter to Winthrop was a falling-out between Massachusetts, proud of her status as the leading New England colony, and Connecticut, jealous of her newly won independence, over a plan of confederation put forward by Winthrop and the Massachusetts magistrates in 1638. Winthrop worried the chief bone of contention in the pages of his *Journal,* belaboring Connecticut for refusing to trust their commissioners to the confederacy with "absolute power" to make important decisions, for asserting that the people at home should be constantly informed and requested for advice, and—here Winthrop makes a rare show of petulance—for choosing "divers *scores* men, who had no learning nor judgment." This brought to the surface the disagreement between Hooker and Winthrop over the relative importance of people and magistrates in the conduct of civil affairs. In an exchange of letters, each of these worthy men seized the opportunity to express his basic philosophy. What we have of this historic debate is Winthrop's summary of an opening letter to Hooker, the full text of Hooker's reply, and a rough draft of Winthrop's conciliatory answer. Winthrop, as generations of historians will happily attest, saved his correspondence; Hooker, as they will sadly lament, did not.

Had Hooker thought more consciously in a political vein, he might well have written out for publication the sermon to the General Court of May 1638. The few precious scraps of information that we possess of this lecture have come down to us in the form of ciphered notes in the manuscript notebook of Henry Wolcott, jr., of Windsor. This treasure was discovered in the nineteenth century and was deciphered by the noted Hartford antiquarian, J. Hammond Trumbull. Wolcott's outline of Hooker's sermon reads thus:

BY MR. HOOKER, AT HARTFORD, MAY 31, 1638

Text: Deut. i:13. "Take you wise men, and understanding, and known among your tribes, and I will make them rulers over you." Captains over thousands, and captains over hundreds—over fifties—over tens, &c.

Doctrine. I. That the choice of public magistrates belongs unto the people, by God's own allowance.

II. The privilege of election, which belongs to the people, therefore must not be exercised according to their humours, but according to the blessed will and law of God.

III. They who have power to appoint officers and magistrates, it is in their power, also, to set the bounds and limitations of the power and place unto which they call them.

Reasons. 1. Because the foundation of authority is laid, firstly, in the free consent of the people.

2. Because, by a free choice, the hearts of the people will be more inclined to the love of the persons [chosen] and more ready to yield [obedience].

3. Because, of that duty and engagement of the people.

Uses. The lesson taught is threefold:

1st. There is matter of thankful acknowledgment, in the [appreciation] of God's faithfulness toward us, and the permission of these measures that God doth command and vouchsafe.

2dly. Of reproof—to dash the conceits of all those that shall oppose it.

3dly. Of exhortation—to persuade us, as God hath given us liberty, to *take* it.

And lastly—as God hath spared our lives, and given us them in liberty, so to seek the guidance of God, and to choose *in* God and *for* God.

This election sermon, surely one of the most influential ever preached in New England, set the stage for the adoption of the Fundamental Orders.

There is little to be said about the sources of Hooker's thought, which were almost exclusively theological. Like other leading exponents of early New England Congregationalism, he had gone to school with Augustine, Calvin, Beza, Parker, and Ames, and especially with the Continental logician, Petrus Ramus. At the same time, he did a good deal of digging on his own into Scripture; many passages in his sermons are plainly those of an original mind. He was apparently untouched by winds of political doctrine. What little politics he expressed was transcribed ecclesiasticism. Charles M. Andrews once implied that Roger Williams might have had a good deal of influence on Hooker during a visit the latter made to Providence in 1637, and confessed himself "tempted to believe" that some of the ideas later expounded by Williams in *The Bloudy Tenent* found their way into the election sermon.

The notion that Hooker was loosened up politically by the Rhode Island subversive is tempting indeed, but must remain forever in the realm of pleasant speculation.

V

The core of Hooker's political thought was the core of all speculation about the structure of church and state in Puritan New England: the covenant. He could no more have escaped from the grasp of this concept than he could have from a belief in hellfire and damnation. Yet there were several notable differences between Hooker's version of the covenant and that of Cotton and Winthrop, and for these differences we hail him as the leading spokesman for this idea in seventeenth-century America. For one thing, the covenant was for Hooker a living concept in a way that it was not for Winthrop. The Fundamental Orders of 1639, in whatever light we care to read them, were a long step forward from the Massachusetts charter of 1629. For another, what was in Hooker's philosophy an article of faith was in many another Puritan's a convenient hypothesis with about as much popular substance as the contract of Hobbes. And in *The Summe of Church-Discipline* Hooker went a good deal further than any of his contemporaries in discussing the covenant as the basis for all forms of social organization.

Hooker's theory of the covenant was quite unsophisticated. Had he ever been asked directly to account for the formation of civil society, he might have drawn on his scriptural and historical knowledge for such explanations as that of conquest or of the expanding family. When he was asked directly how such a society *ought* to be formed —as he apparently was at least once in his life—he replied, "In the free consent of the people." Let us hear of the

covenant from Hooker himself. Though the style is primitive, the spelling casual, the logic opaque, and the issues
long dead, the meaning of *The Summe of Church-Discipline* cannot be misread. Hooker could have written Chapters 7 and 8 of Locke's *Second Treatise.*

Mutuall covenanting and confoederating of the Saints in the
fellowship of the faith according to the order of the Gospel, is
that which gives constitution and being to a visible Church. . . .
  Its free for any man to offer to joyn with another who is fit
for fellowship, or to refuse. Its as feee for another to reject or
receive such who offer, and therefore that they do joyn, it is
by their own free consent and mutuall ingagement on both
sides; which being past, that mutuall relation of ingagement, is
as it were the sement, which soders the whole together: or like
the mortising or brazing of the building, which gives fashion
and firmnesse to the whole.
  Whence it is evident, First, that it is not every relation, but
such an ingagement, which issues from free consent, that makes
the covenant.
  Secondly, This ingagement gives each power over another,
and maintains and holds up communion each with other, which
cannot but be attended, according to the termes of the agreement.
  And lastly it being of persons, who were wholly free, each
from the other. There can no necessary tye of mutuall accord
and fellowship come, but by free ingagement, free (I say) in
regard of any humane constraint. . . .
  This Covenant is dispensed or acted after a double manner.

Either $\begin{cases} \text{Explicitely,} \\ \quad \text{or} \\ \text{Implicitely.} \end{cases}$

An Explicite Covenant is, when there is an open expression and
profession of this ingagement in the face of the Assembly, which
persons by mutuall consent undertake in the waies of Christ.
  An Implicite Covenant is, when in their practice they do that,
whereby they make themselves ingaged to walk in such a society,

according to such rules of government, which are exercised amongst them, and so submit themselves thereunto: but doe not make any verball profession thereof. . . .

3. Its most according to the compleatnesse of the rule, and for the better being of the Church, that there be an explicite covenant. . . .

3. *The reasons of the Covenant*

I.

The first is taken from that resemblance which this policy hath with all other bodies politick. . . .

The first part of the Argument, hath reason and common sense to put it beyond gainsaying. Each whole or intire body, is made up of his members, as, by mutuall reference and dependence they are ioyned each to the other. . . .

Its that sement which soders them all, that soul as it were, that acts all the parts and particular persons so interested in such a way, for there is no man constrained to enter into such a condition, unlesse he will: and he that will enter, must also willingly binde and ingage himself to each member of that society to promote the good of the whole, or else a member actually he is not. . . .

3. Amongst such who by no impression of nature, no rule of providence, or appointment from God, or reason, have power each over other, there must of necessity be a mutuall ingagement, each of the other, by their free consent, before by any rule of God they have any right or power, or can exercise either, each towards the other. This appears in all covenants betwixt Prince and People, Husband and Wife, Master and Servant, and most palpable is the expression of this in all confoederations and corporations. . . .

Mutuall subjection is, as it were the sinewes of society, by which it is sustained and supported.

In Hooker's homely passages there were several rough deviations from the orthodox theory of the covenant which later generations were to refine into a philosophy of liberty.

These points might be noted in support of Hooker's position as an important precursor of democratic political thought: (1) the flat affirmation of ecclesiastical equality; (2) the equally flat affirmation of the doctrine of free consent, of the unprejudiced liberty of every man "to joyn . . . or to refuse" to join in the covenant; (3) the distinction between the explicit and implicit covenant, and Hooker's popular preference for the former; (4) the attempt to justify the church covenant through its "resemblance . . . with all other bodies politick," as well as through "reason and common sense"—all this in rare anticipation of the democratic notions of John Wise; (5) the emphasis on the covenant as one of man to man, at the expense of the covenant between man and God; (6) the reminder of the duties that "mutuall ingagement" lays upon all participants; (7) the clear assertion that "the good of the whole" is the chief purpose of a covenanted polity; and (8) the constant reiteration of the explosive doctrine, destined to be thundered from hundreds of pulpits:

Mutuall subjection is, as it were the sinewes of society, by which it is sustained and supported.

We can now see the touch of Hooker's hand in the preamble to the Fundamental Orders. Whatever else this primitive charter may have been, it was certainly one of the most outspoken plantation covenants in colonial New England. The counsel of the master was writ large in its words:

Forasmuch as it hath pleased the Allmighty God by the wise disposition of his diuyne providence so to Order and dispose of things that we the Inhabitants and Residents of Windsor, Harteford and Wethersfield are now cohabiting and dwelling in and vppon the River of Conectecotte and the Lands thereunto adioyneing; And well knowing where a people are gathered togather the word of God requires that to mayntayne the peace and vnion of a such people there should be an orderly and

decent Gouerment established according to God, to order and
dispose of the affayres of the people at all seasons as occation
shall require; doe therefore associate and conioyne our selues to
be as one Publike State or Commonwelth; and doe, for our selues
and our Successors and such as shall be adioyned to vs att any
tyme hereafter, enter into Combination and Confederacõn togather. . . .

VI

Hooker was the most constructive exponent among orthodox Puritans of two other forward-looking doctrines that
proceeded from the concept of the covenant: the sovereignty of the people, which is the logical foundation of the
theory of free association, and limited magisterial authority,
which is its most logical extension. On these two issues he
parted company with Winthrop and thereby heralded the
democratizing of the New England Way. And on these
two issues he showed himself to be a more genuine Congregationalist than Cotton. Again we must recall that the
disagreements among these men were a matter of emphasis
—especially over the relative importance to be accorded
elders or magistrates on one hand, and congregation or
citizenry on the other. Hooker never in his life gave countenance to straight-out democracy. Yet he did stress the
ultimate power of the whole congregation, and he did
oppose the autocratic notion of a magistracy elected for
life and unrestricted by written law. He was the more
influential because he chose to speak within the system of
Puritan orthodoxy, if not within the borders of Massachusetts.

A passage in the preface to *The Summe of Church-Discipline* expresses Hooker's advanced definition of "the people": the congregation in the visible church, the "Inhabitants and Residents" in the civil community.

But whether all Ecclesiasticall power be impaled, impropriated and rightly taken into the Presbytery alone: Or that the people of the particular Churches should come in for a share, according to their places and proportions; This is left as the subject of the inquiry of this age, and that which occasions great thoughts of heart of all hands. . . .

These are the times when people shall be fitted for such priviledges, fit I say to obtain them, and fit to use them. . . .

And whereas it hath been charged upon the people, that through their ignorance and unskilfulnesse, they are not able to wield such priviledges, and therefore not fit to share in any such power. The Lord hath promised: To take away the vail from all faces in the mountain, the weak shall be as David, and David as an Angel of God. The light of the Moon shall be as the Sun, and the Sun seven times brighter, when he hath not only informed them, but made them to be ashamed of their abominations, and of all that they have done, then he will shew them the frame of his house, and the patern thereof, the going out thereof, the coming in thereof, the whole fashion thereof, and all the ordinances thereof, all the figures thereof, and laws thereof. . . .

These are the words of a man with faith in the right and capacity of the whole congregation to exercise the sovereign authority that God has bestowed upon it. To be sure, Hooker's ecclesiastical democracy was a democracy of the Saints, who were apparently few in early Connecticut, just as his political democracy was restricted to the godly, sober, and respectable. "The people" in Hooker's doctrine was a limited body, yet not nearly so limited as in Winthrop's or Endicott's. And surely he hoped that all men in time would deserve full ecclesiastical and political citizenship. Despite his orthodox persuasion concerning predestination, despite his eloquent despair with the crudeness and ignorance in men, he stressed repeatedly the reasonableness present in every man's mind and soul. There was nothing in this preacher's theology that made him, like some of his colleagues, *want* to believe that most men never could be Saints; there was nothing in his politics that led him to believe that participation in government would always be the responsibility of the few. In announcing the sovereignty of all those who had subscribed to the compact, in proclaiming that ecclesiastical and political authority should come from below and not from above, Hooker prepared the way for later messengers of the belief that all men are qualified for free association. He was a better prophet than he realized of the Revolutionary doctrine of popular sovereignty.

Hooker's opinion of the authority of the magistrates in civil affairs and of the elders in the church is most plainly read in the letters that he exchanged with Winthrop in 1638-1639. The sweeping and discretionary power of the magistracy was the marrow of the noble governor's political theory. Although Winthrop, too, was imbued with the covenant idea, his version of this Puritan belief was free of any popular taint. The reins of a decent form of government were firmly in the hands of ruling magistrates, just as the government of a true church was in the safekeeping of elders. With consistency and courage Winthrop proclaimed his doctrine of magisterial oligarchy to the restless inhabitants of Massachusetts. In his famous lay sermon to the company aboard the *Arbella*—*A Modell of Christian Charity* (1630)—he declared that God had called some people to be "highe and eminent in power and dignitie; others meane and in subieccion." Fifteen years later, in the "little speech" to the General Court that had just acquitted him of a charge of exceeding his magisterial authority, he could still maintain with dignity and candor that the only true liberty of man was his liberty "quietly and cheerfully [to] submit to that authority which is set over" him.

In his letter to Hooker, Winthrop expounded his doctrine
of the stewardship of a hand-picked magistracy over a
people charged by heaven to obey cheerfully and submit
permanently. In his notes the chief argument is summarized
thus:

I expostulated about the unwarrantableness and unsafeness of
referring matter of counsel or judicature to the body of the
people, quia the best part is always the least, and of that best
part the wiser part is always the lesser. The old law was, choose
ye out judges etc. and thou shalt bring the matter to the judge
etc.

Winthrop also warned, as we learn from a passage in
Hooker's letter, that "to referr the dicision of a civill quaestion or controversy to whole churches cannot be safe."

To this blunt dismissal of the people's claims to political
participation Hooker made a testy and unequivocal rejoinder. The revealing portions of his letter are these:

I fully assent to those staple principles which you sett downe:
to witt: That the people should choose some from amongest them:
that they should referr matter of counsell to ther counsellours,
matter of Judicature to ther iudges: Only the quaestion here
growes: what rule the Judge must have to iudge by: 2ly who
those counsellors must be.

That in the matter which is referred to the iudge the sentence
should lye in his breast, or be left to his discretion according to
which he should goe: I am afrayd it is a course which wants
both safety and warrant: I must confesse I ever looked at it as
a way which leads directly to tyranny, and so to confusion, and
must playnly professe: If it was in my liberty, I should choose
nether to live nor leave my posterity vnder such a government:
Sit liber judex as the Lawyers speake: 17 Deut. 10, 11: Thou
shalt observe to do according to all that they informe according to the sentence of the Law Thou shalt seek the law at his
mouth: not ask what his discretion allowes, but what the law
requires: And therfore the Apost[les] when the rulers and high

preist passed sentence agaynst ther preaching as preiudiciall to the state, The Apost[le] Peter made it not daynty to professe and practise contrary to ther charge, because ther sentence was contrary to law, though they might have pretended discretion and depth of wisdome and policy in ther charge.

And we know in other Countryes, had not the law overruled the lusts of men, and the crooked ends of iudges many tymes, both places and people had beene in reason past all releif in many cases of difficulty: you well knowe what the Heathen man sayd by the candell light of common sense: The law is not subiect to passion, nor to be taken aside with self seeking ends, and therfore ought to have cheif rule over rulers them selves.

Its also a truth that counsell should be sought from counsellors: but the quaestion yet is, who those should be: Reserving smaller matters, which fall in occasionally in common course to a lower counsell: In matters of greater consequence, which concern the common good, a generall counsell chosen by all to transact businesses which concerne all, I conceave vnder favour most sutable to rule and most safe for releif of the wholl This was the practise of the Jewish church directed by God Deutr. 17:10:11; 2 Cron: 19 and the approved experience of the best ordered states give in evidence this way: Salomons one wise man, and the one wise woman in Abell that delivered the city showes the excellency of wisdome and of counsell where it is, but doth not conclude that one or few should be counsellors, since in the multitude of counsellors ther is safety.

Here is evidence, which can hardly be misread, that Hooker was well launched on the course from autocracy to liberty. He rejected flatly the essence of Winthrop's politics, the doctrine that government is most wisely committed to the very few, who must be allowed to govern according to their own discretion. He had already proved the earnestness of his resolve "nether to live nor leave my posterity vnder such a government," and he now made clear why it was in Connecticut, which was about to adopt the Fundamental Orders and a definite code of laws, that he was pleased to live. "If I was to choose I would be where I am."

Hooker's thinking about the magistrates was at odds
with Winthrop's in at least four essentials: They were to
be chosen by the people at regular intervals; they were to
govern not at their own discretion but in accordance with
written law; they were to consult the people and defer to
their measured judgment in all "matters of greater consequence, which concern the common good"; and they
were to act subject to the authority of the people "to set
the bounds and limitations of the power and place" to
which they had been called. If we add to these tenets the
generous definition of "the people" toward which Hooker
assuredly looked, we have arrived at an acceptable definition
of representative, constitutional democracy.

VII

Hooker died at Hartford July 7, 1647, the victim of "an
epidemical sickness" that had swept the northern colonies.
His eleven years in Connecticut had been devoted in full
measure to the needs of his people, and in all his labors he
had been generous and self-effacing. It is almost unbeliev-
able how few scraps of direct or even hearsay evidence we
have of his ministry in Hartford. The Connecticut records
scarcely acknowledge his existence, except in such passages
as this:

> Walter Gray, for his misdemeanor in laboring to inueagle the
> affections of Mr. Hoockers mayde, is to be publiquely corrected
> the next lecture day.

In this light, it is somewhat amusing to read the eighteenth-century jeer of Samuel Peters, "Hooker reigned
twelve years high-priest over Hertford," or the twentieth-

century observation of Perry Miller and T. H. Johnson, "For the rest of his life he was the virtual dictator of Connecticut." These remarks do little justice to the character of men like Ludlow, Haynes, Stone, and, if I may be pardoned the gesture, Dr. Rossiter of Windsor. Hooker was neither high priest nor dictator, but a preacher whose fusion of benevolence and eloquence sustained the colony through the first awkward decade. The fact that only one person in his church was excommunicated during his ministry bears witness to the tenacity of his lifelong conviction that, "If men would be tender and careful to keep off offensive expressions, they might keep some distance in opinion, in some things, without hazard to truth or love." When he did go out of his way to keep dissent in check, he did it in the knowledge that one ill-tempered controversy like those provoked by Roger Williams and Anne Hutchinson would have been enough to rend asunder the infant experiment. Stability, too, has its uses for freedom.

There is little else to add to this account of the masterful life and selfless preaching of the man whom Mather saluted as "the Light of the Western Churches." He was neither democrat nor constitutionalist but a child of his time and place. He was not an advocate of religious freedom or toleration but a staunch believer in the oneness of church and state. Certainly he had no such modern notions as that of "the state as a public-service corporation," which Parrington bestowed on him in a transport of liberal rapture. Yet in his primitive encounters with the magnificent theories of the social compact, the sovereignty of the people, and the authority of the electors to set limits upon the elected, Hooker took such a conspicuous step toward the democracy of the future that he must always be celebrated in the annals of American liberty. He first planted in New

England soil the seeds of liberty hidden away in the brittle
pod of Puritanism. He first proved, all unwittingly, that
the New England Way contained the means of its own
liberation.

2

ROGER WILLIAMS

Apostle of "Soul Liberty"

IN THE YEAR 1654, a certain windmill in the Low Countries, whirling round with extraordinary violence, by reason of a violent storm then blowing; the stone at length by its rapid motion became so intensely hot, as to fire the mill, from whence the flames, being dispersed by the high winds, did set a whole town on fire. But I can tell my reader, that above twenty years before this, there was a whole country in America like to be set on fire by the rapid motion of a windmill, in the head of one particular man.

With these quaint words Cotton Mather of Boston paid his orthodox respects to Roger Williams of Providence. Since Mather was the chief apologist for the Massachusetts oligarchy and Williams the "first rebel against the divine church-order established in the wilderness," we might have expected the author of the *Magnalia* to be more caustic in his sketch of the great heretic. Yet Mather, like many another orthodox New Englander, could not help paying this remarkable man a grudging compliment. Of Williams's life in Providence he remarked:

It was more than forty years after his exile that he lived here, and in many things acquitted himself so laudably, that many judicious persons judged him to have the root of the matter in him, during the long winter of his retirement.

Modern writers, too, have had trouble putting Williams in his place and have found him the most slippery of candidates for definitive biography. He has, of course, long since received his due from the historians, theologians, orators, and school children of a grateful nation. He has been depicted, quite properly, as the founder or at least chief colonist of Rhode Island, one of the noblest white friends of the Indians, the "apostle of complete religious liberty," and the rod and staff of the most popular system of government in the colonial period. Yet he remains a puzzling figure; before him the modern mind stands for a while in wonder, then retreats into shameless hyperbole.

This chapter makes no attempt to bring perfect order out of the perplexities of Williams's life and mind. Rather, it is a severely limited evaluation of his political thought and practice that may perhaps help others to present him as a whole man. It pictures him as the embodiment of certain ideas and techniques that were to take fast root in American soil. And it salutes him, without hyperbole, as the first great democrat of the colonial era.

I

The story of Roger Williams begins exactly as that of an authentic folk-hero should begin: in a pall of uncertainty about his ancestry and origin. The records of his birth and early years went up in the smoke of the great London fire of 1666, and it has required the most intense application of antiquarian scholarship to dispel a good deal of nineteenth-century misinformation about him. It is now agreed that he was born in 1603 in the parish of St. Sepulchre's, London, the third of four children of James Williams, "citizen and merchant tailor," and his wife Alice Pemberton of the "lesser landed gentry." As a boy he lived with his well-established parents in Cow Lane, witnessed some of the stirring events of the reign of James I, and, by his own testimony, was "persecuted even in and out of my father's house" for early and unexpected dissent from accepted religious ideas. We know nothing of his early education, except for the providential fact that he somehow acquired a skill that was to change the whole course of his life. Like many a famous American of later times, young Roger Williams attracted the attention of a distinguished public figure because he had learned to take shorthand. Years later an English lady testified:

This Roger Williams, when he was a youth, would, in a short hand, take sermons and speeches in the Star Chamber and present them to my dear father. He, seeing so hopeful a youth, took such liking to him that he sent him in to Sutton's Hospital . . . full little did he think that he would have proved such a rebel to God, the king, and his country.

The "dear father" whom Williams served as court stenographer, and who "was often pleased to call" him "his son," was that great man of the law, Sir Edward Coke. James I himself could hardly have been a more eminent and useful patron to a young man anxious to be something more than a merchant tailor. From "Sutton's Hospital," where he was a scholar of celebrated Charterhouse, Williams went in 1624 as pensioner to Pembroke Hall, Cambridge. Having received his bachelor's degree in 1627, he passed two additional years at Cambridge as a graduate student in theology, where he was doubtless stuffed with the mixed fare of scholasticism, classicism, and Puritanism that the tutors of Cambridge were serving up in his college days. Already a person of pronounced nonconforming views, and therefore excluded from preferment in the England of Charles and Laud, he withdrew from the university before completing requirements for his second degree and took a position as chaplain to Sir Edward Masham, a leading Puritan gentleman of Otes in Essex.

His short residence with this family was almost as fortunate a turn of events as his service with Coke, for he made the solid acquaintance of several men who were later to rule England and support Rhode Island in her struggles with greedy neighbors. Cromwell, Hampden, and Whalley were all relatives of Lady Masham. The young minister flew a little fast and high, it would seem, for he sued unsuccessfully for the hand of Whalley's sister. Rebuffed by the maiden's guardian, although not by the maiden, he found a lifetime of solace and devotion in Mary Barnard, a young lady of his own class, whom he married at High Laver December 15, 1629.

The call to New England had already sounded. In the summer of 1629 Williams had attended a meeting at Sempringham of persons interested in the Bay enterprise. He had ridden there in the memorable company of Thomas Hooker and John Cotton, and had doubtless been asked to cast his lot with the prospective emigrants. Finally, in late 1630, still too young and unimportant to invite Laud's close attention, yet old and knowing enough to imagine what would befall him when his own turn came due, he made for Bristol and Massachusetts. Winthrop's *Journal* has this entry for February 5, 1631:

The ship *Lyon*, Mr. William Peirce, master, arrived at Nantasket. She brought Mr. Williams, (a godly minister), with his wife.

The arrival of Williams was an event of some importance, for most of the famous men of God who were to hold sway in Massachusetts and Connecticut had not yet come over. We have testimony of the esteem in which he was held in the fact that he was asked shortly to be teacher to the first church at Boston. He was forced to refuse this position by a conscience already far stronger than any desire for worldly preferment, "because I durst not officiate to an unseparated people, as, upon examination and conference, I found them to be." Dismayed that a dissenting congregation would cling so stubbornly to the Church of England, Williams withdrew to the more amiable atmosphere of Salem. Here, too, he was "called to the office of a teacher," and here, too, he found himself out of step with the elders. Under pressure from the oligarchs in Boston, who were further appalled by Williams's opinion "that the magistrates might not punish . . . a breach of the first table," the Salem congregation retracted its offer. Once again Williams withdrew, this time to Plymouth.

For two years Williams lived quietly at Plymouth and "wrought hard at the hoe" for his bread. Bradford set him down as "a man godly and zealous, having many precious parts, but very unsettled in judgment," who "exercised his gifts among them" by teaching in a manner somewhat unsettling yet "well approved." In late 1633 Williams returned to Salem, there to assist the pastor, Samuel Skelton, "by way of prophecy," and Cotton arrived in Boston, there to accept the position that Williams had refused. Winthrop tells the story of the next two years:

(November, 1633) The ministers in the bay and Sagus did meet, once a fortnight, at one of their houses by course, where some question of moment was debated. Mr. Skelton, the pastor of Salem, and Mr. Williams . . . took some exception against it, as fearing it might grow in time to a presbytery or superintendency, to the prejudice of the churches' liberties.

(December 27, 1633) The governor and assistants met at Boston, and took into consideration a treatise, which Mr. Williams (then of Salem) had sent to them, and which he had formerly written to the governor and council of Plymouth, wherein, among other things, he disputes their right to the lands they possessed here, and concluded that, claiming by the king's grant, they could have no title, nor otherwise, except they compounded with the natives.

(November 27, 1634) It was likewise informed, that Mr. Williams of Salem had broken his promise to us, in teaching publickly against the king's patent, and our great sin in claiming right thereby to this country, etc., and for usual terming the churches of England antichristian.

(April 30, 1635) The governor and assistants sent for Mr. Williams. The occasion was, for that he had taught publicly, that a magistrate ought not to tender an oath to an unregenerate man, for that we thereby have communion with a wicked man in the worship of God, and cause him to take the name of God in vain. He was heard before all the ministers, and very clearly confuted.

(July 8, 1635) At the general court, Mr. Williams of Salem was summoned, and did appear. It was laid to his charge, that, being under question before the magistracy and churches for divers dangerous opinions, viz. 1. that the magistrate ought not to punish the breach of the first table, otherwise than in such cases as did disturb the civil peace; 2, that he ought not to tender an oath to an unregenerate man; 3, that a man ought not to pray with such, though wife, child etc.; 4, that a man ought not to give thanks after the sacrament nor after meat, etc.; and that the other churches were about to write to the church of Salem to admonish him of these errors; notwithstanding the church had since called him to [the] office of a teacher. Much debate was about these things. The said opinions were adjudged by all, magistrates and ministers, (who were desired to be present,) to be erroneous, and very dangerous, and the calling of him to office, at that time, was judged a great contempt of authority.

(July 12, 1635) Salem men had preferred a petition, at the last general court, for some land in Marblehead Neck, which they did challenge as belonging to their town; but, because they had chosen Mr. Williams their teacher, while he stood under question of authority, and so offered contempt to the magistrates, etc., their petition was refused till, etc.

(August, 1635) Mr. Williams, pastor of Salem, being sick and not able to speak, wrote to his church a protestation, that he could not communicate with the churches in the bay; neither would he communicate with them, except they would refuse communion with the rest; but the whole church was grieved herewith.

(October, 1635) At this general court, Mr. Williams, the teacher at Salem, was again convented. . . . Mr. Hooker was appointed to dispute with him, but could not reduce him from any of his errors. So, the next morning, the court sentenced him to depart out of our jurisdiction within six weeks, all the ministers, save one, approving the sentence, and his own church had him under question also for the same cause; and he, at his return home, refused communion with his own church, who openly disclaimed his errors, and wrote an humble submission to the magistrates, acknowledging their fault in joining with Mr. Williams in that letter to the churches against them, etc.

Here are set down the facts of Williams's expulsion from Massachusetts: the "divers new and dangerous opinions" with which he challenged the authority of magistrates and ministers; the attempts, in which the best minds in the colony joined, to argue him into submission; the extent to which many plain people had been "much taken with the apprehension of his godliness"; the calculating manner in which the church at Salem was threatened and bribed in an effort to turn it against Williams; his final decision to separate from all churches and stand alone and unyielding before the General Court; the sentence of banishment; and the reduction of the Salem recalcitrants.

Here, too, is evidence of the confusion that has marked the controversy whether Williams was "enlarged" out of Massachusetts primarily for religious or for political reasons. He was enlarged for both: for subverting the peace and order of a community in which state and church, religion and politics, were thoroughly and deliberately merged in one ideal and institutional pattern. In challenging the authority of Winthrop, he denied the teachings of Cotton; in questioning the logic of Hooker, he undermined the position of Haynes. In flouting the majesty of an untrustworthy king, several of whose highborn subjects had already moved in hostile array against the charter, he tampered capriciously with the unreliable but essential foundation of the holy experiment. And in proclaiming the sinful doctrine of unqualified separatism, in asserting as a practical consequence that the state might not punish errors and shortcomings in religion, he questioned not only the essence of the Puritan purpose but one of the most ancient assumptions of Christendom itself. While his ideas were none too ordered in his own mind, the danger they offered to the Bay colony was clear and present. Though we like to applaud Williams and hoot at his persecutors, we must agree that one outspoken man proclaiming separation, the invalidity of the King's grant of lands, and civil immunity of breaches of the first table—all this from a prominent pulpit—was one rebel too many for a Bible commonwealth. He was neither the first nor the last, but simply the most famous, to be ordered out of the Bay for what must have appeared to the elders as calculated subversion. In our light, they were guilty of bigotry and persecution; in theirs, which burned as brightly and a good deal more fiercely, they were engaged in an act of simple self-preservation.

II

Since Williams was too sick to travel and his wife was pregnant, the magistrates granted him leave to remain in Salem until spring, under severe injunction "not to go about to draw others to his opinions." The gesture was lost on Williams, however, for word soon filtered back to Boston that he was preaching the same old heresy to "company in his house." More dangerous still, "he had drawn about twenty persons to his opinion, and they were intended to erect a plantation about the Narragansett Bay, from whence the infection would easily spread" into Massachusetts. "Whereupon," writes Winthrop,

a warrant was sent to him to come presently to Boston, to be shipped, etc. He returned answer, (and divers of Salem came with it,) that he could not come without hazard of his life, etc. Whereupon a pinnace was sent with commission to Capt. Underhill, etc., to apprehend him, and carry him aboard the ship, (which then rode at Natascutt;) but, when they came at his house, they found he had been gone three days before; but whither they could not learn.

Winthrop must have set down these last words with a dissembling pen, for the outcast was later to give "that ever honored Governor" full credit for advising him "to steer [his] course to Narragansett Bay and Indians, for many high and heavenly and public ends." From Salem Williams and one or two companions fought their way through the wilderness snows to the half-starved hospitality of the Indians to the south. Some time in May,

I first pitched, and began to build and plant at Seekonk, now Rehoboth, but I received a letter from my ancient friend, Mr. Winslow, then Governor of Plymouth, professing his own and others love and respect to me, yet lovingly advising me, since

I was fallen into the edge of their bounds, and they were loath to displease the Bay, to remove but to the other side of the water, and then, he said, I had the country free before me, and might be as free as themselves, and we should be loving neighbors together.

Once more he moved on, leaving the year's planting behind, and came by canoe in June 1636 to a spring near the meeting of the Moshassuck and Woonasquetucket rivers. Here at last he found the refuge of his years, in a place that he named Providence, "in a Sence of Gods mercefull providence unto me in my destresse." By winter perhaps eight families had been settled in houses, a pattern of farming, trading, and hunting had begun, and a primitive form of town democracy had been instituted for regulating their few public affairs. With the planting of Portsmouth in 1638, Newport in 1639, and Shawomet (Warwick) in 1643 by other heretics, troublemakers, and backsliders from the Bay area, another English colony had become a visible if not yet legal reality. All four settlements were legal in Williams's sight, however, for in each instance the white man had made good his occupation with a solemn deed from Canonicus and Miantonomo, great sachems of the Narragansett.

Here in Rhode Island and Providence Plantations, removed in space and doctrine from the two worlds he had tilted at in vain, Williams lived strenuously for almost a half century. Except for two excursions to England in behalf of friends and neighbors, he wrought his legendary deeds within the bounds of this tiny colony, which at his death in 1683 counted not more than four thousand persons. The record of his life in and about Providence bears striking witness to the truth that great men not only can live in small places, but often must. Williams and his colleagues were able to break radically with centuries of

doctrine and build their new society without bloodshed
only because their lands were spare and remote. Rhode
Island could not have been much larger and richer and
still have served as a laboratory for the future.

Despite the studied refusal of early New England historians to give the first rebel his due, we know a surprising
number of well-documented facts about his life and deeds
—as planter, proprietor, statesman, envoy and friend to
the savage, religious pioneer, and visitor to England. His
years in Rhode Island remind us that the famous men of
early New England, with few exceptions, spent most of
their days in backbreaking toil. Williams was first of all
farmer and trader. "I know what it is to Study, to Preach,
to be an Elder, to be applauded; and yet what it is also
to tug at the Oar, to dig with the Spade, and Plow." He
could honestly say that he had "digged as hard as most
diggers in Old and New England for a living." He knew
what it was, too, to provide for a wife and six children.

As first proprietor of the lands about Providence Williams showed unique solicitude for the needs of those who
arrived with him and after him to seek refuge from intolerance and autocracy. His historic services in more dramatic affairs have obscured his actions and agitations in
behalf of a liberal land policy. He spiked the schemes of
land-grabbers like William Harris and Humphrey Atherton,
and at the same time ceded graciously, with scant compen-
sation, his prior rights to the land conveyed to him as an
act of "love and favor" by Canonicus and Miantonomo.
Although he was not altogether successful in stemming the
onrushing tide of speculation, he did achieve conspicuous
victories in applying his doctrine of "liberty and equality,
in land and government." There is no more impressive evidence of his generosity and foresight than his solemn protest, delivered some time around 1662, against the plans of

his forgetful neighbors in Providence to divide among themselves certain lands still held in common:

. I have one only motion and petition, which I earnestly pray the town to lay to heart . . . it is this, that after you have got over the black brook of some soul bondage yourselves, you tear not down the bridge after you, by leaving no small pittance for distressed souls that may come after you.

. Williams participated in the political affairs of town and colony from his first days as proprietor to his last as simple citizen. He was called upon repeatedly by his fellow out-casts to discharge some office of the greatest or smallest trust. As arbitrator, moderator, constitution-maker, town councilor, assistant, "chief officer" (1644-1647), president (1654-1657), peacemaker, captain of the trainband, com-mitteeman, special envoy to red man and white, scribe, and general handyman for Providence and the colony, he gave years of his many-sided life to public service. Few political thinkers have had so many practical opportunities to test their theories, or have drawn so many new ideas from experience. Not content to spin out fine notions and watch them float off to agitate Massachusetts and England, he put the doctrines of popular republicanism and religious liberty to work in the Rhode Island commonwealth. Not content to draw all his ideas out of books and "right rea-son," he arrived at some of his most cherished beliefs along the hard road of experience.

His chief visible services, not only to his own colony but to all New England, were his labors for peace and order among and with the Indians. The story is an old one, well and often told. It should be enough to sum up his half century as the leading white man in the world of Nar-ragansett and Wampanoag under these three headings: his Indian diplomacy, which he pursued at tremendous cost to his health and wealth and often in peril of his life; the publication, in London in 1643, of the justly famed *Key into the Language of America;* and his shrewd but honest activities as a trader who refused to traffic with the savage in liquor and guns. Williams achieved his most notable triumph in Indian diplomacy in his first year in Providence, when "the Lord drew the bow of the Pequod war against the country." In successfully detaching the Narragansetts from an alliance with the Pequots, he may well have saved New England from war to the knife.

Williams is best remembered as religious pioneer, as one who roamed from Anglicanism through Puritanism and Baptism to Seekerism, spending his last forty-odd years in search of the religious truth that he probably never expected to find on earth. A thoroughgoing Calvinist in his personal theology, Williams was none the less sufficiently unsure about the five points—and completely unsure about problems of church organization—to find Seekerism the most comfortable platform on which to take his stand. Through all his years, and largely because of him, Rhode Island clung in law and spirit to the doctrines of absolute separation and liberty of individual conscience. The acid test of the sincerity of Williams's views came with the arrival after 1657 of large numbers of Quakers. Although he shrank in disgust from their excesses and debated caustically with their leaders, never by word, deed, or counsel did he lend the slightest dignity to the common cause of persecution that harried these difficult people in England and the colonies. Rather, he joined with his fellow colonists in spurning the peremptory demand of the United Colonies that Rhode Island cast out her Quakers. Later in his life, when they had become so numerous as to capture the government, he withdrew not an inch from his consistent submission to the doctrine of majority rule. His public record in connection with the Jews is no less liberal and honorable. Williams helped persuade Cromwell in 1652 to readmit them to England and called upon rulers "to break down that superstitious wall of separation (as to Civil things) between us Gentiles and the Jews." When the first Jews came to Rhode Island in 1658, he welcomed them as he did all victims of oppression. For the elders of Boston this was just one more reason to look upon Rhode Island as a pit of anarchy and bestiality.

A word should be said about his two visits to England. The first, on which he embarked at New Amsterdam in early 1643 and from which he returned (with the aid of a safe-conduct) through Boston in late 1644, was occasioned by the struggling colony's need of legal sanction for union and independence. Thanks to his wide and sympathetic acquaintance among the parliamentary party, Williams was able to secure a patent from the Warwick commission which strengthened the hand of Rhode Island against her traducers without and seducers within. He also published several important books and engaged heavily in the religious and political controversies that were shaking all England. He was gone from Providence a second time, from November 1651 to the summer of 1654, to petition the council of state to confirm the patent of 1644 and vacate a damaging commission it had granted William Coddington in April 1651. In this quest, too, he made shrewd diplomatic use of his friendship with the great men of England and their distaste for the "lord brethren" of Massachusetts to score a victory for Rhode Island. During this visit he apparently saw a good deal of Cromwell, Milton, and Sir Harry Vane, and again took advantage of his presence in civilization to publish tracts on issues of great moment.

In all these trials and exploits—in the fields at home, the meeting-houses at Portsmouth and Newport, the public

places of England, and the "filthy smoky holes" of the
Indians—Williams displayed an extraordinary character. All
the adjectives that we like to pin on our great men—
generous, sincere, decent, public-spirited, honest, brave,
warmhearted, unselfish—applied to him as to few other
persons of prominence in colonial America. That he was
human, too, and could complain, quarrel, boast, and beg
is likewise evident in the records and letters that remain.
Perhaps the most important visible trait of his triumphant
character was his perpetual search for truth and willingness to argue openly and freely about it. If there was any
single event in his wonderful life that tells us of the way
he chose to live it, it was the occasion in 1672 when he
rowed with his "old bones" from Providence to Newport
to debate with three leading Quaker orators before a hostile
audience.

III

We cannot understand Williams's political thought without some knowledge of the government of seventeenth-
century Rhode Island, a political theater in which his
principles had profound influence, and in which they in
turn were tried and found good. The vicissitudes of Rhode
Island government during this first half-century in the
wilderness are significant in their own right: They provide
an interesting case-study in the interaction of English
habits and frontier conditions, and they prove that it was
no easy matter to set up a polity dedicated to the reconcili-
ation of liberty and order.

Through most of Williams's life Rhode Island was in
political difficulties. It was repeatedly menaced from within
by disunion, treason, and straight-out anarchy, and from
without by the grasping schemes of powerful neighbors who

hated its principles and coveted its lands and harbors. More
often than not, internal dissension and external encroachment went hand in hand, for its malcontents learned early
to appeal to Boston or London for support against Williams.
Other factors that frustrated orderly government were the
intense land-hunger of certain inhabitants, most notoriously
the testy William Harris of Providence and Pawtuxet, and
a reputation, carefully nurtured by all the old wives and
preachers of Boston and New Amsterdam, as the "sewer"
of New England, where riffraff ran wild and women gave
birth to horned monsters. The despised colony was several
times denied admittance to the New England Confederation on the ground that it lacked a stable government.
Yet Rhode Island managed to endure through all this
turmoil, slander, and isolation with surprisingly little dam-
age to the principles of religious liberty, equality in land,
and popular government on which it was founded.

The political chronology of early Rhode Island is roughly
this: the establishment of Providence (1636) as a primitive
form of householders' democracy; the establishment of
Portsmouth (1638), Newport (1639), and Warwick
(1643) according to various political impulses ranging
from democracy to neo-feudalism, yet all like Providence
on the basis of a compact; the union of these autonomous
towns in the patent of 1644; the creation, after three more
years of separatism, of the first real government, which
lasted until the secession of Aquidneck (Portsmouth and
Newport) in 1651; the re-establishment of the union in
1654; and the winning in 1663 of a royal charter, which
altered a few but preserved most of the techniques the
Rhode Islanders had created for their own governing.

The first rude government in Providence was shaped almost completely to the notions of Roger Williams. It was
based squarely on two explicit compacts—one among the

first heads of families, the other, adopted a year or two later, admitting certain newcomers and single men. The authority of the rulers extended "only in civill things." The core of government was the town meeting, which began when "the masters of families . . . met once a fortnight and consulted about our common peace, watch, and planting." The executive and judicial machinery was extremely simple—hardly more than a clerk, a treasurer, and, after 1640, five "Disposers," who were elected every three months to settle disputes by arbitration. This primitive pattern of popular government was grounded upon an unusually liberal land policy, for which Williams fought without respite. Under it newcomers were to be admitted "into the same fellowship and privilege" with the first inhabitants. The stake-in-society principle underpinned and limited the democracy of Providence, but it was one town in which the stake was open to all on equal terms.

The other towns were established on principles that varied from general accord with those of Williams to flat contradiction. The island of Aquidneck was purchased with his aid from the Narragansetts and settled by several leading Antinomians who had departed or been banished from Boston—most notably William Coddington, John Clarke, and William Hutchinson. The first government at Portsmouth was a curious combination of theocracy and feudalism, in which principal authority was lodged in a single "Judge," the former Boston oligarch, Coddington. The arrival of such malcontents as Anne Hutchinson and Samuell Gorton and the example of Providence conspired shortly to upset Coddington's little dictatorship. In early 1639 he withdrew in anger with his followers to found a new town at Newport. The popular-minded yeomen remaining at Portsmouth entered into a second compact for a "civill body politicke." In 1640 the two Aquidneck settlements united for certain general purposes, and a year later a new popular movement forced the adoption of these forward-looking orders:

> It is ordered and unanimously agreed upon, that the Government which this Bodie Politick doth attend unto in this Island, and the Jurisdiction thereof, in favour of our Prince is a DEMOCRACIE, or Popular Government; that is to say, It is in the Powre of the Body of Freemen orderly assembled, or the major part of them, to make or constitute Just Lawes, by which they will be regulated, and to depute from among themselves such Ministers as shall see them faithfully executed between Man and Man.
>
> It was further ordered, by the authority of this present Courte, that none bee accounted a Delinquent for *Doctrine:* Provided, it be not directly repugnant to ye Government or Lawes established.

Thus were two of Williams's great principles, popular government and religious liberty, established in the towns about Narragansett Bay. They were likewise established, although with more interference from outside detractors, at Warwick in 1643.

The colony of Rhode Island began its formal existence in March 1644, when Williams secured his precious patent from the Commissioners of Plantations. Unlike Massachusetts, Plymouth, and Connecticut, Rhode Island was formed in the union of independent towns. What had brought them together to send Williams to England was exactly what has brought discordant autonomies together since the beginning of history: fear of designing and more powerful neighbors. The patent itself was all that Williams could have asked for, except in the loose delineation of the colony's boundaries. It incorporated Providence, Newport, and Portsmouth as an independent and united plantation; gave them authority to rule themselves and future settlers by whatever "Form of Civil Government, as by voluntary consent of all, or the great Part of them, they shall find most suitable to their Estate and Condition"; recognized therewith the principle of separation of church and state; ordered that laws "be conformable to the Laws of England," but only "so far as the Nature and Constitution of the place will admit"; and reserved to England the right to supervise external relations between Rhode Island and the other colonies.

Not for another three years did the necessities of union become sufficiently pressing to force the organization of government under the patent. Then, in May 1647, at a meeting of the three older towns and Warwick at Portsmouth, the charter was accepted and a popular type of government adopted. The most interesting features of the new government were these: (1) it was adopted by an assembly attended by "the major parte of the Colonie" and was thus one of the few constitutions in history to proceed directly from the people; (2) it was couched in the language of an explicit civil compact; (3) the form was declared to be "DEMOCRATICALL; that is to say, a Government held by ye free and voluntarie consent of all, or the greater parte of the free Inhabitants"; (4) it recognized the rights of the originally independent towns by establishing a pattern of incipient federalism that was strengthened by subsequent laws and town charters; (5) it made further concessions to the towns by inaugurating a primitive system of initiative, referendum, and recall; and (6) it instituted an extensive code of laws and liberties based directly on those of England.

The code in turn embodied several notable features: an affirmation of Chapter 29 of Magna Charta, the concept of public office as not only a trust but a duty, a strain of leniency not found in the codes of neighboring colonies, a careful organization of courts to enforce the laws, and finally this noble statement:

These are the Lawes that concerne all men, and these are the Penalties for the transgression thereof, which by common consent are Ratified and Established throwout this whole Colonie; and otherwise than thus what is herein forbidden, all men may walk as their consciences perswade them, every one in the name of his God.

The officers of the new government, all elected annually by the court of election, were a president, four assistants (one to each town), recorder, treasurer, and sergeant. The duties of president and assistants were both executive and judicial, but in no sense were they "magistrates" on the Massachusetts model. The core of government remained, of course, the General Court, which became a representative body for legislative purposes—with six "commissioners" chosen from each town—but remained a primary gathering when convened as court of election.

This popular scheme of government continued until 1663 with several changes and one conspicuous break. The changes were the addition of several new executive officials, the further liberalization of many fundamental laws, the repeated use of Williams's cherished principle of arbitration, and the institution of ad hoc committees for executive duties. The break lasted from 1651 to 1654 and was chiefly the work of that dissident aristocrat, William Coddington, who did everything in his power, including overtures to the New England Confederation and a trip to England for a commission to govern Aquidneck for life, to frustrate the patent of 1644. Only after the joint voyage to England of Williams and John Clarke, emissary of the anti-Coddington forces in Newport and Portsmouth, was Coddington finally brought to earth.

The restoration of Charles II in 1660 presented a new

threat to Rhode Island's independent status. Thanks, however, to the quick submission of the colony and devoted diplomacy of John Clarke, a royal charter of astounding liberality was passed through the seals July 8, 1663. It confirmed the scheme of government existent in Rhode Island, with some change in the number and title of officials and with provisions looking to a stronger central government. Most important, Clarke had included in his petition a specific request "to hold forth a lively experiment, that a flourishing civill State may stand, yea, and best be maintained, and that among English spirits, with a full liberty in religious concernments." Charles II, whose persecuting tendencies were softened in this instance by a desire to make his colonies attractive to would-be settlers, granted this request with a gallant sweep that must have stunned the elders of Massachusetts.

Our royall will and pleasure is, that noe person within the sayd colonye, at any tyme hereafter, shall bee any wise molested, punished, disquieted, or called in question, for any differences in opinione in matters of religion, and doe not actually disturb the civill peace of our sayd colony; but that all and everye person and persons may, from tyme to tyme, and at all tymes hereafter, freelye and fullye have and enjoye his and theire own judgments and consciences, in matters of religious concernments, throughout the tract of lande hereafter mentioned; they behaving themselves peaceablie and quietlie, and not useing this libertie to lycentiousnesse and profanenesse, nor to the civill injurye or outward disturbeance of others.

This charter endured as the foundation of government in colony and state for almost two centuries.

The record of Rhode Island politics in Roger Williams's lifetime is obviously spotty, especially when contrasted with the stability of Massachusetts or Connecticut. Yet those historians who have concluded that government in Rhode Island was a failure have been noticeably wide of the mark. When we recall the factors that militated against its success—the pre-existence of the towns, the open hostility of its neighbors, the speculative schemes of Harris and Atherton that Williams refused to suffer gladly, the designs of Coddington, the lack of geographic unity, the virtual nonexistence of a hortatory clergy, the leniency of the code, the free play accorded all manner of heterodoxies, and the general spirit of populism which several times erupted in barefaced anarchy—we may wonder how it survived at all to win its independence within the British colonial system. Yet it did survive, with no more actual bloodshed than a few battered heads and with its libertarian principles in a remarkable state of preservation. Nor should it be forgotten that while Harris agitated, Gorton posed, Coddington plotted, and overheated zealots ran naked about the streets, most of the colony's good people tilled their lands and plied their trades with no interference from magistrates, preachers, or other persecuting oligarchs.

"Possibly," wrote Williams to Vane in 1654,

a sweet cup hath rendered many of us wanton and too active, for we have long drunk of the cup of as great liberties as any people that we can hear of under the whole heaven.

Possibly, yet no more wanton and active than could be expected of men who had hardly suspected that orderly government could exist without severe regulation and legalized inequality. The colonial records testify that Rhode Island was the closest thing to democracy in seventeenth-century America. They testify also that Roger Williams was the one man most responsible for this triumph of liberty.

IV

Williams stands alone and unchallenged among colonial thinkers. Populist, libertarian, skeptic, and seeker, advocate of a future that is yet to come, he was by all odds the most exciting character in the story of colonial liberty. We must not be surprised or chagrined to learn that he was also the most lonely. It is the business of prophets to be lonely.

Several facts about Williams's political philosophy should be established at the outset. First, an unusually close connection between thought and practice marked both his mind and career. It is popular among historians to eulogize him as thinker and write him off as practitioner, but this is to underestimate grossly the success with which he converted doctrine into fact. He stamped his personality emphatically upon the society in which he lived, and the society in turn gave form and support to some of his most fine-spun ideas. It also taught him a few hard truths that he would never have learned in England or Massachusetts.

Although Williams produced a sizable body of doctrine, he was no doctrinaire. In politics as in religion he was always the seeker. As sponsor of an actual political experiment he could speak with a good deal more authority than other seventeenth-century republicans, yet he shied away from proclaiming political and social dogma. Although he arrived at many of his basic ideas at an early date and championed them loudly to the end of his life, he stood always ready to abandon them should more workable principles be found to take their place.

Williams serves as a reminder that the first settlers were not only English but English-minded, men who had worked up their theories in the mother country and had brought them over to be tested in a strange land. Only by courtesy, and for the sake of national pride, can we call a man like Williams an American. The debate between Cotton and Williams over the nature of church and state was carried on in England, through the medium of English presses, and as an attempt to influence English rather than colonial opinion.

Williams did not expound a systematic political theory, and we must search at length through his tracts and letters for ideas that can be properly termed political in character. His writings were occasional, polemic, and framed in the idiom of his age, all of which is another way of saying that he was the father of all American political thinkers. Although he had an inclusive political philosophy, he never attempted to present it in an organized, discriminating manner.

We must look in two categories of Williams's writings for his political ideas: the numerous books and pamphlets that he contributed to the great Anglo-American debate on the nature of church and state, and a handful of extant letters, especially four public lectures to the town of Providence on the manner in which his fellow citizens were disregarding the noble purposes of the original settlement. The most important of his formal writings were:

Mr. Cottons Letter Lately Printed, Examined and Answered (London, 1644), in which Williams first proclaimed in print his doctrines of separatism, sectarianism, and freedom of conscience.

Queries of Highest Consideration (London, 1644), a direct contribution to the presbyterian controversy then agitating England.

The Bloudy Tenent of Persecution for Cause of Conscience (London, 1644), his most celebrated and influential work, in which he launched an all-out assault on the closely related ideas of a national church and persecution of religious nonconformity. Williams addressed *The Bloudy Tenent* to Parliament, which repaid the unsolicited compliment by ordering the common hangman to burn the book. Three years later Cotton published a reply, *The Bloudy Tenent Washed White in the Blood of the Lambe* (London, 1647), which justified the ways of Massachusetts against the disruptive nonsense of religious liberty.

The Bloody Tenent Yet More Bloody (London, 1652), Williams's answer to Cotton's "Fig-leave Evasions and Distinctions."

The Hireling Ministry None of Christs (London, 1652), a powerful indictment of the national church.

The Fourth Paper, Presented by Major Butler (London, 1652), a plea for liberty of conscience, even for non-Christians.

Experiments of Spiritual Life and Health (London, 1652), a tract on piety in which he evidenced an essentially humanistic opinion of the nature of man.

George Fox Digg'd out of his Burrowes (Boston, 1676), in which he made clear that there are limits to what men can do to disturb the peace in the name of religious liberty.

In all these works, as their titles quaintly proclaim, Williams had the relationship of church and state as his primary concern. Yet in advancing his own revolutionary solutions to the problems this relationship had generated, especially in advocating rigid separation and freedom for all well-behaved religions, he was forced into an attitude toward political authority hardly less radical than his theology. His life and thought provide one more illustration of the historic manner in which the struggle against autocracy in the state followed naturally from, or even moved step by step with, the struggle against autocracy in the church. Although there have been several bold attempts

to secularize Williams's thought, to draw a sharp line between his politics and ecclesiasticism and give primacy to
the former, these ignore the whole tenor of his writings and
the limitations on speculation and debate characteristic of
the age in which he lived. Not only were religious nonconformity and political liberalism inseparable parts of his
total philosophy, but it was about the former that he
thought first, hardest, and most influentially.

V

The strictly political aspects of Williams's philosophy—
which we consider "strictly political" at the risk of misreading his seventeenth-century mind—were so casually
proclaimed that we would do him a disservice were we to
regard them as either the hard core of his thought or his
chief contribution to the evolution of democratic thought.
Here and there in his writings he expressed his adherence to
all well-known refinements of early republicanism, but he
rarely if ever paused to explain any one of them. He saved
his powers of analysis for the more pressing questions of
persecution and "soul liberty." Though he was a devoted
exponent of the liberating doctrines of popular sovereignty
and the social compact, he had pondered neither profoundly
nor originally about the noble philosophy that was in time
to dominate the American mind. It should therefore be
sufficient to list briefly, with the aid of a few quotations,
the various elements of seventeenth-century republicanism
that he carried across the sea, followed dutifully but not
fanatically in his experiments at state-building, and flung
at Cotton in an offhand manner in the debate over persecution.

Civil government, wrote Williams, though ultimately of
divine origin, springs immediately from the body of the

people, "who have fundamentally in themselves the Root of Power, to set up what Government and Governours they shall agree upon." Agreement on the form of government is reached through explicit techniques of popular consent. The records of Providence and Rhode Island reveal that Williams regarded government, though not necessarily society, as the artificial creation of an open covenant. The purpose of government is altogether popular: "the preservation of the peace and welfare of the state" and of all the people in it. Peace, which Williams defined in the broadest terms as liberty and security for all men, was the favorite word in his political lexicon. Civil government brings peace and is therefore good and necessary.

If the sword and balances of justice (in a sort or measure) be not drawn and held forth, against scandalous offenders against civil state, that civil state must dissolve by little and little from civility to barbarisme, which is a wilderness of life and manners.

It makes no difference, said Williams, what form of government the people decide upon so long as all those in authority look upon themselves as "eyes and hands and instruments of the people," recognize that any "Minister or Magistrate goes beyond his commission, who intermeddles with that which cannot be given him in commission from the people," and remain answerable to the unprejudiced power of recall vested in the community at large. The fundamental organ of government is the assembly of the citizens, primary or representative according to circumstance, and operating under the doctrine of majority rule.

Most of these principles are expressed in a famous passage from *The Bloudy Tenent*:

That the Civill Power may erect and establish what forme of civill Government may seeme in wisedome most meet, I acknowledge the proposition to be most true, both in it self, and also considered with the end of it, that a civill Government is an Ordinance of God, to conserve the civill peace of people, so farre as concernes their Bodies and Goods, as formerly hath been said.

But from this Grant I infer, (as before hath been touched) that the Soveraigne, originall, and foundation of civill power lies in the people, (whom they must needs meane by the civill power distinct from the Government set up.) And if so, that a People may erect and establish what forme of Government seemes to them most meete for their civill condition: It is evident that such Governments as are by them erected and established, have no more power, nor for no longer time, then the civill power or people consenting and agreeing shall betrust them with. This is cleere not only in Reason, but in the experience of all commonweales, where the people are not deprived of their naturall freedome by the power of Tyrants.

Williams was extremely hazy about natural or fundamental law and therefore about the whole concept of natural rights. He certainly cannot be cited as an early Anglo-American exponent of the right of resistance or revolution. The rights that Williams emphasized in his writings were civil and English, not natural and universal. A notable passage from an admonitory letter to the town of Warwick in 1666 expresses this clearly:

The whole summ and scope of his Majesties Royall graunt and charter to us is to bestow upon us 2 inestimable Jewells.

The first is peace, commonly calld among all men the Kings peace (among) ourselues and among all the Kings subjects and Friends in this Countrey and wheresoeuer. . . .

The 2 Jewell is Libertie: the first of our spirits which neither Old nor N. Eng: knowes the like, nor no part of the World a greater.

2. Libertie of our persons: no Life no Limbe taken from us: No Corporall punishment no Restraint, but by knowne Lawes and Agreements of our own making.

3. Libertie of our Estates, Howses catle, Lands, Goods, and not a peny to be taken by any rate, without euery mans free debate by his Deputies, chosen by himself and sent to the General Assembly.

4. Libertie of Societie and Corporacion: of sending or being sent to the Gen: Assembly: of choosing and being chosen to all offices, and of making or repealing all Lawes and Constitutions among us.

5. A Libertie, which other Charters haue not, to wit of attending to the Lawe of Eng: with a favourable mitigacion viz: not absolutely but respecting our Wilderness Estate and Condicion.

VI

Roger Williams made his chief contribution to liberty with brave new solutions to bitter old problems that had been agitating Christendom since the beginning of the Reformation. By proclaiming in *The Bloudy Tenent* and underwriting in Rhode Island the doctrines of religious liberty that he had dimly perceived at Cambridge and was still groping for at Salem, Williams swept away, almost too impudently, a formidable barrier to political liberty; at the same time, he furnished an object lesson that men of good will in other Christian countries could ponder and apply. The portrait of Williams as religious figure has been painted and repainted in so many hundreds of books and articles —often faithfully and as often too heroically—that we may confine this exposition to the political implications of his explosive teachings. More precisely, we must examine two related aspects of his religious doctrines: where they fixed the line between authority of state and liberty of individual, and what their formulation and successful application actually contributed to the rise of American liberty.

Williams's religious teachings were essentially negative in character, for he denied just about every important principle of church and state that men had been asserting for more than a thousand years: that there was one true religion, that there was one true church, that the central purpose of the divinely ordained state was to defend the church, that prince and bishop or minister and magistrate must support each other with the sanctions at their command, that the civil power must protect the true religion by punishing errors of doctrine and shortcomings of religious performance, and that it might rightfully persecute for cause of conscience. In short, Williams rejected categorically the concept of unity of church and state that had dominated the Middle Ages and was even then dominating Massachusetts and Connecticut, "that commonly received and not questioned opinion, viz. That the civill state and the spirituall, the Church and Commonweale, they are like Hippocrates twinnes, they are borne together, grow up together, laugh together, weepe together, sicken and die together."

In practical terms, this meant that church and state were to be cleanly separated, that no religion was to be preferred or nourished by the civil power, that each church was to be treated as just another private organization with the usual corporate rights, that liberty of conscience was to be guaranteed to each individual, and that no man was to be molested by his government or fellow citizens for his religious opinions—so long as he did not express them in such manner as to disturb the civil peace. The purpose of government was "the preservation of the peace and welfare of the state," not the propagation of one religion or all. The authority of the state was to extend only to a man's behavior, never to his conscience.

Williams's own words, however archaic they may seem

to us, expressed these ideas with an intensity that must
have amazed the General Court in Boston and Parliament
in London.

All Civill States with their Officers of justice in their respective constitutions and administrations are . . . essentially
Civill, and therefore not Judges, Governours or Defendours of
the Spirituall or Christian State and Worship.

It is the will and command of God that (since the comming
of his Sonne the Lord Jesus) a permission of the most Paganish,
Jewish, Turkish, or Antichristian consciences and worships, bee
granted to all men in all Nations and Countries: and they are
onely to bee fought against with that Sword which is only (in
Soule matters) able to conquer, to wit, the Sword of Gods
Spirit, the Word of God.

God requireth not an uniformity of Religion to be inacted
and inforced in any civill State; which inforced uniformity
(sooner or later) is the greatest occasion of civill Warre, ravish-
ing of conscience, persecution of Christ Jesus in his servants,
and of the hypocrisie and destruction of millions of souls.

The permission of other consciences and worships then a state
professeth, only can (according to God) procure a firme and
lasting peace, (good assurance being taken according to the
wisdome of the civill State for uniformity of civill obedience
from all sorts.) . . .

The government of the civill Magistrate extendeth no further
then over the bodies and goods of their subjects, not over their
soules, and therefore they may not undertake to give Lawes
unto the soules and consciences of men.

The Church of Christ doth not use the Arme of secular power
to compell men to the true profession of the truth, for this is to
be done with spirituall weapons, whereby Christians are to be
exhorted, not compelled.

His most famous and oft-quoted words were these:

Hence it is that so many glorious and flourishing cities of
the World maintaine their Civill peace, yea the very Americans

and wildest Pagans keep the peace of their Towns or Cities; though neither in one nor the other can any man prove a true Church of God in those places, and consequently no spiritual heavenly peace: The Peace Spiritual (whether true or false) being of a higher and farre different nature from the Peace of the place or people, being meerly and essentially civill and humane.

The Church or company of worshippers (whether true or false) is like unto a Body or Colledge of Physitians in a Citie; like unto a Corporation, Society, or Company of East-Indie or Turkie-Merchants, or any other Societie or Company in London: which Companies may hold their Courts, keep their Records, hold disputations; and in matters concerning their Societie, may dissent, divide, breake into Schismes and Factions, sue and implead each other at the Law, yea wholly breake and dissolve into pieces and nothing, and yet the peace of the Citie not be in the least measure impaired or disturbed; because of the essence or being of the Citie, and so the well-being and peace thereof is essentially distinct from those particular Societies; the Citie-Courts, Citie-Laws, Citie-punishments distinct from theirs. The Citie was before them, and stands absolute and intire, when such a Corporation or Society is taken down.

It is plain to see what Williams thought about the authority of the state in religious matters. He opened up a whole new field of liberty for the individual, or rather set up a fence between ruler and ruled that the former had no power—from nature, Scripture, principle, or expediency—to break down or push beyond. At the same time, he did not advocate that the state adopt a completely laissez-faire attitude toward religion. It could punish outrages against the civil peace by persons whose religion moved them to violence or obscenity. It could defend one person professing an unpopular faith against the active intolerance of another.

Through his bold advocacy of the twin doctrines of separation of church and state and liberty of conscience, and through his endorsement of their trial-by-ordeal in despised Rhode Island, Williams reached two centuries or more into the American future. He asserted and proved that a moral, stable society could exist without the support and sanctions of a national church. With one bold stroke—by thrusting them out of the area of political intervention—he disposed of several questions that had muddied and bloodied Western society for generations and had repeatedly fractured the peace so necessary for the effective working of free institutions. He added new dignity and meaning to individualism by telling men that they could think and teach as they pleased, even irreligiously and anti-Christianly, without answering to any earthly authority. And he gave impetus to good government by reminding those in authority of their proper and primary tasks. In short, he solved the most perplexing political problem of his age by insisting that it was not political at all. And he did all this, as good Americans have done ever since, with the help of arguments that were derived from expediency. He assaulted *The Bloudy Tenent* with a benumbing array of citations from Scripture and applications of reason, but his most telling accusation was that "there is no Doctrine, no Tenent so directly tending to break the Cities peace, as this Doctrine of persecuting or punishing each other for the cause of conscience or Religion." Contrary to the opinions of the persecutors of old and New England,

The free permitting of the *consciences* and *meetings* of *conscionable* and *faithful people* throughout the *Nation,* and the free permission of the *Nation* to frequent such *assemblies,* will be one of the principal Means and expedients (as the present state of Christianity stands) for the propagating and spreading of the Gospel of the Son of God.

There is a surprisingly modern and utilitarian note in Williams's case for separation and "soul liberty."

Williams was not, as many writers and orators have loosely insisted, an advocate of toleration. This concept implies the superiority of one belief over others, and the willingness of those who hold it to tolerate those who refuse to conform. Williams pushed well beyond the boundaries of mere toleration to proclaim religious liberty as the consequence of the essential equality of all faiths. Here again he made little sense to most men of his age, especially because he was, in the words of Miller and Johnson, "pious with a fervor and passion that went beyond most of his contemporaries," and not, like Jefferson, "a man to whom theology and divine grace had become stuff and nonsense." To reduce the matter to simplest terms, Williams wanted separation because he feared that state would contaminate church, Jefferson because he feared that church would contaminate state.

As first theoretical and practical exponent of the American doctrine of religious liberty, Roger Williams is rightly considered an authentic folk-hero. While ideas and realities of this sweep are the gift of many men, Williams surely comes as close as any American to being the embodiment of a fundamental principle of democracy.

VII

Williams is well and wisely celebrated for his doctrines of popular republicanism and religious liberty. In discussing these two categories of his thought, I have done little more than recall and reshape the paramount facts in a record that has long been public property. Yet there was a third category that his biographers do not touch upon with sufficient emphasis or enlightenment: a half-dozen tenets of political authority and organization which he neither brought with him out of England nor deduced from first principles, but rather hammered out on the anvil of experience during his long public service. These were the lessons in political science that he found through experience to be helpful or essential to free and orderly government:

Free inquiry and free expression of the results. Speaking, in *The Bloody Tenent Yet More Bloody,* to "the several respective General Courts, especially that of the Massachusetts in N. England," Williams noted with sorrow that "Liberty of searching out Truth [was] hardly got, and as hardly kept." In this writing, of course, he was concerned primarily with the search for religious truth, but excerpts from his letters and incidents in his career prove that he was as much the seeker in politics as in religion. He came to the conclusion that in statecraft as in theology authority grounded in doctrine would harden into tyranny grounded in dogma, and that open-minded investigation was therefore the only trustworthy technique for reaching adequate solutions to social problems. Free men, argued Williams, must have free minds, and he spent his life trying to convince friends and neighbors that Rhode Island's unique government and way of life depended for continued success on their cultivation of the habits of intellectual freedom.

At the same time, he made clear that a man must be prepared to discuss his conclusions openly and responsibly with his fellow citizens—without fear of official interference or private intolerance. "Free Conferrings, Disputings and Preachings" were, as he testified in his debates with the Quakers at the end of his life, the main cog in the mechanism of freedom.

None shall see the Truth but the Soul that loves it, and digs for it as for treasures of gold and silver, and is impartial, patient, and pitiful to the opposers.

Williams was uniquely anxious to accord freedom of expression to opinions that he found stupid or even dangerous. The only "ism" against which he set his face intolerantly seems to have been that interesting practice of certain early Quakers, nudism. Williams learned from experience in the wilderness—at the assembly in Portsmouth, the town meeting in Providence, and the council fire in the Narragansett country—what he could only have assumed in England and Massachusetts: that men who will search openly for the truth and talk freely and humbly about their conclusions with their fellows are the stuff of political liberty.

Arbitration. In keeping with his everlasting emphasis on peace among men, Williams put a high value on the spirit of compromise. He had learned to recognize this spirit as the magic wand that turns license into liberty and thus brings stability to free society. Writing to the inhabitants of Providence in 1648, he had this to say about the squabbles then convulsing the Rhode Island towns:

WORTHY FRIENDS, that ourselves and all men are apt and prone to differ, it is no new thing. In all former ages, in all parts of the world, in these parts, and in our dear native country and mournful state of England, that either part or party is most right in his own eyes, his cause right, his carriage right, his arguments right, his answers right, is as woefully and constantly true as the former. . . . And since, dear friends, it is an honor for men to cease from strife; since the life of love is sweet, and union is as strong as sweet and since you have been lately pleased to call me to some public service and my soul hath been long musing how I might bring water to quench, and not oil or fluid to the flame, I am now humbly bold to beseech you . . . to be willing to be pacifiable, willing to be reconcilable, willing to be sociable, and to listen to the (I hope not unreasonable) motion following: To try out matters by disputes and writings, is sometimes endless; to try out arguments by arms and swords, is cruel and merciless; to trouble the state and Lords of England, is most unreasonable, most chargeable; to trouble our neighbors of other colonies seems neither safe nor honorable. Methinks, dear friends, the colony now looks with the torn face of two parties, and that the greater number of Portsmouth, with other loving friends adhering to them, appear as one grieved party; the other three towns, or greater part of them, appear to be another: Let each party choose and nominate three . . . let authority be given to them to examine every public difference, grievance, and obstruction of justice, peace and common safety: let them, by one final sentence of all or the greater part of them, end all, and set the whole into an unanimous posture and order, and let them set a censure upon any that shall oppose their sentence.

Here is a tribute to arbitration, the technique that Williams considered the most sensible way for free men to solve their problems and compromise their differences. "Agreed," stated the plantation covenant adopted by Providence in 1640, "that after many Considerations and Consultations of our owne State and alsoe of States abroad in way of government, we apprehend, no way so suitable to our Condition as government by way of arbitration. But if men agree themselves by way of arbitration, no State we know of disallows that, neither doe we." This was a clear recognition of the efficacy of a procedure that Williams had learned something of in Massachusetts and had made one of the most dependable props of the Rhode Island way of life. All his life he clung to a conviction that peacefully minded men could settle their own differences without recourse to governmental sanctions, by referring them to fellow citizens who were prepared to examine the facts objectively and give reasoned judgment.

The necessity of authority. It has been written that in the beginning Massachusetts had law without liberty and Rhode Island liberty without law. This is, as we have seen, a gratuitous insult to the people of seventeenth-century Rhode Island, most of whom tilled their fields, paid their

taxes, and discharged their duties faithfully as citizens of
a free state. Nevertheless, there were some who found any
kind of authority distasteful and preached the gospel of
all-out anarchy. "We enjoy liberties of soul and body,"
Williams lamented in a letter to John Winthrop, jr., "but
it is license we desire." To them and to all others who would
wreck free government by defying even the most legitimate
and needful authority, Williams made answer in 1655
through a public letter to the town of Providence. In it he
made clear that it was the civil liberty of men under a
government of their own making, not the irresponsible
license of beasts in a jungle, that he had always championed.

That ever I should speak or write a tittle, that tends to such
an infinite liberty of conscience, is a mistake, and which I have
ever disclaimed and abhorred. To prevent such mistakes, I shall
at present only propose this case: There goes many a ship to sea,
with many hundred souls in one ship, whose weal and woe is
common, and is a true picture of a commonwealth, or a human
combination or society. It hath fallen out sometimes, that both
papists and protestants, Jews and Turks, may be embarked in
one ship; upon which supposal I affirm, that all the liberty of
conscience, that ever I pleaded for, turns upon these two hinges
—that none of the papists, protestants, Jews, or Turks, be forced
to come to the ship's prayers or worship, nor compelled from
their own particular prayers or worship, if they practice any.
I further add, that I never denied, that notwithstanding this
liberty, the commander of this ship ought to command the ship's
course, yea, and also command that justice, peace and sobriety,
be kept and practiced, both among the seamen and all the passengers. If any of the seamen refuse to perform their services, or
passengers to pay their freight; if any refuse to help, in person
or purse, towards the common charges or defence; if any refuse
to obey the common laws and orders of the ship, concerning
their common peace or preservation; if any shall mutiny and
rise up against their commanders and officers; if any should

preach or write that there ought to be no commanders and officers; because all are equal in Christ, therefore no masters nor officers, no laws nor orders, nor corrections nor punishments;— I say, I never denied, but in such cases, whatever is pretended, the commander or commanders may judge, resist, compel and punish such transgressors, according to their deserts and merits.

This was the courageous message of a persecuted individualist to those of his fellow refugees who, perhaps understandably, could not rid themselves of the notion that all authority was evil and oppressive. Not only was it an important contribution to the working theory of one of our first free governments; it stands even today as a uniquely toughminded testament of a man who had learned through the hardest kind of experience that liberty without law and government without authority are swamps in which true freedom sinks without a trace.

Rights and duties. Along with this clear-eyed apology for authority went another of Williams's pragmatic beliefs about the place of the individual in the political community, one that was not to be acknowledged officially outside Rhode Island until the French constitution of 1792: the idea of reciprocity of rights and duties. Williams's individualism was suprisingly modern in flavor. His writings stressed the social fact that men found the fullest expression of their liberty in fulfilling their functions in the community. A free man had duties as well as rights; indeed, he had no claim to the latter unless he was prepared to execute the former.

Again we read in the record of Williams's years in Providence that he came to this unusual notion through saddening experience, and again we have evidence that the colony itself accepted the great man's teaching. The Acts and Orders of 1647 embody the concept of reciprocal rights and duties. For example,

In case a man be called unto Office by a lawfull Assemble, and refuse to beare office, or be called by an officer to assist in the execution of his office, and refuse to assist him, he shall forfeit as much again as his wages would have amounted unto, or be otherwise fined by the judgment of his Peers, and to pay his fine or forfeiture. . . . But in case of eminent danger, no man shall refuse.

The trials of friendless Rhode Island, menaced by white enemies and red from without, weakened by anarchists and Quakers from within, taught Williams and his co-workers the necessity of individual participation in public life.

Equality. Three centuries ago in Providence Roger Williams practiced another belief that many Americans are still content to preach: the principle of equality, perhaps the firmest spiritual and practical foundation of democratic society. If Williams had a less exalted notion of equality than some of the natural-law philosophers of the eighteenth century, he had a far more intimate working knowledge of its prime importance for the merging of liberty and order through free institutions. He arrived first at a belief in religious equality, in the parity of all faiths in the eyes of the state. In time and through experience he moved further in the direction of democracy by extending this concept to at least three other essentials: equality in law (which was realized in the code of 1647), equality in land (which he sponsored with a selflessness unmatched in colonial America), and equality in government (which spurred his relentless campaign against the pattern of feudalism that Coddington insisted on transplanting to America). There were limits to his understanding of equality—for example, the status of inferiority in which he seemed content to leave women—but he could hardly have been expected to cast loose completely from the values and prejudices of his age. It is enough to point out that Wil-

liams, thanks to an overflowing humanity and a shrewd
perception of conditions in England, Massachusetts, and
his own colony, was far ahead of his age in proclaiming
equality as both right and necessity in these four fundamentals—religion, law, land, and government. Most unusual, of course, was his insistence on land for all on equal
terms—for the latecomer as well as for the original home-
steader. The peculiar American doctrine of equality of opportunity has at least one of its roots in Williams's land
policy.

It is not at all surprising that many historians and political scientists have explained Williams's mind in overly
modern terms, for it takes little imagination to picture
him as the seventeenth-century prophet of several momentous twentieth-century principles. For one thing, there
is evidence that in his comprehension of the workings of
political, religious, and corporate institutions he came very
close to the concept of pluralism. For another, he had a
primitive understanding of the way in which economic arrangements shape political institutions, which explains his
emphasis on "liberty and equality, both in land and government." And he seems to have perceived, thanks to his freedom from dogma and from respect for prescriptive authority, that social and political institutions are ever in a
state of change, and that it is therefore both inexpedient
and unnatural to enforce a rigid pattern of law and government upon any society. "Nor can your most prudent
Heads, and potent hands," he warned Parliament in 1652,
"possibly erect that Fabrick, which the next Age (it may
be the next Parliament) may not tumble down." Actually,
he did not say enough about these matters to justify our
considering him their early expounder. It would be a mistake to read too much Laski, Beard, and Herbert Spencer
into this searching colonial mind.

Yet it would be a mistake, too, not to recognize in Williams an early exemplar of the American tradition of political pragmatism. Even when he seemed to his contemporaries to be most hopelessly impractical, as in his enthusiastic advocacy of separation and "soul liberty," he was arguing from experience rather than contemplation of eternal verities. Some of his half-dozen working principles have been absorbed into the great body of American thought, some have not. But all were the product of a general technique that unnumbered Americans, most of whom never heard of Roger Williams, were to make the leading article of their political faith: No idea is sound until it has been tested through experience; if it has been learned through experience, so much the sounder. To this extent at least Williams was the first *American* political thinker.

VIII

Roger Williams died in Providence some time between January 27 and March 15, 1683, survived by his wife and six children. Although he was mourned by his friends and neighbors, who buried "the Venerable remaines of Mr. Roger Williams, the Father of Providence, the Founder of the Colony, and of Liberty of Conscience" with "all the solemnity the colony was able to shew," his passing stirred hardly a ripple of interest in old or New England. He left a living monument to political and religious liberty in Rhode Island, but not until almost two centuries later did his words and deeds become generally known in the United States and Europe.

The reason is, of course, that his mind had far outrun the understanding of all but the most imaginative of his fellow colonials. His radical solutions to the great problems of the age, which to us seem eminently sound and workable, were looked upon by most of his contemporaries as sheerest nonsense. Yet we can see plainly that his books and letters, for all their thorny verbiage and interminable wranglings, were a memorable stage in the rise of a theory of liberty. In giving practical application to the concepts of popular sovereignty and social compact; in concluding almost pragmatically that reciprocity of rights and duties, the spirit of compromise, equality in land and government, and a certain minimum of order and authority were requisites of successful free government; and above all in proclaiming separation of church and state and liberty of conscience on grounds of social expediency, Williams left a legacy of ideas and accomplishments that persuades us to look upon him as the first American democrat. Perhaps his finest achievement was that he came to know better than any man of his age—better than the autocrats in London and Boston, better than the nihilists in Providence and Pawtuxet—just where to draw the line between the freedom of the individual and the sanctions of the state. An English thinker, G. P. Gooch, has written, "If democracy . . . in its ultimate meaning be held to imply not only a government in which the preponderant share of power resides in the hands of the people, but a society based on the principles of political and religious freedom, Rhode Island beyond any other of the American Colonies is entitled to be called democratic." The debt of Rhode Island the democracy to Williams the democrat is one that can hardly be overstated. If the colony, as it grew and prospered, retreated noticeably from Williams's original program for a popular government and equitable land-policy, it retreated hardly at all from his program for religious liberty. Thanks to Roger Williams and his "impractical notions," Rhode Island led all the world in the practice of this vital principle of human liberty.

Williams's life was heroic, and we are stirred by his triumphs. It was simple, and we are refreshed by his lack of pretension. Above all it was an act of faith, and we are astonished by his sense of destiny.

It hath pleased the Most High to carry me on eagles' wings, through mighty labors, mighty hazards, mighty sufferings. . . . In my poor span of time, I have been oft in the jaws of death, sickening at sea, ship-wrecked on shore, in danger of arrows, swords and bullets: and yet, methinks, the most high and most holy God hath reserved me for some service to his most glorious and eternal majesty.

3

JOHN WISE

"A Star of the First Magnitude"

VERNON L. PARRINGTON once described the seventeenth
century in America as a *saeculum theologicum,* the eighteenth as a *saeculum politicum.* No one is likely to cavil at
this neat bisection of colonial intellectual history. An im-
mense gulf separates the crabbed fields of the Puritan divines
from the lush meadows of Otis, the Adamses, Jefferson, and
Hamilton. At the same time, this generalization, like others
of its type, demands qualification. We must remember that
there were many bridges across the gulf, that one age passed
into the other without too rough a detour in our social and
literary development. These two centuries did, after all, have
an intellectual unity.

Of all the bridges from the age of theology to that of
politics, the most convenient and plainly marked is the life
and writings of John Wise, pastor of a church in Chebacco
(then part of Ipswich, now of Essex) in Massachusetts. The

dates of Wise's ministerial career, 1675 to 1725, are symbolic of the manner in which his thinking spanned the two ages. A relentless warrior for both ecclesiastical and political liberty, he was a companion-at-arms to all the Separatists who had gone before and to all the Revolutionists who were to come after. A fellowship with Wise brings Samuel Adams and Jonathan Mayhew into company with Robert Browne and John Robinson; his life and work persuade us to look upon the debate between Daniel Leonard and John Adams as a projection of the debate between John Cotton and Roger Williams. From the Cambridge Platform to Wise and from Wise to the Declaration of Independence the road lies open and is plainly marked.

Yet Wise is an obscure figure. Although there have been several brilliant efforts to bring him forward to the front rank of the champions of American liberty, he continues to receive only passing mention in the histories of our political thought and none at all in the histories of our democracy. He has not been without witnesses to his "valor and great deeds." His own generation looked upon him as a public figure of special stature:

He was of a Generous and Publick Spirit, a Great Lover of his Country, and our happy Constitution, a studious Assertor, and faithful Defender of its Liberties and Interests.

Moses Coit Tyler called Wise "the first great American democrat." The eminent Congregational theologian, Williston Walker, not to be outdone by an ex-Congregationalist from the West, presented his spiritual forebear as "the first conspicuous American opponent of taxation without representation," and Parrington thought that Wise had "the keenest mind and most trenchant pen of his generation of New Englanders." Yet Charles E. Merriam ignored him completely in his *History of American Political Theories,* and for even the most perceptive historians he remains the forgotten saint in the hagiology of American democracy.

Wise was a far too noble friend of liberty in practice, a far too compelling student of liberty in theory, to be forever indulged the oblivion that has been his usual lot. His life is a rare testament to all that is good and decent in human hearts and minds; his political philosophy is a sure sign that the essentials of liberty were taking fast hold in the New England villages. Let us therefore turn to a brief account of his life and a more extended analysis of his political ideas.

I

John Wise, as befits a man nominated for the title of "the first great American democrat," was of humble, even plebeian origin. He was born in Roxbury, Massachusetts, probably in July 1652, the fifth of thirteen children of Joseph Wise. His father had come to Massachusetts Bay about 1635 as an indentured servant of Dr. George Alcock. The death of the master in 1640 gave freedom to the servant. Alcock's will bequeathed to Joseph Wise "my young heifer, and the rest of his time from after midsomer next." Joseph celebrated his good fortune by marrying Mary Thompson, probably of Braintree, on December 3 of his first year of freedom.

After receiving his early education in the "Free Schoole" in Roxbury and the church of John Eliot, apostle to the Indians, John Wise entered Harvard in 1669, the first son of an indentured servant to be admitted to the college. He took his first degree in 1673, his second in 1676, maintaining as his commencement part the affirmative of the spacious question: *"An impossibile sit Mundum fuisse ab aeterno?"* He apparently loved good fun (college style) as

much as philosophical debate, for he was arrested and
censured along with several of his friends for feasting on a
turkey stolen from Captain Daniel Gookin.

Following brief intervals of preaching in the Connecticut towns of Branford and Hatfield, Wise came to Ipswich,
one of the leading settlements in the Bay colony, as minister of the Second Church. The good people who lived in
the part of Ipswich known as Chebacco had been finding it
increasingly difficult to travel the six or seven miles to
meeting in Ipswich, and in 1677 had petitioned the town
for liberty to call a minister to preach among them. After
a lengthy struggle with the Saints of Ipswich, the Saints
of Chebacco finally won permission from the General
Court to establish a church of their own. With the gathering of the church and final withdrawal of the objections
of the Ipswich meeting, Wise was formally ordained August 12, 1683. With him to his new parish he brought
his wife, Abigail Gardner of Roxbury, whom he had married December 5, 1678. Wise had seven children, three of
whom were graduates of Harvard.

Until his death in 1725 Wise labored for the Lord in
this single vineyard. Without pretension to fame or ambition for power, he was content to live and work in relative obscurity, leaving to others, notably the Mathers, the
questionable glory of provincial leadership. From our point
of view, he carried his quest for oblivion too far. It is
regrettable that he declined the General Court's invitation
to deliver the election sermon in 1719, even more regrettable that he left no diary to complement those of Samuel
Sewall and Cotton Mather. Only on rare occasions does
Wise's noble figure suddenly appear in the pages of colonial
histories. We see him for a moment taking vigorous sides
in an issue that agitates the colony; then, just as suddenly,
.we see him no more until several years have passed and a

new issue has arisen. He was apparently uninterested in permanent leadership or power. His few appearances, however, were Homeric, for when he did decide to come forth from Chebacco and strike a blow for justice, he fought with brilliance and tenacity. It is remarkable and gratifying to find Wise so consistently right about the issues of his time, issues that found many a man no less intelligent and humane than he far over the wrong side of the fence and deep in fields of error.

To his quiet life in Ipswich and occasional sallies into colonial prominence Wise brought a physical presence fully as powerful as his intellect, which was, as we shall see, unique in his time. We unfortunately have no likeness of him, but we have ample testimony that he was a man "of a majestic form, and of great muscular strength and activity." Tyler writes, "He had almost every quality that gives distinction among men. He was of towering height, of great muscular power, stately and graceful in shape and movement; in his advancing years, of an aspect most venerable." He was accounted by his fellow townsmen "a superior wrestler," this being a reputation, according to the town's nineteenth-century antiquarian, "much more respectable in his day than ours." The story is told that late in Wise's life the leading sport of Andover, Captain John Chandler, came over to Ipswich to challenge him for the championship of the area. Wise, although at first pleading age and infirmity, finally agreed to grapple with Chandler. In a very few seconds he threw Chandler completely over his front wall, whereupon the champion of Andover arose and announced that he would be on his way just as soon as Mr. Wise threw his horse over after him. The connection between Wise's big body and big spirit was not missed by his friends and neighbors:

The graceful Structure of his Manly Body, Majestick Aspect,.

and sweet Deportment, were but an Emblem of the mighty
Genius & brighter Excellencies of his Superior Soul.

His parishioners were convinced that the power of his
prayer was equal to that of his muscles. On one occasion
a boat's crew from Chebacco fell among pirates. At Sunday meeting Wise prayed for their deliverance, ending with
an impassioned "Great God! if there is no other way, may
they rise and butcher their enemies." The next day the
crew, having risen and butchered their enemies, returned to
Chebacco. The parish was persuaded of the efficacy of
prayer.

Wise's first sally into colonial affairs pitted him against
Sir Edmund Andros, royal governor of the Dominion of
New England under James II. The plans of the Crown for
a united, well-governed, subordinate New England failed
to reckon with the spirit of self-government that animated
many of the Massachusetts towns. It was one thing for
Sir Edmund simply to do away with the General Court,
quite another to exercise its powers by laying a tax on the
towns without legislative consent. In 1687 Andros and
his council, acting pursuant to royal commission, re-enacted
the old Massachusetts revenue law. Included in this public
levy was the "country rate," a tax of one penny on one
pound to be collected in the several towns by commissioners of their own choosing. The town of Ipswich, aroused
to stubborn rebellion by Wise, refused to elect a commissioner to collect the tax and lectured the council "that no
taxes should be levied upon the subject without the consent
of an Assembly, chosen by the Freeholders for assessing the
same." Wise, who seems to have been a spiritual forebear
of Samuel Adams, had won the leading citizens of Ipswich
to this stand in an extraordinary conclave the night before

town meeting. The town's defiance was a preview of things to come:

At a Legall Towne Meeting August 23d 1687.

Assembled by vertue of an order from John Usher Esq. Treas^er, for choosing a Commiss^er to join wth ye Selectmen to assess ye Inhabitants, according to an act of his Excellency ye Governor & Counsill, for Levying rates.

Then considering that the s'd act doth infringe their Liberty as Free borne English subjects of his Majes^tie, by interfearing wth ye statutory Laws of the Land, By wch it is enacted, that no taxes shall be Levied on ye Subjects w^thout consent of an assembly chosen by ye Freeholders for assessing ye same.

They do therefore vote, that they are not willing to choose a Commiss^er for such an end, w^thout s'd previledges.

And morover consent not that the Selectmen do proseed to lay any such rate, until it be appointed by a General assembly, concurring wth ye Govern^er, and Counsell,—Voted by the whole assembly twisse.

Sir Edmund was no man to brook interference with his application of Stuart prerogative to Massachusetts Bay, especially since he realized that a soft policy toward Ipswich would encourage the whole colony to resist. He therefore seized Wise and twenty-seven others and, having grilled them in council, placed six of them on trial before judges thoroughly prejudiced and a jury firmly packed. Wise led the defense, quoting Magna Charta, the statutes, and "the rights of Englishmen" in denial of the council's arbitrary assessment. For his pains in asserting his privileges before the council he was told, "Mr. Wise, you have no more privileges left you, than not to be sold for Slaves." And for his unyielding attitude in court he was punished with a fine of fifty pounds, suspension from the ministry, and payment of a £1,000 bond for one year's good behavior. Wise was allowed to resume his preaching, and after the expulsion of Andros the next year, he brought suit against his former fellow townsman Joseph Dudley, who as chief justice had denied him a writ of habeas corpus. Legend tells us that he collected damages.

At this time Wise received evidence of the esteem in which he was held by town and colony. In 1689 he went as a representative from Ipswich to the meeting in Boston at which the General Court was reorganized, and in 1690 he marched against Quebec as chaplain of the ill-conceived expedition under Sir William Phips, having been appointed to this position of trust by the General Court itself. He carried himself with distinction throughout the unpleasant fiasco before Quebec, "where not only the Pious Discharge of his Sacred Office, but his Heroick Spirit, and Martial Skill and Wisdom, did greatly distinguish him." Wise left a pungent account of the expedition and of the reasons for its failure. This document, discovered in Paris in the late nineteenth century, was in the form of a letter to Increase Mather, who was in England as agent for Massachusetts during the intercharter period. Not so brilliant as Caesar, Trotsky, or Churchill in reporting the campaigns in which he took part, Wise is a good deal more humble and bluntly honest.

Wise's consistent stand for common sense in the witchcraft persecution of 1692 moves him even further toward the front rank of the company of colonial friends of religious and political liberty. The historian of the Salem craze, Charles W. Upham, wrote of him as "a learned, able, and enlightened man. He had a free spirit, and was perhaps the only minister in the neighborhood or country, who was discerning enough to see the erroneousness of the proceedings from the beginning." Whether he was composing a petition to the Assistants to save John Procter's life, commending Increase Mather's testimony against "spectral evidence," or signing an address to the General Court to remove "the infamy and reproach" from the names and posterity of those convicted of witchcraft, Wise demonstrated a total lack of fear of the persecutors of his time.

Other issues claimed Wise's attention. For example, he took part in the controversy over singing by note that excited the colony around 1720. He wrote to Thomas Symmes, the leader of the movement to substitute congregational singing for the primitive method of chanting a line at a time behind a precentor, "that when there were a sufficient number in a Congregation to carry away a Tune Roundly, it was proper to introduce that Tune." Wise, like Symmes, was unimpressed by cries of "Popery!" A more serious affair was the question of inoculation against smallpox. Wise was one of a handful of ministers who advocated this radical innovation of which the Mathers were the chief proponents. The currency problem was another of his interests. The arguments of Sewall and the rising merchant-aristocracy for the maintenance of a metallic currency found a cold reception among the country folk of Ipswich. Convinced, with his parishioners, of the merits of paper money, Wise entered the lists under the pseudonym "Amicus Patriae" with *A Word of Comfort to a Melancholy Country*, "Humbly Dedicated to the Merchants in Boston." While his economic musings were not altogether sound, his sympathies were once again at the disposal of the rising agrarian democracy.

II

Despite his excursions into the political, economic, social, medical, and musical contentions of his time, Wise was first and last a minister. It is therefore not surprising that

the controversy into which he plunged with the most
vigor and consequence was primarily religious in character.
Throughout the last twenty years of his life he carried on
a running fight with the Mathers and others who sought
to impose more order on the constitution of the New
England churches. This skirmish was, of course, only one
episode in the long struggle in the Congregational churches
between "Barrowism," the semi-presbyterianism advanced
by Henry Barrowe, and "Brownism," the doctrine of virtual
autonomy in the local church. Although not exactly an
uncritical follower of Robert Browne and his extreme views,
Wise was a zealous believer in democracy in the church,
which to him meant church government in the hands of
the individual congregation and only loose bonds of "mutual watch and brotherly helpfulness" between the churches
of the colony.

The decline of the Puritan oligarchy, symbolized and
made certain by the withdrawal of the charter in 1684,
ushered in a period of unrest in the affairs of the New
England churches. The clergy, feeling political power slip-
ping from its fingers, did what most clergies have done
under similar circumstances: It set out to bolster its ecclesiastical power. Specifically, it became the avowed purpose of the Mathers and their sympathizers to effect a
closer union of the churches and to institute active control
of the different congregations through the so-called Ministerial Convention of Massachusetts. This was an annual
gathering of the ministers of the province at the time of
the May General Court, "which had begun," according to
Walker, "in the informal coming together of the ministers
in the earliest days of the colony, and had crystallized
sufficiently by about 1680 to have a moderator, a dinner,
and a sermon." In addition to the Convention, several

ministerial associations, voluntary groupings of the ministers of a particular area, had arisen in the Bay colony.

The most significant action of the "Presbyterian Party"
was that of nine prominent ministers—among them Samuel
Willard, Ebenezer Pemberton, and Cotton Mather—who
met in Boston in September 1705 and drew up sixteen
proposals. These proposals, which would have imposed a
synodal form of government upon hitherto autonomous
churches, were transmitted to the various associations November 5, 1705, and were approved by the Ministerial
Convention that met in Boston in May 1706. There can be
no question that the centralizing plans of the Mather group,
quite innocuous when viewed from our secular age, would
have worked substantial alterations in the Congregational
polity of colonial New England. They were a pronounced
step toward union and conciliar control, and thus were
hostile to the principle of autonomy in the local churches.
The threat was the more pronounced because of the excellent persons who had originated or approved the sixteen
proposals. A majority of the Massachusetts pastors, many
of them perhaps unwittingly, had signified acquiescence
in this plan.

Not John Wise, however. As two gentlemen of Gloucester were later to point out, "All our Watchmen were
not asleep, nor the Camp of Christ surprized and taken,
before they had Warning." Wise thought that the proposals "smelled very strong of the infallible chair," and
his warning to the camp was immediate and vociferous.
The New England method of ministerial licensure may be
said to date from these recommendations of 1705, and
certainly the ministerial associations were further stimulated. Otherwise the proposals, especially those looking to
the establishment of a standing council with power to dis-

cipline the member churches, were received with hostility
or disdain and had little success in altering the government of the churches.

Wise spoke out sharply to his parishioners and correspondents in defiance of this scheme, but apparently had
nothing immediate to say for publication. The opposition
of the more self-contained churches hardly needed stimulation. When, however, the churches of Connecticut embarked in 1708 on a similar presbyterian adventure—by
adopting the Saybrook Platform, a series of elaborate articles based on the Massachusetts proposals of 1705—he took
up his pen and advanced to do battle for democracy in the
churches. Here was "mischief, mischief in *summo gradu;*
yea exorbitant mischief," and Wise would have none of it.

His contribution to this decisive contest consisted of two
small volumes. The first, *The Churches' Quarrel Espoused*
(1710), was a "Reply in Satire" to the sixteen proposals of
the Mather faction. Printing the proposals without comment in the first pages of his book, Wise proceeded to
destroy them one by one with shrewd, witty, even abusive
satire. He wrote a limited treatise for a limited purpose, and
the whole production was purely occasional. Nevertheless,
it was a superlative exposition of ecclesiastical democracy
and a convincing rejection of the presbyterian idea as un-
suitable for the churches of Christ, "especially in such a
country and climate as this."

In 1717 Wise returned to combat with a second book, *A
Vindication of the Government of New-England Churches.*
This work, the product of several years of painstaking reading and reflection, was his most brilliant literary performance. Indeed, it was probably the outstanding piece of
polemical writing in the first 150 years of the American
settlements. As a systematic defense of ecclesiastical democracy *A Vindication* was several cuts above *The Churches'*

Quarrel Espoused. Where the first book had been negative, destructive, and satirical, *A Vindication* was positive, constructive, and sober. Since the day of its publication it has been a powerful force in Congregational thought.

A Vindication was something more than an ecclesiastical tract. Wise was not content to base his defense of congregational autonomy on the Word of God alone. Although he was careful to find support for his arguments in Scripture, the "Providence of God," and the example of the primitive churches, his case for what he understood as democracy in the church rested most heavily upon its similarity to what he understood as democracy in the state. Wise reversed completely the line of argument of those who had praised political liberty as a reflection of ecclesiastical liberty and had championed the social contract as the logical extension of the church covenant. The spectacle of a Puritan minister examining "the Light of Nature" to discover that democracy was the form of government most favored by the precepts of natural law, then grounding his case for democracy in the church on "the near affinity our constitution holds" with political democracy, was truly astounding—not least to Cotton Mather, who had already branded Wise "a furious Man" and had preached against his attitude as a "Satanick insult, twice over." Wise's approach was a revolution in our intellectual history, for he was the first New England preacher to free himself from the restrictions of the *saeculum theologicum* and enter into literary controversy without primary reliance on the weapons of Scriptural disputation or Ramean logic. Thus, whatever Wise may have set forth to prove, his second book is a work in political rather than ecclesiastical thought.

III

Wise was not an original political thinker. He would have
been the first to admit that his argument from the law of
nature, uncommon as it must have seemed to many of his
adversaries, was simply a reshaping to his own purposes of
a system of thought that had long since swept over Europe,
and that he had read for himself in the writings of one of
its leading exponents. Nevertheless, he must be accorded
full credit for applying the principles of natural law to the
problems of New England and for phrasing them in language that his compatriots could understand and repeat.

Wise himself acknowledged his primary debt: "And I
shall principally take Baron Puffendorf for my chief guide
and spokesman." The baron, of course, was the eminent
German jurist Samuel von Pufendorf (1632-1694), a
major figure in the natural-law school. His great work, *De
Jure Naturae et Gentium*, a persuasive exposition of natural
law, particularly in its application to international law, had
been published in 1672 and republished many times over.
An English translation had been printed in London in 1703.
It is impossible to determine the year in which Wise first
came upon Pufendorf's work, or to discover whether his
copy was in the Latin original or English translation. A
careful comparison of the language of Wise's two books
suggests that he first studied Pufendorf thoughtfully after
1710. By the time he came to write *A Vindication*, he had
absorbed completely the philosophy and phraseology of the
natural-law school.

Wise did not rely on Pufendorf alone. He was a learned
man, and his pages are spiced, but fortunately not cloyed,
with quotations and lessons from all manner of writers and
schools—the ancients (Plato, Aristotle, Virgil, Plutarch,

Cicero, Cato); the church fathers (especially Tertullian
and Eusebius of Caesarea); the early and late leaders of the
Reformation (Luther, Benedict Turretin, William Ames,
John Owen); fellow New Englanders (the Mathers,
Nicholas Noyes, Cotton); such diverse political and philosophical figures as Boethius, Ulpian, Machiavelli, Richard
Hooker, and Sir Edward Coke (whose name he also gives,
with the cavalier disregard of his age for the niceties of
spelling, as Cook and Cooke); Greek, Roman, church, and
English history; and Aesop's fables. Despite this impressive
list of authorities, his books owe a good deal to his own
reasoning about the conformity to nature of the New
England churches. He could say with Hobbes that he had
used his brains more than his bookshelves. He did not, it
should be noted, cite Calvin or Locke.

Wise's style merits some mention. The substance of his
two books was muscular enough to overwhelm the arguments of his presbyterian adversaries, but when clothed in
the mailed fist of his vivid prose its effect was positively
crushing. A contrast of *The Churches' Quarrel Espoused*
with such thorny offerings as Williams's *Bloody Tenents,*
Hooker's *Survey of the Summe of Church-Discipline,* Cotton's *The Way of the Congregational Churches Cleared,*
or any of the many hundred items in the Mathers' well-
padded bibliography would make an instructive study in
American literary development. The prose of his occasional
or unpublished writings—the complaint against Andros,
the account of the expedition to Quebec, the paper-cur-
rency tracts, his *Instructions for Emigrants from Essex
County, Mass., to South Carolina* (1697)—was loose and
undistinguished, brilliant only in flashes and spelled with
abandon. It was still a great improvement over Hooker or
Williams. The two major works are of a far different order.
His imagery is fresh and far-ranging; intensive order marks

the progression of his arguments; and he alternates sobriety
and satire, learning and wit, eloquence and plain talk, with
a skill that would be exceptional in any time and place.
Considering his time and place, it is evidence of natural
genius.

Examples of his forceful prose will fill the pages from
here on. A few other phrases, not particularly germane to
his political thought, should be recorded here in testimony
to his skill and for the delight of the reader. Of controversy he writes: "I neither desire, nor design to hurt any
man, no, not so much as a hair on his head, but I solely
aim at *error,* that is the butt I level for." Of order and
disorder: "Order is both the beauty and safety of the uni-
verse; take away the decorum whereby the whole hangs
together, the great frame of nature is unpinned and drops
piece from piece; and out of a beautiful structure we have
a chaos." Of duty: "The dream of an embroilment can
never counterpoise duty; if men are trusted with duty, they
must consult that, and not events. If men are placed at
helm to steer in all weather that blows, they must not be
afraid of the waves or a wet coat." Of the state of New
England: "There is no want in this country, unless it be
the want of good and honest hearts." Of Harvard: "That
artillery garden from whence we receive our most expert
soldiers in Christ." At another point he cautions his readers against "an implicit faith in the stark naked *ipse dixits*
of any men." This sort of writing, many times more striking when read in the context of Wise's two books than
when sifted here, led Moses Coit Tyler to acclaim Wise as
"the one American who, upon the whole, was the most
powerful and brilliant prose-writer produced in this country during the colonial time." With this judgment we can
warmly agree.

Wise's political philosophy was as simple as it was unusual. There was nothing of the Mephistopheles in this country pastor, and we do not have to rummage through piles of confused verbiage for his few direct and comprehensible ideas. Although Wise in his modesty warned, "I shall go out of the common road, and take into an unusual and unbeaten path, wherein possibly I may fall into some thickets now and then, and be somewhat entangled," the reader is never for a moment led astray. Let us turn to the chief tenets of his political thought.

IV

A simple, even artless faith in the existence of higher law was the foundation of Wise's political thought. So comfortably at home was he with this ancient doctrine that he hardly paused to explain its significance or content. He seems to have assumed that his readers would understand exactly what he was talking about, and that they, too, would subscribe to the concept of a law of nature "written on men's hearts." This law of nature, wrote Wise, could be discovered and applied to current problems. It was for man, who was "most properly the subject of the law of nature" and "the favorite animal on earth," to employ "right reason" in the search for its principles.

That which is to be drawn from man's reason, flowing from the true current of that faculty, when unperverted, may be said to be the law of nature, on which account, the Holy Scriptures declare it written on men's hearts. For being endowed with a soul, you may know from yourself, how, and what you ought to act. (Rom.2:14.) These having not a law, are a law to themselves. So that the meaning is, when we acknowledge the law of nature to be the dictate of right reason, we must mean that the understanding of man is endowed with such a power, as to be able, from the contemplation of human condition to discover a necessity of living agreeably with this law;

and likewise to find out some principle, by which the precepts of it, may be clearly and solidly demonstrated. The way to discover the law of nature in our own state, is by a narrow watch, and accurate contemplation of our natural condition and propensions.

And to what final definition of natural law would the application of *recta ratio* lead Wise's average man? The Golden Rule—this was for Wise the sum of nature's rules for human conduct.

Others say this is the way to find out the law of nature, namely, if a man any way doubts, whether what he is going to do to another man be agreeable to the law of nature, then let him suppose himself to be in that other man's room, and by this rule effectually executed. A man must be a very dull scholar to nature not to make proficiency in the knowledge of her laws.

The law of nature, as it appeared in Wise's system, was of divine origin. He might have agreed with Grotius that God, once he had established the law of nature, could not alter its content or terms—"Just as even God, then, cannot cause that two times two should not make four, so He cannot cause that that which is intrinsically evil be not evil"—but as a Puritan divine he could not have subscribed to a secularized version of the higher law.

God has provided a rule for men in all their actions, obliging each one to the performance of that which is right, not only as to justice but likewise as to all other moral virtues, the which is nothing but the dictate of right reason founded in the soul of man.

The contrasting philosophies of Hobbes and Locke, or of Calhoun and Jefferson, demonstrate that any particular system of political thought is a reflection of the opinion held by its author about the nature of man. It should come as no surprise, then, that Wise, like Locke and Jefferson a believer in popular government, considered man to be inherently good and reasonable. Although "a principle of self-love and self-preservation is very predominant in every man's being," he is also possessed of "a sociable disposition" and "an affection or love to mankind in general." Wise seems to have freed his thinking completely from the harsh compulsions of the Calvinistic view of human nature. He would not even be drawn into a discussion of this matter.

In this discourse I shall waive the consideration of man's moral turpitude, but shall view him physically as a creature which God has made and furnished essentially with many ennobling immunities, which render him the most august animal in the world, and still, whatever has happened since his creation, he remains at the upper end of nature, and as such is a creature of a very noble character.

The most important of man's qualities was "sociableness"; if he lacked this characteristic, "every government would soon moulder and dissolve."

Man is a creature extremely desirous of his own preservation; of himself he is plainly exposed to many wants, unable to secure his own safety and maintenance without assistance of his fellows; and he is also able of returning kindness by the furtherance of mutual good; but yet man is often found to be malicious, insolent, and easily provoked, and as powerful in effecting mischief as he is ready in designing it. Now that such a creature may be preserved, it is necessary that he be sociable; that is, that he be capable and disposed to unite himself to those of his own species, and to regulate himself towards them, that they may have no fair reason to do him harm; but rather incline to promote his interests, and secure his rights and concerns. This then is a fundamental law of nature, that every man as far as in him lies, do maintain a sociableness with others, agreeable with the main end and disposition of human nature in general. For this

is very apparent, that reason and society render man the most
potent of all creatures. And finally, from the principles of
sociableness it follows as a fundamental law of nature, that man
is not so wedded to his own interest, but that he can make the
common good the mark of his aim; and hence he becomes
capacitated to enter into a civil state by the law of nature; for
without this property in nature, namely, sociableness, which is
for cementing of parts, every government would soon moulder
and dissolve.

No statement of Wise's was more central to his political
thought than this observation "that man is not so wedded
to his own interest, but that he can make the common
good the mark of his aim." Again and again he returned to
acclaim this quality as the basis of popular government,
often calling it "sociableness" and as often "fraternity." It
is good to hear from this son of the wilderness settlements
so powerful an exposition of the fraternal attitude. In our
latter-day efforts to proclaim liberty and equality through
all the lands—or to sit at home and ponder the fundamental contradiction of these two requisites of democracy
—we have tended to forget that there is a third element
in the celebrated trinity, fraternity, without which democracy would be little better than a mediocre anarchy. A
century and a half before Walt Whitman, Wise bore witness to the need for fraternal sympathy in free society, and
with a good deal less beating of his breast.

Wise was an enthusiastic believer in natural rights. Man
in a state of nature was "a free-born subject under the
crown of heaven, and owing homage to none but God
himself." To him belonged "an original liberty enstamped
upon his rational nature." Wise, like the other writers of
his time and school, did not attempt to catalogue the
contents of this liberty. It was enough for him to define
man's natural liberty as the "faculty of doing or omitting

things according to the direction of his judgment," with the qualification that "this liberty does not consist in a loose and ungovernable freedom, or an unbounded license of acting."

Such license is disagreeing with the condition and dignity of man, and would make man of a lower and meaner constitution than brute creatures, who in all their liberties are kept under a better and more rational government by their instincts. Therefore, as Plutarch says: Those persons only who live in obedience to reason, are worthy to be accounted free: they alone live as they will, who have learned what they ought to will. So that the true natural liberty of man, such as really and truly agrees to him must be understood, as he is guided and restrained by the ties of reason and laws of nature; all the rest is brutal, if not worse.

These were notions that Wise had taken from Pufendorf. From the *De Jure Naturae*, too, came Wise's radical assertion of natural equality, a doctrine of no particular currency in colonial New England. This concept was a corollary of the idea of natural rights, just as the latter was in its turn a corollary of the law of nature.

The third capital immunity belonging to man's nature, is an equality amongst men; which is not to be denied by the law of nature, till man has resigned himself with all his rights for the sake of a civil state, and then his personal liberty and equality is to be cherished and preserved to the highest degree, as will consist with all just distinctions amongst men of honor, and shall be agreeable with the public good. . . . Since, then, human nature agrees equally with all persons, and since no one can live a sociable life with another that does not own or respect him as a man, it follows as a command of the law of nature, that every man esteem and treat another as one who is naturally his equal, or who is a man as well as he.

And to his support he called Boethius by name and

Horace by implication. One of his most forceful sentences
appears to have been a literal translation of that magnificent

> *Pallida Mors aequo pulsat pede pauperum tabernas*
> *regumque turris.*

In Wise's thinking there was a close identity of natural
and civil rights, the second being simply that portion of
the first which men retained upon entrance into government, with adaptions to meet the conditions of organized
society.

It is certainly a great truth, namely, that man's original
liberty after it is resigned (yet under due restrictions) ought to
be cherished in all wise governments; or otherwise a man in
making himself a subject, he alters himself from a freeman into
a slave, which to do is repugnant to the law of nature. Also the
natural equality of men amongst men must be duly favored; in
that government was never established by God or nature, to
give one man a prerogative to insult over another, therefore, in
a civil, as well as in a natural state of being, a just equality is
to be indulged so far as that every man is bound to honor every
man, which is agreeable both with nature and religion, (1
Pet.2:17); Honor all men.

In turn, civil rights were for Wise "the rights of Englishmen." The Ipswich minister was a loyal colonial, and
the pages of his books are full of laudatory remarks about
Magna Charta and "the ancient liberties of the English
nation."

All Englishmen live and die by laws of their own making . . .
they are never pleased with upstart law-makers.

Englishmen hate an arbitrary power (politically considered)
as they hate the devil.

The very name of an arbitrary government is ready to put
an Englishman's blood into a fermentation; but when it really

comes and shakes its whip over their ears, and tells them it is their master, it makes them stark mad.

Wise, needless to say, considered himself very much an Englishman. Yet he was also a zealous New Englander. He could have cried with William Stoughton, "God sifted a Whole Nation that he might send Choice Grain over into this Wilderness," for he found on every side evidence of the particular solicitude that God indulged for Massachusetts and her sisters. Later American statesmen and writers were to assert that God had singled out this country for peculiar blessings, but in bestowing His grace had also bestowed a particular responsibility for the success of free government. Wise, no less proud and hortatory of New England than they were to be of all America, called upon his readers to give "recognition of what God has done for these famous English colonies" by following His way and that of nature with reverence and good example.

V

We have already noted that Wise considered "sociableness" to be a dominant trait of natural man. It was this "inclination to society" that caused men, acting in obedience to the dictates of nature, to seek out one another for mutual protection and support.

Every man, considered in a natural state, must be allowed to be free and at his own disposal; yet to suit man's inclinations to society, and in a peculiar manner to gratify the necessity he is in of public rule and order, he is impelled to enter into a civil community, and divests himself of his natural freedom, and puts himself under government, which amongst other things, comprehends the power of life and death over him, together with the authority to enjoin him some things to which he has an utter aversion, and to prohibit him other things for which he may have as strong an inclination—so that he may be often, under this authority, obliged to sacrifice his private for the public good; so that though man is inclined to society, yet he is driven to a combination by great necessity. For that the true and leading cause of forming governments and yielding up natural liberty, and throwing man's equality into a common pile to be new cast by rules of fellowship, was really and truly to guard themselves against the injuries men were liable to interchangeably; for none so good to man as man, and yet none a greater enemy.

Still following Pufendorf, but simplifying him greatly, Wise continues:

Let us conceive in our mind a multitude of men, all naturally free and equal, going about voluntarily to erect themselves into a new commonwealth. Now their condition being such, to bring themselves into a politic body they must needs enter into divers covenants.

1. They must interchangeably each man covenant to join in one lasting society, that they may be capable to concert the measures of their safety, by a public vote.

2. A vote or decree must then nextly pass to set up some particular species of government over them. And if they are joined in their first compact upon absolute terms to stand to the decision of the first vote concerning the species of government, then all are bound by the majority to acquiesce in that particular form thereby settled, though their own private opinions incline them to some other model.

3. After a decree has specified the particular form of government, then there will be need of a new covenant, whereby those upon whom sovereignty is conferred engage to take care of the common peace and welfare; and the subjects, on the other hand, to yield them faithful obedience; in which covenant is included that submission and union of wills by which a state may be conceived to be but one person.

Here is as precise a rendition of the social contract as

any political theorist has ever presented. Certainly Locke, who was later to get most of the credit for popularizing this notion, never expressed it in such plain terms as these. The contract as an explanation of the nature of government and society has long since been driven from the stage of political philosophy under a hail of ridicule and abuse. We now seek other, more sophisticated explanations of political obedience. Yet we should not impute to Wise too much naïveté in his political thought. Far more "subtile" men than he—Plato, Epicurus, Cicero, St. Augustine, Althusius, the Monarchomachs, Grotius, Locke, Hobbes, and Pufendorf—had subscribed to some version of this antique concept. And for Wise, it must be remembered, the mutual agreement of free men to form a community was no mere figment of the imagination. He had known men who had come in the beginning and had actually signed their names to church and plantation covenants. When the Mayflower company undertook to "covenant and combine our selves togeather into a civill body politick, for our better ordering and preservation," they were putting this theory to practical use. Moreover, the covenant was the foundation of the New England churches. All in all, it was for Wise a concept of compelling historical and logical force. And it is still, for all its *lacunae*, the noblest answer ever made to the perplexing question: Why should men who call themselves free owe their allegiance, obedience, and even their lives to government? If only for the purposes of our democratic dialectic, it is comforting to think of the "consent of the governed" as the foundation of government. Wise, in this instance, was a true American political thinker, one who pointed ahead to the Revolution by asserting that "English government and law is a charterparty settled by mutual compact between persons of all degrees in the nation."

Since all men were naturally free and equal, and since they had contracted one with another to form a society for the protection of an important residuum of that freedom and equality (so much as "shall be agreeable with the public good"), all political power rested in the keeping of the people. While they could commission others to exercise it for them, they alone could be said to possess it. "The first human subject and original of civil power is the people." Respectfully aware of the presence of God at all levels of human endeavor, Wise nevertheless refused to have anything to do with the Puritan fiction of God as the repository of political sovereignty. He could say, "It must needs be allowed as a fundamental principle relating to government, that (under God) all power is originally in the people," yet God was no part of the mechanics of establishing and maintaining civil government. The people were the focus of Wise's attention.

VI

Many Puritan ministers, most prominently Wise's old pastor John Eliot in *The Christian Commonwealth,* expressed a belief that God had ordained a definite type of government, although not all of them could agree on the identity of the divinely favored form. Wise did not share this point of view. "Nothing can be God's ordinance, but what he has particularly declared to be such; there is no particular form of civil government described in God's word, neither does nature prompt it. The government of the Jews was changed five times."

His own catalogue of the types of civil polity was the time-honored trinity—democracy, aristocracy, monarchy:

The forms of a regular state are three only, which forms arise from the proper and particular subject in which the supreme power resides. As,

1. A democracy, which is when the sovereign power is lodged in a council consisting of all the members, and where every member has the privilege of a vote. . . .

2. The second species of regular government is an aristocracy, and this is said then to be constituted when the people or assembly, united by a first covenant, and having thereby cast themselves into the first rudiments of a state, do then by common decree devolve the sovereign power on a council consisting of some select members; and these having accepted of the designation, are then properly invested with sovereign command, and then an aristocracy is formed.

3. The third species of a regular government is a monarchy, which is settled when the sovereign power is conferred on some one worthy person. It differs from the former, because a monarch, who is but one person in natural as well as in moral account, and so is furnished with an immediate power of exercising sovereign command in all instances of government; but the forenamed must needs have particular time and place assigned, but the power and authority is equal in each.

He also recognized that there could be "mixed governments." Indeed, being a loyal if colonial Englishman, he had kind words for the British Constitution:

Mixed governments, which are various and of divers kinds (not now to be enumerated), yet possibly the fairest in the world is that which has a regular monarchy, settled upon a noble democracy as its basis; and each part of the government is so adjusted by pacts and laws that render the whole constitution an elysium. It is said of the British empire, that it is such a monarchy as that, by the necessary subordinate concurrence of the lords and commons in the making and repealing all statutes or acts of parliament, it hath the main advantages of an aristocracy and of a democracy, and yet free from the disadvantages and evils of either. It is such a monarchy as, by most admirable temperament, affords very much to the industry, liberty, and happiness of the subject, and reserves enough for the majesty and prerogative of any king who will own his people as subjects, not as slaves. It is a kingdom that, of all the kingdoms of the world, is most like to the kingdom of Jesus Christ, whose yoke is easy and burden light.

For pure monarchy or aristocracy, in church or state, Wise had nothing but contempt. A constitutional monarchy, one in which the king "will own his people as subjects, not as slaves," and will rule in association with popular institutions, held no fears for him. But as for an absolute monarchy, of which the Papacy was this New England Puritan's horrid example, "God and wise nature were never propitious to the birth of this monster." He could conceive of excellent rule by a "select company of choice persons," but he saw clearly the inherent danger of aristocratic government: the fact that a small ruling group must eventually be corrupted by power and substitute "private will" for common weal as "the rule of their personal and ministerial actions."

For what is it that cunning and learned men cannot make the world swallow as an article of their creed, if they are once invested with an uncontrollable power, and are to be the standing orators to mankind in matters of faith and obedience?

And so, Wise concluded, "Considering how great an interest is embarked, and how frail a bottom we trust," we must shun the monarchical and aristocratic solutions to the problems of ecclesiastical and civil polity, "especially if we can find a safer way home." The way, of course, was democracy. Wise was by experience and reason a true (if doubtless somewhat unsophisticated) democrat. Thanks to his training in the town meeting and his belief in popular sovereignty, he could not have been otherwise. "A democracy in church or state is a very honorable and regular government according to the dictates of right reason." Equally important:

This form of government appears in the greatest part of the world to have been the most ancient. For that reason seems to show it to be most probable, that when men (being originally in a condition of natural freedom and equality) had thoughts of joining in a civil body, would without question be inclined to administer their common affairs by their common judgment, and so must necessarily, to gratify that inclination, establish a democracy; neither can it be rationally imagined that fathers of families, being yet free and independent, should in a moment or little time take off their long delight in governing their own affairs, and devolve all upon some single sovereign commander; for that it seems to have been thought more equitable that what belonged to all should be managed by all, when all had entered by compact into one community.

Democracy for Wise was, of course, a simple concept, the philosophical reflection of a simple form of government, the town meeting.

A democracy is then erected, when . . . the right of determining all matters relating to the public safety is actually placed in a general assembly of the whole people; or by their own compact and mutual agreement, determine themselves the proper subject for the exercise of sovereign power. And to complete this state, and render it capable to exert its power to answer the end of a civil state, these conditions are necessary.

(1) That a certain time and place be assigned for assembling.

(2) That when the assembly be orderly met, as to time and place, that then the vote of the majority must pass for the vote of the whole body.

(3) That magistrates be appointed to exercise the authority of the whole for the better despatch of business of every day's occurrence, who also may, with more mature diligence, search into more important affairs; and if in case any thing happens

of greater consequence, may report it to the assembly, and be
peculiarly serviceable in putting all public decrees into execution,
because a large body of people is almost useless in respect of
the last service, and of many others as to the more particular
application and exercise of power. Therefore it is most agreeable
with the law of nature, that they institute their officers to act
in their name and stead.

Wise seems to have had little grasp of the idea of representative democracy. It is safe to say, however, that he
looked upon the General Court, if not the royal governor,
as an instrument of popular government, since its members were the elected representatives of the town meetings.
As a matter of dialectic, Wise was in no position to argue
too warmly for representative democracy. His primary
concern was to defend congregational autonomy. The General Court may have been an essential part of civil government, but he did not want, indeed wrote his books directly
against, an ecclesiastical version of this provincial assembly.

VII

Wise was no leveler or doctrinaire populist. Like Jefferson, he not only conceded but pointed with satisfaction to
the existence of an *aristoi*. Yet the "best men" were not
best by reason of wealth or blood; the only aristocracy that
a free man could recognize was that of learning or virtue
or wisdom. Wise went back to Aristotle for support of
the principle that "nothing is more suitable to nature, than
that those who excel in understanding and prudence, should
rule and control those who are less happy in those advantages." Yet he, again like Jefferson, left it to the people to
determine by free suffrage whether or not such men were
actually to govern, and he granted them the power of
recall along with that of election. "Nor does natural fitness

for government make a man presently governor over another. . . . It would be the greatest absurdity to believe, that nature actually invests the wise with a sovereignty over the weak." Wise developed this point even further by insisting that it was the business of society to keep the road open for others, to preserve a real equality of opportunity. Himself a natural aristocrat who had risen from the bottom of a stratified society, Wise could write with sincerity, "The parity of our descent inclines us to keep up the like parity by our laws, and to yield the precedency to nothing but to superior virtue and wisdom."

We have heard enough from Wise to know that he was a strong advocate of "the venerable major vote." The simplicity of his political thought is manifest in his uncritical acceptance of this doctrine and apparent incapacity to comprehend its dangers. But Locke, too, was oblivious to the perils that John Adams, Hamilton, and Calhoun—all of them skeptics, it should be noted—never wearied of voicing. In a political entity as homogeneous as that of colonial Ipswich there was little danger of a tyranny of the majority. Even Calhoun, it must be remembered, considered majority rule a sufficient support of constitutional government "if the whole community had the same interest." Wise had one splendid passage concerning majority rule, in which he made clear his democratic dedication to the rule of "one person, one vote":

But in every distinct house of these states, the members are equal in their vote: the most ayes make the affirmative vote, and most noes the negative. They do not weigh the intellectual furniture, or other distinguishing qualifications of the several voters, in the scales of the golden rule of fellowship; they only add up the ayes and the noes, and so determine the suffrage of the house.

At one point at least Wise disagreed sharply with the

more radical adherents of the natural-rights school of the
late eighteenth century. Thomas Paine, for example, believed that "Society in every state is a blessing, but Government, even in its best state, is but a necessary evil."
Wise, to the contrary, took a more traditional view of the
character of civil government. So necessary, such "an incomparable benefit to mankind" was government, that
natural man was "driven" into it willy-nilly. Yet this was
no hardship, for:

> Government is the greatest blessing in the world, of a worldly
> nature; it is felony, cheaper by far to the loosers, to plunder men
> of their estate and wealth, nay, and of their lives too, then to
> despoil them of government; for by the latter you harass and
> worry them in the world with plagues and miseries, worse than
> death itself, that the basest is far better than no government; a
> churlish tyranny is better than an insolent anarchy, where
> men are without law, and all hail fellows, not well, but badly
> met.

Every defender of a particular political theory must be
prepared to answer the question: What are the true ends of
the government you advocate? Wise had a reply that arose
naturally from his theories of compact and consent, and it
was a far cry from that of the Puritan oligarchy. The protection of the free man and preservation of his freedom
and equality, not the maintenance of the true religion, were
the purposes for which government was instituted. In this
respect Wise echoed Locke and anticipated the Declaration
of Independence.

> The end of all good government is to cultivate humanity,
> and promote the happiness of all, and the good of every man
> in all his rights, his life, liberty, estate, honor, etc., without
> injury or abuse done to any.

One of the oldest devices in political theory is the comparison of the state with the human body. Wise presented his version thus quaintly:

A civil state is a compound moral person . . . which may be conceived as though the whole state was now become but one man; . . . And by way of resemblance the aforesaid being may be thus anatomized.

(1) The sovereign power is the soul infused, giving life and motion to the whole body.

(2) Subordinate officers are the joints by which the body moves.

(3) Wealth and riches are the strength.

(4) Equity and laws are the reason.

(5) Counsellors the memory.

(6) *Salus Populi*, or the happiness of the people is the end of its being, or main business to be attended and done.

(7) Concord amongst the members and all estates, is the health.

(8) Sedition is sickness, and civil war death.

The right of resistance had an inferior standing in Wise's political thought. This was certainly not true of most prominent writers of the natural-law school. Locke, for example, devoted his longest chapter to "The Dissolution of Government," and the right of resistance, even of revolution, is openly proclaimed in the Declaration of Independence. But Wise, who had come forth to defend an established church-democracy against an encroaching aristocracy, was neither by nature nor purpose a revolutionary political thinker. If anything, he was an unabashed traditionalist. Had he been questioned about his purpose, he would have proclaimed simply: *stare super antiquas vias*. And for him the ancient ways upon which New England stood were the ways of ecclesiastical democracy. In his interpretation of the Cambridge Platform of 1649 as the foundation of democracy in the New England churches he was reading a few too many popular principles into a theocratic constitution, yet he was apparently quite sincere in his belief that it sponsored congregational autonomy. "And this is our constitution, and why cannot we be pleased?"

His conception of the right of resistance or revolution was therefore not at all well defined. Like others of his school he maintained that "the prince who strives to subvert the fundamental laws of the society is the traitor and rebel," but he made no attempt to fix standards for determining when the contract had been broken and the people thus entitled to reassert their constituent power. Wise cannot be cited as an authority in favor of the right of resistance. Had he written his tracts in 1688, he would doubtless have given more attention to this important corollary of the contract theory. Had he written them in 1765 or 1776, he might have outdone Paine and Jefferson in proclaiming the necessity of resistance and revolution. Like all American political thinkers he shaped theory to fact.

VIII

All these major and minor principles add up to a coherent and impressive system of thought, the more impressive by reason of the time and place in which it was expounded. Writing in defense of a form of ecclesiastical government that he considered to be the established order, Wise ranged far afield from his original purpose and ended up by rendering a magnificent apologia for political liberty. Like Hooker and Williams, he saw clearly what Cotton, Winthrop, Davenport, and the Mathers refused to acknowledge: the bridge leading from the church covenant to the social contract, from congregational autonomy to self-government, from democracy in the church to democracy in the state. Unlike his liberal or radical predecessors, he retraced the course their minds had traveled and justified

Congregationalism by its similarity to the first and most "natural" of civil governments—democracy. In doing all this—in linking up ecclesiasticism and politics and arguing from the latter toward the former—he made a notable contribution to American intellectual history, one that has never been properly acknowledged.

Wise claims the attention of the historian of ideas for at least three other reasons. First, he was not just a libertarian but, as much as one could be in that time and place, a thoroughly democratic thinker. No other colonist, whether writer or man of affairs, was so bold in his use of words like "democracy" and "equality" or so genuinely willing to champion the radical concepts they expressed. Second, he was the model of all the hundreds of New England preachers who received and reaffirmed the liberating principles of natural law and rights. His books are evidence that the political thought of the Revolution had been part of men's thinking for several generations before 1765. Few men moved so far as Wise into the radical wing of the natural-law school, but many of his ideas about higher law and the contract were widely accepted articles of political faith. Finally, the fact that Wise, the most prominent of early American exponents of natural law, went to Pufendorf rather than Locke for his lessons in political theory, proves that the latter was not, after all, the exclusive oracle of the American libertarians. They were heirs of a great tradition of which Locke was only one of many eminent apostles.

It would be pleasant to report that Wise's teachings, even if forgotten today, were a vital force in the American Revolution. The fact is that his ideas were quite without effect, even upon the minds of the Massachusetts patriots. Although his two books were reprinted in 1772 and purchased in large quantities by such celebrated Revolutionary figures as Timothy Pickering (6 copies), Ebenezer Dorr (3), William Dawes (100!), Artemas Ward (6), Rev. Edward Emerson of Concord (24), John Scollay (4), and Tapping Reeve of Litchfield, rarely do we find Wise's name quoted in the leading tracts and pamphlets of the time. Rarely, of course, do we find the rebellious colonists calling any of their fellow countrymen to witness, for they were far too pleased with the advice tendered by Locke, Sidney, Cicero, and St. Paul to pay much attention to native prophecy. There were two special reasons for Wise's oblivion. First, his books were out of print until 1772, while those of the others, especially Locke's *Civil Government*, were available in numerous editions. Even when reprinted, Wise's works seem to have been invoked largely for Congregational purposes. Second, the point has already been made that Wise's purpose, the defense of the Congregational principle, persuaded him to say as little as possible about the right of resistance. For this reason more than any other he was ignored by a people for whom the most useful principle of the natural-rights theory was the right of resistance.

Forgotten by the late eighteenth century, Wise has been forgotten ever since. That he will remain a shadowy figure in the political and intellectual history of American democracy, a formidable person with a lesser reputation than he doubtless deserves, seems altogether probable. History plays strange jokes, and just as we will never celebrate July 2 as Independence Day, so we will never see Wise taught in high school. This is unfortunate, for he has as valid a claim to our patriotic attention as Roger Williams or any other figure in colonial history. There were brave democrats before Samuel Adams and Thomas Jefferson, none braver than John Wise.

Wise died on April 8, 1725, less than two months after

the death of his wife. He remained strong to the end in the principles he had so passionately embraced. "He told me in the beginning of his Sickness," said his son-in-law, John White, "that he had been a Man of Contention, but the State of the Churches making it necessary; upon the most serious Review, he could say he had *Fought a Good Fight;* and had comfort in reflecting upon the same." Wise was buried in the yard of his church and rests there to this day under a stone that proclaims:

> For Talents, Piety and Learning he shone
> As a Star of the first magnitude.

Since Wise never did care for praise, it would be more to his liking were we to conclude with his own words of good cheer for his and this and every other generation of American democracy:

Hold your hold, brethren! *Et validis incumbite remis,* pull up well upon your oars, you have a rich cargo, and I hope we shall escape shipwreck; for according to the latest observation, if we are not within sight, yet we are not far from harbor; and though the noise of great breakers which we hear imports hazard, yet I hope daylight and good piloting will secure all.

4

JONATHAN MAYHEW

Herald of Revolution

In his last doughty years John Adams of Quincy was much given to reminiscing about the coming of the Revolution, particularly with Southern correspondents who refused to acknowledge gracefully the primacy of Massachusetts. Although the old man of 1818 is not always to be trusted as he recreates the events of 1765 and 1776, many of his observations have stood up bravely under the battering of modern scholarship. One such musing about men long dead and events forgotten was this enumeration of the men of Massachusetts chiefly responsible for the "awakening and revival of American principles and feelings" in the early 1760's:

The characters the most conspicuous, the most ardent and influential in this revival, from 1760 to 1766, were, first and foremost, before all and above all, James Otis; next to him was

116

Oxenbridge Thacher; next to him, Samuel Adams; next to him, John Hancock; then Dr. Mayhew.

The most instructive lesson that we learn from this heroic muster is one that Adams himself apparently overlooked: the fact that of the five Massachusetts colonials most prominent in the first overt phase of the Revolution four were men of affairs (two lawyers, a politician, a merchant) and only one a man of God—and he the fifth in line. Had any such roll of Commonwealth leaders been drawn up in 1650 or 1700, or even so late as 1750, the influence of the pulpit would surely have been more pronounced. The first and second of these names indicate a major transformation in the character of colonial leadership which took place in the decades immediately preceding the Revolution. By 1760 the pulpit had lost much of its direct political influence, for a variety of reasons upon which most historians agree: the growth of science and humanistic learning, the expansion of trade and population, the establishment of the popular press, and the abrupt rise of the legal profession. The day of the preacher was at an end; the day of the lawyer had dawned. Yet at least one minister stood fast in the great tradition. As Adams wrote:

Another gentleman, who had great influence in the commencement of the Revolution, was Doctor Jonathan Mayhew, a descendant of the ancient governor of Martha's Vineyard. This divine had raised a great reputation both in Europe and America, by the publication of a . . . sermon in 1750, on the 30th of January, on the subject of passive obedience and nonresistance, in which the saintship and martyrdom of King Charles the First are considered, seasoned with wit and satire superior to any in Swift or Franklin. It was read by everybody; celebrated by friends, and abused by enemies. During the reigns of King George the First and King George the Second, the reigns of the Stuarts, the two Jameses and the two Charleses were in general disgrace in England. In America they had always been held in abhorrence. The persecutions and cruelties suffered by their ancestors under those reigns, had been transmitted by history and tradition, and Mayhew seemed to be raised up to revive all their animosities against tyranny, in church and state, and at the same time to destroy their bigotry, fanaticism, and inconsistency. . . . To draw the character of Mayhew, would be to transcribe a dozen volumes. This transcendent genius threw all the weight of his great fame into the scale of his country in 1761, and maintained it there with zeal and ardor till his death, in 1766.

This is high praise, yet Mayhew surely earned it. For nineteen years his pulpit was the storm center of Boston theology, and for almost as long the religious outpost of colonial resistance to British political and ecclesiastical encroachment. One of the last of the great colonial preachers, he was at the same time the rough-voiced herald of a new day for religious and political liberty. Rationalism and Whiggery had no more outspoken an exponent.

I

Jonathan Mayhew was born at Chilmark, Martha's Vineyard, October 8, 1720. He was the third of four sons of the Reverend Experience Mayhew and his wife Remember, daughter of Shearjashub Bourne of Sandwich. The Mayhews of the Vineyard were a family "respectable in all its stages." Jonathan's great-great-grandfather, Thomas Mayhew, had acquired title to Martha's Vineyard in 1641 under both the Stirling and Gorges patents and had lived there from 1646 to 1682 as proprietor, magistrate, and missionary. His son, Thomas, Jr., had come to the island from the mainland in 1642 as the first permanent settler and had served, even before John Eliot, as an apostle to the Indians. Their immediate descendants, John and his

son Experience, were like them tillers of the soil and con-
verters of the "salvages." The last of this line was rewarded
for his labors in 1720 with one of the first Harvard honorary degrees.

The education of Jonathan Mayhew came from three
sources: his father, Harvard, and himself. From Experience (and doubtless from Remember, too) proceeded the
better part of his early schooling, in which he acquired a
satisfactory acquaintance with Greek and Latin, an aston-
ishing knowledge of "the inspired writings," and a profound mistrust of religious and political Calvinism. From
Harvard in 1744 he received his degree, the outward sign
of an intense formal education for which he had paid
dearly. A lack of funds several times interrupted his residence at Cambridge, and the effort to make up for lost
time and studies played havoc with his health. (It did not,
on the other hand, seem to interfere with his youthful
relish for alcoholic sport.) This was the Harvard of Edward
Holyoke, that "polite Gentleman, of a noble commanding
presence," called "Guts" by his devoted students and worse
things by the orthodox clergy, for whom the college, especially after Leverett's famous presidency (1708-1724), was
a liberal thorn in the side of expiring Calvinism. Holyoke,
who reigned for thirty-two years (1737-1769), had an
abiding influence on his students. The roll of those who
learned of truth and freedom from this eminent divine is
a *dramatis personae* of the Massachusetts phase of the
American Revolution: Samuel and John Adams, James
Otis, James Bowdoin, Oxenbridge Thacher, John Hancock,
Timothy Pickering, Joseph Warren, Robert Treat Paine,
and Jonathan Mayhew. Finally, from himself Mayhew received a continuing education that ceased only with death.
Throughout his career he studied with peculiar intensity,
ranging the fields of polite and polemic learning from

Hebrew grammar to the latest sermons from London, from
Harrington to Voltaire, from Genesis to Revelation. At
one stage in his ministerial progress he studied himself into
a state of physical collapse.

In March 1747 the West Church in Boston, which had
already achieved some notoriety for unorthodox tendencies
in its ten-year existence, invited Mayhew to become its
second pastor. In the interval since his graduation from
Harvard he had been moving steadily away from the five
points of Calvinism, thanks to study of Samuel Clarke and
Locke at Cambridge and a mutually fruitful and liberaliz-
ing residence with the celebrated Dr. Ebenezer Gay of
Hingham. Mayhew's reputation had run before him: Although eleven ministers, including Mayhew's father and
Dr. Gay, assembled from the country churches to welcome
the new minister at his ordination, no representative of a
Boston church put in an appearance. Mayhew eventually
came to cordial social and even ecclesiastical terms with
several of the city's clergy, but he was always catalogued
as an "amiable heretic." He never joined the Boston Association of Congregational Ministers.

Mayhew's pastorate was short but honorable. For nineteen years he served his large and distinguished congregation with warmth and imagination, and his passing was
mourned with unforced grief. "In this Charge he continued
'till his death, loving his people, and by them beloved."
However much his more peace-loving parishioners might
have protested against the advanced and acid observations
that he delivered almost every Sunday, they recognized in
him a man of superior attainments as pastor, teacher, and
friend. At his death it was written:

In him, *it may be truly said,* his disconsolate Widow has
lost a kind and affectionate Husband, his children a tender and
faithful Parent, his Family a humane and indulgent Master;

the Poor *of all Denominations* a charitable and constant Friend; his Church a worthy, learned, social, virtuous and religious Pastor; this Continent a resolute and strong Defender of its religious Independency; and Mankind a bold and nervous Assertor of their rights, and that Liberty wherewith Christ has made them free.

Mayhew's congregation supported him loyally in his daring forays into unexplored ecclesiastical country. He could write his father without cant or conceit, "My people are united, attentive, and kind." His character shines through his sermons and letters in a pattern that cannot be misconstrued, and what his own words withhold those of his friends and enemies convey. Here was a man quite comprehensible to the modern mind—candid, sincere, diligent, amiable, publicity-conscious, supremely aware of his many powers and few limitations, and constantly "on the run." To the meek, mild, and decent he was a gentle friend and counselor; to the "hypocritical, and the dogmatical and censorious" he was "bold and severe," at least in print. More than one literary antagonist came through a joust with Mayhew feeling that Old Nick himself had thrown acid in his face. His style is straightforward if not exactly dazzling, while from all accounts he was a speaker of genuine eloquence.

From his first day in the West Church pulpit Mayhew was a man with a name and mission. His liberal preaching and pamphleteering won him immediate fame. His very first book, *Seven Sermons . . . Preached as a Lecture in the West Meeting House,* brought him an Aberdeen D.D., in February 1750. As a conscientious and effective member of the Harvard Board of Overseers he won the respect if not always the approval of such colleagues as Thomas Hutchinson. He corresponded widely with persons in England sympathetic to the causes of independency and colo-

nial liberty, most notably from 1759 to his death with the
third of those gentlemen named Thomas Hollis who were
so pleasantly and purposefully philanthropic to Harvard
College. To James Otis, Samuel Adams, James Bowdoin,
R. T. Paine, John Winthrop, Stephen Sewall, and Harrison
Gray he was a valued friend. His radical theology and
liberal politics made him one of the most controversial yet
respected figures in all New England.

II

Mayhew's lifelong campaign against New England orthodoxy was little more than a series of opportunistic raids on
a once-mighty army left defenseless by desertion. Another
of his ecclesiastical struggles, waged in 1763-1764 over a
definite issue with a proudly armed band of adversaries, was
at once more dramatic and historically significant. This
was the celebrated literary debate between Mayhew and
certain Anglican apologists over the designs of the Church
of England upon the American colonies. The "Mayhew
Controversy," as it is known in the history of the Episcopal
Church in America, was actually three battles in one. At
first simply an exchange of broadsides over the activities
of the Society for the Propagation of the Gospel in Foreign
Parts, it soon turned to a more fundamental issue: the
propriety of establishing an American episcopate. And at
bottom, of course, it was yet another phase of the conflict
between American political independence and British authority.

A word of background will set the stage of the Mayhew
Controversy. For almost a century and a half the most
awesome bogey under the Puritan bed had been the vision
of an Anglican Bishop of Boston. Even such elementary
attempts to bring the Church of England to New England

as the scheme of Governor Andros to use the South Meet-inghouse for Anglican worship were enough to give the Puritan clergy nightmares of an American Laud. Most of the time this issue lay dormant, but only because conditions in the colonies and England rendered impractical any general extension of the episcopal system. By the middle of the eighteenth century, however, the establishment of an American episcopate seemed a distinct possibility. Leading colonial Episcopalians, beset from the North by the never-flagging hostility of independence and from the South by the growing autonomy of their own parishes, were outspoken in their desire for one or more bishops. At the same time, the Society for the Propagation of the Gospel, established in 1701 to carry on missionary work in those corners of the King's dominions where provision for a ministry was inadequate, had aroused much anxiety in New England by settling its missionaries in populated regions rather than on the frontier. By 1760 there were thirty Anglican ministers propagating their own version of the gospel in New England towns. Finally, many New Englanders of 1760 suspected that schemes for strengthening the colonial position of the Church of England were tied in with the Crown's determination to reassert its power over the increasingly headstrong Americans. From 1763 to the outbreak of Revolution this question was paramount in the minds of many Americans, for whom an Anglican bishop and a Stamp Tax collector were co-villains in a plot to subvert their ancient liberties. Actually, the threat from this quarter was not half so perilous as Mayhew and his colleagues believed. This, however, is a judgment made with the assistance of hindsight.

The principal stages in the Mayhew Controversy were these: (1) a newspaper article published in Boston in February 1763, which seized upon the death of an Anglican

missionary in Braintree as an excuse for attacking the
practice of the Society for the Propagation of the Gospel
of placing its missionaries in settled towns; (2) a return
to these aspersions by the Rev. East Apthorp, missionary
in Cambridge, entitled *Considerations on the Institution
and Conduct of the Society;* (3) a quick retaliation by
Mayhew, *Observations on the Charter and Conduct of the
Society;* (4) a series of replies to Mayhew, one of them
from England; (5) two further rejoinders by Mayhew,
A Defence of the Observations in reply to the most important American attack, and *Remarks on an Anonymous
Tract* in reply to the British pamphlet; (6) a final pamphlet by Apthorp, in which he reviewed the entire controversy and got in a few last blows for the Church of England and the Society. Mayhew thought it unworthy of an
answer and put an end to this war of words by ignoring it.

He is a brave scholar indeed who can read over these
mildewed pages with any feeling other than exasperated
boredom. Both Mayhew and his opponents are guilty a
thousand times over of all the sins of eighteenth-century
pamphleteering, especially the practice of endless repetition
of a simple and easily stated major premise. Only the British
An Answer to Doctor Mayhew's Observation, which was
eventually traced back to Thomas Secker, Archbishop of
Canterbury, and Mayhew's *Remarks* are sufficiently well-
ordered and well-mannered to merit modern consideration.
In this tract Mayhew rose above the secondary questions
whether the Society had, as he claimed, misread its charter,
misapplied its funds, and misrepresented the state of religion in New England, for he challenged the Anglican
hierarchy to deny that the real purpose of planting bishops
in America was to establish the Church of England. In
his *Remarks* he asked in more polite and therefore more

convincing fashion what he had already asked with passion in the *Observations:*

> Will they never let us rest in peace, *except where all the weary are at rest?* Is it not enough, that they persecuted us out of the old world? Will they pursue us into the new to convert us here?—*compassing sea and land to make us proselytes,* while they neglect the heathen and heathenish plantations! What other new world remains as a sanctuary for us from their oppressions, in case of need? Where is the COLUMBUS to explore one for, and pilot us to it, before we are consumed by the flames, or deluged in a flood of episcopacy?

We cannot pass this off as the fulmination of a New England dissenter ready to believe anything of Canterbury or Rome. For Mayhew, even in his most detached moments, the danger of the established church was clear and present, and he echoed faithfully the fears of like-minded countrymen. Again we hear from John Adams:

> Where is the man to be found at this day, when we see Methodistical bishops, bishops of the church of England, and bishops, archbishops, and Jesuits of the church of Rome, with indifference, who will believe that the apprehension of Episcopacy contributed fifty years ago, as much as any other cause, to arouse the attention, not only of the inquiring mind, but of the common people, and urge them to close thinking on the constitutional authority of parliament over the colonies? This, nevertheless, was a fact as certain as any in the history of North America. The objection was not merely to the office of a bishop, though even that was dreaded, but to the authority of parliament, on which it must be founded. . . . All sensible men knew that this system could not be effected but by act of parliament; and if parliament could do this, they could do all things; and what security could Americans have for life, liberty, property, or religion?

In this passage the discerning old patriot gives the most plausible explanation for the intensity of Mayhew's loudly voiced convictions: the tight connection between the aspirations of the Anglican bishops and designs of the Tory ministers. Certainly it was known to all men that the established church was heavily committed to the prerogative state, that it had supported various plans to subject corporate and proprietary governments to the control of the Crown, and that Parliament claimed the final power to legislate religions in and out of the colonies (as it demonstrated in 1774 with the passage of the Quebec Act). Mayhew was perhaps more vocal than the people about him, but not much more alarmed. If we smile at him for baiting the Church of England, we must also smile at Otis for assailing the writs of assistance, at Samuel Adams for bombarding the Boston press, and at Henry for striking his poses in the House of Burgesses.

One joke that history played on Mayhew is too edifying to be consigned to a footnote. Elizabeth Mayhew, his daughter and only surviving child, was married after the Revolution to Peter Wainwright of Liverpool. Their son, who bore the proud dissenting name of Jonathan Mayhew Wainwright, was from 1852 to 1854 Episcopal Bishop of New York. This grandson of the man who had no use for bishops answered Rufus Choate's remark that the Pilgrims had founded "a state without a king and a church without a bishop" with the lofty rebuke, "There cannot be a church without a bishop."

There is little that need be said of Mayhew's other labors for religious and political freedom except to point out that no controversy with British authority was too trifling to enlist his tongue and pen. Twice he was at the front of those struggling for colonial liberties. In 1762 he was the penman, orator, and chief strategist of the Harvard Board

of Overseers in its successful resistance to the establishment
of a second college in Hampshire County. This was an
engagement particularly to Mayhew's liking, for he was
able to deliver stout blows to both Calvinists, who had
begun the movement for a new college out of discontent
with Harvard's "liberal" tendencies, and Anglicans, whose
natural leader, the newly arrived Governor Bernard, seized
this heaven-sent opportunity to embarrass and even under-
mine the citadel of Congregationalism.

The resistance of Massachusetts to the ill-begotten Stamp
Act needed no Mayhew to goad it into action. Indeed, had
the Boston mob listened more attentively to the strong but
moderate counsels of men like Mayhew, this exciting affair
would have made a far prettier chapter in the history of
American patriotism. In any case, the kind of leadership
offered by Otis and Adams on the political front was
matched by the exhortations of Mayhew, Charles Chauncy,
and Samuel Cooper from their famous pulpits. No sermon
did more to stiffen resistance than Mayhew's memorable
discourse of August 25, 1765, on Galatians v, 12-13. ("I
would they were even cut off which trouble you. For,
brethren, ye have been called unto liberty; only *use* not
liberty for an occasion to the flesh, but by love serve one
another.") No sermon expressed more exultantly yet humbly the sense of popular relief over the repeal of the Stamp
Act than *The Snare Broken*, May 23, 1766, which Mayhew,
always thoroughly respectful of the power of the press, had
in print within six days of delivery. The first of these won
Mayhew an undeservedly bad reputation among those ready
to believe the worst of him. A leader of the mob that
sacked Hutchinson's house August 26, 1765, dropped an
offhand remark to the effect that he had been aroused by
Mayhew's sermon; and although Mayhew and the Lieu-
tenant-Governor immediately exchanged cordial letters of

sympathy and respect, the outspoken minister was tarred
with the brush of inciting mob violence.

III

The fact that most of Mayhew's friends were secular in
vocation and political in taste tells us a great deal about
his life, work, and thought. He saw more clearly than any
other man in New England that the fight for "private
judgment" in religion and for personal liberty in politics
was one grand battle in which all patriots could join with
a will. Mayhew's political philosophy was the natural corollary of the liberal gospel he preached. Before we can ex-
plore his politics we must understand his religion.

Mayhew's place in theology is most precisely fixed by
saluting him as an important forerunner of American Unitarianism. Samuel A. Eliot devoted the first volume of his
history of Unitarianism, *Heralds of a Liberal Faith,* to the
"period of Protest," which he found "to begin with the
ordination of Jonathan Mayhew in 1747 and to last until
the election of Henry Ware to the Hollis Professorship of
Divinity at Harvard in 1805." John Adams wrote to
Ebenezer Morse in 1815, "Sixty years ago my own minister, Rev. Lemuel Briant, Dr. Jonathan Mayhew, of the
West Church in Boston, Rev. Mr. Shute, of Hingham, Rev.
John Brown, of Cohasset, and, perhaps equal to all, if not
above all, Rev. Dr. Gay, of Hingham, were Unitarians."
Whether Gay or Briant or Mayhew was the first Unitarian
is impossible to state, for Unitarianism was the outgrowth
of a process to which many men contributed their doubts
and talents. In any case, within a few years of his ordination Mayhew was recognized as New England's most outspoken Arian, as a preacher who, if he could never satisfy
his own mind and soul concerning the identity of Jesus

Christ and his relation to God, could none the less insist with conviction that "God was ONE and SUPREME." In a note to a volume of sermons published in 1755 he rejected —somewhat obliquely, to be sure—the doctrine of the trinity.

The impact of Mayhew's religious teachings was felt far beyond the confines of Unitarianism. For most men, after all, the nature of the trinity was a question of doctrinal disputation, and Mayhew's active beliefs would have been the same, and enjoyed the same widespread influence, whether he thought God to be one or three. Mayhew was important because he preached a gospel that rejected flatly the five points of Calvinism. The tenets of orthodox Puritanism—predestination, limited atonement, total depravity, irresistibility of grace, and perseverance of the saints— had no place in his theology. The God of the Mathers, and especially the God of Jonathan Edwards's harrowing Enfield sermon, *Sinners in the Hands of an Angry God,* was not the God of Jonathan Mayhew. Nor did he care for the Calvinism of the Great Awakening any more than for that of the Great Migration. He wrote his father that he had heard George Whitefield preach a sermon "which was a very low, confused, puerile, conceited, ill-natur'd, enthusiastick, etc. Performance as ever I heard in my Life."

Not satisfied with rejecting and ridiculing orthodoxy, Mayhew developed a substitute creed that seemed to him the only plausible religion for the free and thinking man in the good society. First among his principles was his exposition of the nature of God, who for him was as much a God of love and reason as He was for orthodox Puritans a God of anger and whim. He is "a merciful and faithful Creator; a compassionate Parent; a gentle Master,"

who governs his great family, his universal Kingdom, according to those general rules and maxims which are in themselves most

wise and good, such as the wisest and best kings govern by. . . .
Perfect goodness, love itself, is his very essence, in a peculiar
sense; immeasurable, immutable, universal and everlasting love.

As God is a "gentle Master," so is he a "righteous Judge"
who "inspects our conduct" not with the "malice of an *In-
quisitor*" but with "the bowels of a parent." There is a
"natural" difference between right and wrong—"Truth
and moral rectitude are things fixed, stable and uniform,
having their foundation in the nature of things"—and each
of us is fully capable, thanks to a rational nature and free
will, to choose the one over the other. Man's covenant with
God is one of grace *and* works: He who strives consciously
to be good and kind, in the image of Christ, has within
him a full measure of divine grace. The reward, of course,
is eternal life, and there is no man who cannot win it. Indeed, most of us can expect it, for we aim at eternity from
this point of vantage: We are all disposed by nature to
follow the Christian ethic. In defiance of the very core of
the orthodox creed, Mayhew proclaimed the rank absurdity
of the doctrine of total depravity. Man for him was essentially good. This belief permitted him to engage in preaching that was profoundly moralistic. He expected his listeners to behave as circumspectly as their Puritan ancestors
because it was the reasonable rather than necessary thing
to do. In sum, Mayhew expounded a humanistic, liberal,
rational, "natural religion." Only his calling, and an ultimate faith in the God of his New England fathers, restrained him from passing over into an attitude of outright
deism. He was showered with Newtonianism but drenched
with Scripture.

Students of religious philosophy get little satisfaction
from Mayhew, for he was, as his Episcopal contemporary
Samuel Johnson observed, a "loose thinker." Yet he could

hardly have been otherwise—by the nature of his task, which was to grope through the dark fog of centuries of scholastic authoritarianism for a few simple truths about man and God, and by the nature of his religion, which placed emphasis on practice rather than speculation. His opinion of the *cymini sectores*, the splitters of doctrinal hairs, is plain in this passage from one of his first sermons:

It is infinitely dishonorable to the all-good and perfect Governor of the world to imagine, that he has suspended the eternal salvation of men upon any niceties of speculation; or that any one, who honestly aims at finding the truth, and at doing the will of his Maker, shall be finally discarded, because he fell into some erroneous opinions.

In rejecting authority in religion, Mayhew rejected the stuff upon which authority feeds: speculation. The important thing was not to meditate on the size of God's angels but to love God by doing good. What that meant, any man could understand through the use of his own reason and the revealed word, each of which counsels us to love one another. What Samuel Eliot Morison has written of Boston Unitarianism, that it "was not a fixed dogma, but a point of view that was receptive, searching, inquiring, and yet devout," may with peculiar emphasis be written of the religion of this early Boston Unitarian. We are bound to take him as he was, in the words of his friend Harrison Gray, "a great advocate for primitive Christianity." His faith was not expressed in a body of doctrine but in an attitude of mind. And the core of this attitude, the prime rule of action for man in search of God, was the fundamental right of "private judgment."

Did I say, we have a *right* to judge and act for ourselves? I now add—it is our *indispensable duty* to do it. This is a right which we cannot relinquish, or neglect to exercise, if we would, without being highly culpable. . . . God and nature and the gospel of Christ injoin it upon us a duty to maintain the right of private judgment.

Since judgment was a private matter, this meant an end to priestly dictation. Mayhew's religious man was a free individual.

IV

Mayhew's political thought is nowhere expressed in direct, methodical form. He consistently adopted a self-deprecating attitude concerning his right and ability to discuss political problems. Again and again he would approach a point of controversy, go to the root of the matter with a few brilliant observations, and suddenly, with some such remark as, "But these are matters out of the way of my profession," turn off into ten or twelve pages of Scriptural exhortation. As if to refute the accusation of Anglican and Calvinist that he was one of those advanced preachers "who can scarcely be accounted better christians than the Turks," he rarely if ever discussed a subject of secular interest except in terms of Christian principle. The results are extremely irritating to the modern reader, especially when he sees how fertile and influential Mayhew's political ideas actually were. Yet the circumstances under which he announced these ideas were so memorable that he won for himself a solid reputation among America's pre-Revolutionary political thinkers.

Three sermons in particular brought Mayhew a full measure of respect or notoriety in New England and the mother country. The first and most celebrated, *A Discourse Concerning Unlimited Submission and Non-resistance to the Higher Powers,* was delivered less than three years after his ordination, the Sunday after January 30, 1750. It was a

dissenting preacher's refractory answer to the Tory-Angli-
can attempt to memorialize the anniversary of the death
of Charles I and elevate him to "saintship and martyrdom."
It is for this discourse that Mayhew is chiefly remembered
as political thinker and patriot, for it was the first responsible public expression in colonial America of the sacred
right and duty of resistance to tyranny, in J. W. Thorn-
ton's judgment, the "MORNING GUN OF THE REVOLUTION,
the *punctum temporis* when that period of history began."
In his second important lecture on political subjects, the
Massachusetts Election Sermon of 1754, Mayhew expounded to Governor Shirley and the General Court his
conception of political power as something held in trust
for the sovereign people. And finally, on the occasion of
the repeal of the Stamp Act, only a few short weeks before
his unseasonable death, he preached *The Snare Broken*, a
sermon of rejoicing dedicated to America's great friend
Pitt.

The deliberate manner in which Mayhew confused politics with religion and larded all observations on the one
with rambling references to the other becomes especially
evident in an attempt to decipher his sources. On one
hand, he was conversant with the great men of England,
many of whose works had been sent him by Thomas Hollis
—Harrington, Sidney, Milton, Hoadly, *Cato's Letters*, and
Locke. On the other, he rarely quoted one of these secular
writers without supporting him with a passage from the
Bible, without attempting "to examine into the Scripture
account of this matter"—at least into those parts that confirmed his rationalistic politics. Each of his three major
pronouncements on political matters was in the form of a
sermon preached on a particular text. To his listeners, of
course, and even to most of his readers, this technique made
a great deal more sense than it does to modern minds. It

was in this period that Locke and others were elevated to
the status of major prophets by the clergy of Massachusetts and Connecticut, and Mayhew did as much as any
other preacher to introduce their ideas to the colonial audience. He was able to do this without upsetting his congregation by serving these rationalistic doses in a Scriptural spoon. Mayhew is an illuminating example of the
affinity between the philosophy of natural rights and the
postulates of that "primitive Christianity" which had reason for its guide. He was an agreeable synthesis of Locke
and St. Paul.

Central to Mayhew's political philosophy was his pa-
tristic-medieval-Lockean doctrine of political authority as
something held in trust for the people and exercised in their
behalf. This in turn rested squarely upon his opinion of the
nature of man, and of the basis, purpose, and character of
government. Mayhew's natural man we have already met,
and we have found him to be an essentially good, moral,
reasonable, sociable person dwelling at the opposite end of
the spiritual-psychological spectrum from total depravity.
Since God is benevolent and asks not for fear but love,
"The love of God is the love of the divine perfections;
'tis the love of truth, goodness, justice, holiness, and all
moral excellencies."

On men with these qualities rest the good society and
free government, and to both they must be assumed to have
given their consent. "From man, from common consent,
it is that lawful rulers immediately receive their power."
Although Mayhew nowhere expresses a precise theory of
the social contract, it is clear that he entertains no other
view of the ultimate source of power in his kind of polity.
"All besides is mere lawless force and usurpation; neither
God nor nature having given any man a right of dominion
over any society independently of that society's approba-

tion and consent to be governed by him." As for the asser-
tions of the apologists for the divine right of kings, "These
notions are not drawn from the holy scriptures, but from a
far less pure and sacred fountain. They are only the devices
of lawned parasites, or other graceless politicians, to serve
the purposes of ambition and tyranny. And though they
are of late date, yet being traced up to their true original,
they will be found to come, by uninterrupted succession,
from him who was a politician from the beginning"—a
saucy statement indeed to deliver to Governor Shirley's
face.

The purpose of government in this Lockean's philosophy
is, of course, the "happiness of society" or "human felicity"
or the "common good of all, and of every individual, so
far as is consistent therewith." In the election sermon of
1754 Mayhew expressed his humanistic concept of the "sole
end" of political institutions:

> In the SECOND place, we are just to mention the great end
> of government. And after the glory of God, which we usually
> consider as the end of all things in general, that can be no
> other than the good of man, the common benefit of society.
> This is equally evident whether we consider it as a divine, or
> an human institution.
>
> As it is God's ordinance, it is designed for a blessing to the
> world. It is instituted for the preservation of men's persons,
> properties and various rights, against fraud and lawless violence;
> and that, by means of it, we may both procure, and quietly
> enjoy, those numerous blessings and advantages, which are quite
> unattainable out of society.

The nature of civil government is in keeping with these
ends: It is good, "sacred," in its proper form a "blessing"
to all men. Mayhew was no more a friend to the "necessary evil" theory of government than was John Wise. He
believed firmly in the inestimable benefits of a well-ordered

civil polity. Following faithfully in Locke's footsteps, he
found it "a thing of no consequence at all what the particular form of government is" so long as it produced
"good laws—laws attempered to the common felicity of
the governed." At the same time, he was sure that "no
form of government seems so unlikely to accomplish this
end as absolute monarchy." Like other good Americans of
1750 he eulogized the English pattern of mixed government, which was "justly the envy of most other nations."

On these sound foundations Mayhew built his doctrine
of governmental power, expounding at unusual length an
idea that most natural-rights thinkers tossed off briskly or
merely assumed. The core of his doctrine was this: Public
office, and any authority or function or privilege that may
adhere to it, is a public trust, to be exercised exclusively
for the people who created it. The king or magistrate or
legislator, the temporary and conditional possessor of authority, must consider himself only as steward of the people. As such he is to live an exemplary public and private
life. These notions are plain in the unvarnished words of
Mayhew's election sermon, which was preached, be it noted,
on the parable of the talents.

But it is not to be thought merely an office of generosity and
charity, for Rulers to exert themselves in the service of the
public. This is an indispensable duty of justice which they owe
to it, by virtue of their station. They have taken the care and
guardianship thereof upon themselves: yea they are commonly
laid under the solemn obligation of an oath, to study and
pursue its interest. And why are they honoured? why, rewarded
by the public, but that the public may receive benefit from
them? . . .

Rulers, surely, even the most dignified and powerful of them,
should not be so elevated with the thoughts of their power, as
to forget from whom it comes; for what purposes it is delegated

to them; whose impartial eye it is that surveys all their counsels, designs and actions; and who it is that will, one day, exact an account of their stewardship. . . .

As the happiness of men in society depends greatly upon the goodness of their morals, and as morals have a close connection with religion, the latter as well as the former, ought doubtless to be encouraged by the civil magistrate . . . by his own pious life and good example.

In his sermon against *Unlimited Submission* Mayhew also considered the problem of obedience to those in authority:

And here is a plain reason also why ye should pay tribute to them,—for they are God's ministers, exalted above the common level of mankind,—not that they may indulge themselves in softness and luxury, and be entitled to the servile homage of their fellowmen, but that they may execute an office no less laborious than honorable, and attend continually upon the public welfare.

Mayhew's meaning is as clear today as it was two hundred years ago when he went to war against the insolence of authority: There are standards of good behavior for governments as well as individuals. Freedom and order are impossible to achieve except in the *good* society. Mayhew's government was above all a moral government, derived from and conducted by moral men. Lest it be thought that he was content to deal in diffident generalities, it should be recorded that near the end of the election sermon he turned to Shirley and hoped out loud, "You will never forget, Sir, whose minister you are," and that in his sermon of 1750 he took a slap at half of Boston by scolding "all Christians concerned in that common practice of carrying on an illicit trade and running of goods."

V

Mayhew was a courageous if not entirely clear-headed political thinker. Certainly he never pulled up short of a logical conclusion simply because it was likely to be uncommon or unpopular. For him, therefore, as for the famous republicans and Whigs with whom he went to school, the natural consequence of a popular theory of the origin and purpose of government was the doctrine of popular resistance to abuses of public trust. Twenty-five years before Lexington and Concord Mayhew laid down the theoretical premises upon which the Revolution was to be justified, something few other preachers of Lockean principles were yet prepared to do. His clear expression of this doctrine is the more remarkable when set in its historical context, a time of peace, prosperity, and general satisfaction with British rule.

Mayhew began by asserting that under ordinary circumstances obedience to authority is both a natural and Christian duty. He was no radical impatient of all governmental restraints, but a man preaching moderation and civic duty whose text was Romans xiii, 1-8 ("Let every soul be subject unto the higher powers. . . ."), and whose constant admonition was that "a decent regard be paid to those in authority." Such obedience was dictated not only by the Apostle but by reason itself. It was the normal pattern of behavior for any man who had voluntarily surrendered his original freedom in return for the protection of government. "The true ground and reason of our obligation to be subject to the higher powers is, the usefulness of magistracy (when properly exercised) to human society, and its subserviency to the general welfare." Even in 1766 we find Mayhew reminding his audience to adopt "a respectful, loyal and dutiful manner of speech and conduct, respecting his majesty and his government," and to support "his majesty's representatives, the civil magistrates, and all persons in authority, in the lawful exercise of their several offices."

The word "lawful" is the key to the next stage in Mayhew's thought. He was "not in favor of submission to all who bear the title of rulers in common, but only to those who actually perform the duty of rulers by exercising a reasonable and just authority for the good of human society."

If those who bear the title of civil rulers do not perform the duty of civil rulers, but act directly counter to the sole end and design of their office; if they injure and oppress their subjects, instead of defending their rights and doing them good, they have not the least pretence to be honored, obeyed, and rewarded. . . .

When once magistrates act contrary to their office, and the end of their institution,—when they rob and ruin the public, instead of being guardians of its peace and welfare,—they immediately cease to be the ordinance and ministers of God, and no more deserve that glorious character than common pirates and highwaymen.

In fine, "Rulers have no authority from God to do mischief," and citizens have no duty to submit to them if they persist in doing it. Mayhew rejected peremptorily the absolutist doctrines of unlimited submission and nonresistance, which had been bluntly expressed by such thinkers as Luther, James I, and Filmer, and which were to be just as bluntly expressed by Jonathan Boucher and Daniel Leonard on the eve of the Revolution. Instead he asserted the citizen's right not only to ignore and disobey but actively to resist the commands of unlawful authority. He proclaimed it "warrantable and glorious" for the people to disobey the civil powers in certain circumstances, and in cases of very great and general oppression, when humble remonstrances fail of having any effect; and, when the public welfare cannot be otherwise provided for and secured, to rise unanimously even against the sovereign himself, in order to redress their grievances; to vindicate their natural and legal rights; to break the yoke of tyranny, and free themselves and posterity from inglorious servitude and ruin.

To Mayhew's practical way of thinking there were two kinds of tyranny that might evoke resistance:

We may very safely assert these two things in general, without undermining government: One is, that no civil rulers are to be obeyed when they enjoin things that are inconsistent with the commands of God. All such disobedience is lawful and glorious; particularly if persons refuse to comply with any *legal establishment of religion*. . . . Another thing that may be asserted with equal truth and safety is, that no government is to be submitted to at the expense of that which is the sole end of all government—the common good and safety of society.

Mayhew agreed heartily with two of the most venerable refinements of the right of resistance—that in those cases in which resistance is justified it is not only a right but a duty, and that the real rebels are the tyrants who have violated their mandate, not the people who resist them.

If it be our duty, for example, to obey our king merely for this reason, that he rules for the public welfare . . . it follows, by a parity of reason, that when he turns tyrant, and makes his subjects his prey to devour and destroy, instead of his charge to defend and cherish, we are bound to throw off our allegiance to him, and to resist. . . . Not to discontinue our allegiance in this case would be to join with the sovereign in promoting the slavery and misery of that society, the welfare of which we ourselves, as well as our sovereign, are indispensably obliged to secure and promote, as far as in us lies. . . .

The king is as much bound by his oath not to infringe the legal rights of the people as the people are bound to yield subjection to him. From whence it follows, that as soon as the prince sets himself up above law, he loses the king in the tyrant. He does, to all intents and purposes, unking himself by acting out of and beyond that sphere which the constitution allows him to move in; and in such cases he has no more right to be obeyed than any inferior officer who acts beyond his commission. The subject's obligation to allegiance then ceases, of course; and to resist him is no more rebellion than to resist any foreign invader.

Mayhew is no more successful than Locke or Jefferson in being scientific about this unscientific theory, particularly in establishing the degree of illegality or despotism that would call for unpremeditated resistance or concerted revolution. The abuse must be real and "habitual," and arouse a virtually "unanimous" will to resist. Actually, there is little danger that the people will embark on open resistance for trifling causes, for "mankind in general have a disposition to be as submissive and passive and tame under government as they ought to be." In the words that Jefferson borrowed from Locke, a "long train of abuses" is necessary both to incite and to justify active rebellion. In his sermon of 1750 Mayhew did precisely what Jefferson was to do twenty-six years later in the Declaration of Independence: He listed specifically, without too fine a regard for historical truth, the "repeated injuries and usurpations" of the long-dead monarch against whom he was affirming the necessity of revolution.

In the end, of course, the people alone could decide on the necessity for resistance, subject only to the opinion of mankind and the judgment of God. Mayhew defended stoutly the capacity of the people to do the correct and natural thing that circumstance might dictate—obey gladly, submit sullenly, resist passively, or revolt violently.

To say that subjects in general are not proper judges when their governors oppress them and play the tyrant, and when they defend their rights, administer justice impartially, and promote the public welfare, is as great treason as ever man uttered. 'Tis treason, not against one *single* man, but the state—against the whole body politic; 'tis treason against mankind, 'tis treason against common sense, 'tis treason against God. And this impious principle lays the foundation for justifying all the tyranny and oppression that ever any prince was guilty of. The people know for what end they set up and maintain their governors, and they are the proper judges when they execute their trust as they ought to do it.

It is hardly necessary to point out that Mayhew added very little to the great body of political theory. By 1750 the right of resistance or revolution was heavy with age and respectability. Essentially medieval in origin, it had been strengthened and refined by a host of theorists and men of action—Aquinas, Knox, the Huguenots, Buchanan, Mariana, Althusius, and finally Milton and Locke—until it was available and acceptable to any person or community suffering under real or imagined oppression. Nevertheless, Mayhew's place is secure in the development of American political ideas. It was a remarkable accomplishment to have proclaimed a full quarter-century before the Declaration of Independence that a people "really oppressed in a great degree by their sovereign" had the right to have done with him. A thousand orators were to echo these words of Mayhew:

For a nation thus abused to arise unanimously and resist their prince, even to the dethroning him, is not criminal, but a reasonable way of vindicating their liberties and just rights: it is making use of the means, and the only means, which God has put into their power for mutual and self defence.

VI

The fiduciary nature of governmental authority and the right of resistance to those who abuse it are the political principles for which Mayhew is best remembered. To these may be added a third major tenet, which rounds out the circle of his libertarian thought: the unbending belief in personal freedom and accountability that he called "private judgment" in religion and "liberty" in politics, and that we can recognize today as one of the first clear expressions of American individualism. Two passages from sermons delivered in the full vigor of his life will illustrate the intensity of his belief in individual freedom. In the dedication to a volume of eight sermons on *Christian Sobriety* preached to the young men of his church, Mayhew spoke of Cicero as a friend of liberty:

And though he did not fall at last as a martyr directly for true religion; yet he fell as one of the most glorious advocates for LIBERTY, that the world ever saw: An honor next to that of suffering martyrdom for religion; and, in some sort, the same thing; true religion comprising in it the love of liberty, and of One's country; and the hatred of all tyranny and oppression.

And in his sermon on the repeal of the Stamp Act he turned aside to make this autobiographical salute to liberty:

If I may be indulged here in saying a few words more, respecting my notions of liberty in general, such as they are, it shall be as follows. Having been initiated, in youth, in the doctrines of civil liberty, as they were taught by such men as Plato, Demosthenes, Cicero and other renowned persons among the ancients; and such as Sidney and Milton, Locke and Hoadley, among the moderns, I liked them; they seemed rational. Having earlier still learned from the Holy Scriptures that wise, brave and virtuous men were always friends to liberty; that God gave the Israelites a king (or absolute monarch) in his anger, because they had not sense and virtue enough to like a free commonwealth, and to have himself for their king; that the Son of God came down from heaven to make us "free indeed," and that where the spirit of the Lord is, there is liberty; this made me conclude, that freedom was a great blessing. Having, also, from my childhood up, by the kind providence of my God, and the tender care of a good parent now at rest with Him, been educated to the love of liberty . . . I would not, I cannot now, though past middle age, relinquish the fair object of my youthful affections, Liberty . . . the delight of the wise, good and brave; the protectress of innocence from wrongs and oppression, the patroness of learning, arts, eloquence, virtue, rational loyalty, religion!

Again we see the kinship in Mayhew's philosophy of things religious and political—of piety and patriotism, of private judgment and civil liberty, of impatience with speculating bishops and mistrust of overweening kings. The teachings of Samuel Clarke and John Locke fitted together neatly in his humanist mind. In his quest for truth in theology he stripped the forbidding husk of Puritanism with the knife of reason and revealed the latent fruit of private judgment. In his quest for sanity in politics he rejected the simple solutions of Stuart or Puritan authority and embraced with enthusiasm the momentous doctrine of natural rights.

The political and religious liberty that Mayhew preached had a boldly individualistic stamp to it. For him man was above all an individual, free to bring his own reason to the search for political truth and religious peace, accountable for his politics only to his fellow citizens and for his religion only to God. Society was necessary, natural, even beneficial; but it was all these things only when it liberated the powers of the people who composed it. Mayhew's

American, like Mayhew himself, was impatient of pomp, privilege, and legalized inequality. Indeed, it is plain that in 1750 Mayhew had caught sight of "the American, this new man," whom Crèvecoeur and Tocqueville were to observe with wonder and Jefferson and Jackson to lead with pride.

Other aspects of Mayhew's political thought may be disposed of briefly. He may certainly be counted among the foremost colonial advocates of separation of church and state, and also of religious toleration. He made clear his disapproval "of the ancient laws made in the colony, which bore hard on the members of the church of England," and even recommended to the General Court that it consider "whether we have not some laws in force, hardly reconcilable with that religious liberty which we profess." He confessed to Hollis his deep distress that "bigotry in religious matters has far too much place among us; so much, as almost makes one ashamed of my country." It would be asking too much of a dissenting minister of his time and place to criticize him for not extending the hand of friendship to Catholics and for making such a fuss over the dangers of an Anglican invasion. Nevertheless, we may be sure that he was perfectly sincere when he wrote that "persecution and intolerance, are not only unjust, and criminal in the sight of God; but they also cramp, enfeeble, and diminish the state."

He was an early and imaginative herald of the American Mission, of our own version of the concept of the chosen people. He believed that his own state and country held in trust for all nations a peculiar responsibility for the maintenance of political liberty. And he went even further in prophecy of America's destiny by proposing, in *The Snare Broken*, that Americans make ready to offer an asylum to the oppressed and, if ever called upon, to mount a rescue party for freedom in the mother country. Two passages from this splendid sermon are worth quoting in this regard. In his apostrophe to liberty, he ends with the hope:

And if any miserable people on the continent or isles of Europe, after being weakened by luxury, debauchery, venality, intestine quarrels, or other vices, should, in the rude collisions, or now uncertain revolutions of kingdoms, be driven, in their extremity, to seek a safe retreat from slavery in some far distant climate, let them find, O let them find one in America under thy brooding, sacred wings, where our oppressed fathers once found it, and we now enjoy it, by the favor of Him, whose service is the most glorious freedom!

And in almost the very next breath:

The great shock which was lately given to our liberties, may end in the confirmation and enlargement of them. As it is said, the stately oaks of the forest take the deeper root, extend their arms the farther, and exalt their venerable heads the higher, for being agitated by storms and tempests, provided they are not actually torn up, rent in pieces, or quite blasted by the lightning of heaven. And who knows, our liberties being thus established, but that on some future occasion, when the kingdoms of the earth are moved, and roughly dashed one against another by him that taketh up the isles as a very little thing, we, or our posterity, may even have the great felicity and honor to "save much people alive," and keep Britain herself from ruin.

Concerning the emerging constitutional issues of the day Mayhew was not nearly so precise and emphatic as his lawyer friends. He assumed that there were limits to the power of Parliament to legislate for the colonies but never found it necessary to draw the line. While he has occasionally been cited as a prophet of judicial review, the few hints of this doctrine in *The Snare Broken* are pale imitations of Otis's assault upon the writs of assistance. He was an early advocate of some sort of colonial union. One of the last messages from his patriot pen was a letter to Otis in which he urged the formation of committees of correspondence and a "communion of colonies." Finally, Mayhew's plural devotion to the larger communities of which he was a member is an illustration of the three-fold or even four-fold patriotism of the eighteenth-century colonials. Passage on passage may be plucked from his political sermons to prove him a loyal American, a stout son of England, a zealous New Englander, and a man with abiding "faith in Massachusetts." To him, as to his friends, this confusion of loyalties was wholly natural.

VII

Such was the life, character, and teaching of the last of the great colonial preachers. How important a patriot leader he would have been in 1774-1776 we can only guess, for he died July 9, 1766, of "an obstinate nervous disorder in his Head." We may be certain that he would have moved forward step by step with his political friends, for there is evidence enough in his sermons that he looked upon war and independence as justifiable techniques in the struggle for religious and political liberty. And we may be equally certain that he would have won a place, along with Otis, the Adamses, and Hancock, in the brightest galaxy of Revolutionary heroes. As it was, by 1775 his words and deeds were all but forgotten except by his friends. Just after Mayhew's death Edmund Quincy, jr., had expressed his sure hope that God would "send us other Mayhews, as we need them." God sent them, more than enough of them, and the ironic result was to bury Mayhew in undeserved obscurity.

The importance of Mayhew for American political and intellectual history lies as much in what he represented as in what he did or said. First, with his career, and those of Chauncy and Cooper, we bid a sad but preordained farewell to the ancient glory of the Puritan ministry, to that precious band of men who, whether they fought for the future like Hooker or Wise or for the past like Cotton and the Mathers, were leaders of public thought and action as few American ministers have been since the Revolution. Second, Mayhew is easily the most striking representative of the dissenting preachers who from the 1740's onward proclaimed Locke and Sidney from their pulpits and prepared the mind of New England for the Revolution. Like most of these preachers he was a tireless sower of the ideas of English constitutionalism, in John Adams's opinion "a whig of the first magnitude." And surely in his life and thought the tenacious American belief in the interdependence of religious and political freedom, of "democracy in church and state," reached a peak of conviction and candor.

In his own right, too, Mayhew may lay claim to a lasting place among our religious and political thinkers. What he lacked in profundity he redeemed in timing and intensity. It was a memorable achievement for a youthful Boston preacher to have advertised the right of resistance in 1750 and the essentials of Unitarianism in 1755. Even more significant and praiseworthy was his repeated emphasis on the right of private judgment and the use of reason in the solution of all personal and social problems. For this, after all, is the basic postulate of the American intellectual tradition, this optimistic, rationalistic, pragmatic, and ultimately democratic belief that "free examination is the way to truth." This is the rejection of the feudal past, of the right of king or bishop to proclaim dogma to the people, and the assertion of the American future, of the duty of the people to think for themselves. As a youthful poet declaimed at the Harvard commencement in 1792:

> While Britain claim'd with laws our rights to lead,
> And faith was fetter'd by a bigot's creed.
> Then mental freedom first her power display'd,
> And called a MAYHEW to religion's aid.
> For this great truth he boldly led the van,
> *That private judgment was a right of man.*

5

RICHARD BLAND

The Whig in America

THE institutions and values of American democracy are
a rich inheritance to which all manner of men have contributed their lives and talents. Some of our most viable
institutions and liberating values have been the gifts of
men who were not democrats at all. Perhaps the most convincing evidence of this historical truth is the legacy of
law and liberty willed to the new Republic by the men of
the thirteen colonies. In our delight over discovering in
early Virginia and New England a few lonely democrats
(in one or another meaning of that word) born several
centuries too soon, we have given them too much credit
for the ultimate triumph of their splendid doctrines. Roger
Williams, John Clarke, John Wise, and Nathaniel Bacon
were prophets of freedom full worthy of celebration, but
other men than these, men who had no truck with notions

of social and political equality, were the real builders of the half-finished structure of liberty inherited by the Americans of 1776 and altered by their descendants to ever more democratic uses.

The provincial assembly of the eighteenth century was the workshop in which the colonists hammered out the principal tools of liberty. The Whig gentlemen who filled the benches in each assembly—and few of them thought of themselves as anything but Whigs—sought freedom and power for themselves only, displayed undisguised oligarchical tendencies, and certainly found nothing unjust in property qualifications that in many colonies limited the suffrage to one free man in four. Yet in their ceaseless, ill-tempered, often narrow-minded encroachments on the authority wielded by governor and council, they made use of institutions and arguments that were to prove readily convertible to democratic purposes. Their institutions were elective, representative, secular, constitutional, and limited by law; their arguments were framed in terms of "liberty" and "the people." If they knew not what they wrought, they nevertheless wrought well.

The key operator in the shift in the balance of political power in the eighteenth century was the representative in the lower house of the assembly—an aristocratic, liberty-loving, lawmaking moderate rather than a democratic, equality-seeking, stability-shattering leveler. Just such a man was Richard Bland of Virginia, for decades the most active member of America's oldest legislature. Whether in action in the House of Burgesses or in meditation in his library, he was the embodiment of a notable political way of life. His career and philosophy deserve more attention than they have hitherto received, for he was the very model of the American Whig.

I

Richard Bland was an eighteenth-century Virginia aristocrat and was thus about as authentic an aristocrat as
America has produced. Birth, inheritance, and training
placed him at the topmost level of a stratified society.
Character, intelligence, and performance kept him there
throughout a long and useful life.

The Blands were one of Virginia's leading families, and
as such were bound by ties of blood and affection to dozens
of other leading families. The immigrant founder of the
line was Theodorick Bland of Westover, who came to
Virginia from England in 1654 and prospered economically,
politically, and socially until his death in 1671. Successful
planter, eminent squire, Speaker of the House of Burgesses,
and seven years a member of the Governor's Council,
Theodorick Bland was, in the words of a Virginia historian
of the early nineteenth century, "both in fortune and
understanding inferior to no person of his time in the
country." His wife, Ann, daughter of Governor Richard
Bennett, presented him with three sons who survived his
untimely end.

The second of these, Richard Bland, sr., was born at
Berkeley in 1665 and died at Jordan's, Prince George
County, in 1720, having sold the family lands at Westover
to William Byrd I in 1688. He, too, was a public-spirited
Virginia gentleman, serving in his time as burgess and
justice of the peace of both Charles City and Prince George,
vestryman of Bruton Parish, and visitor of the College of
William and Mary. After the death of his first wife and
all their six children (a harsh reminder of the touch-
and-go life led by even the "better sort" in colonial Amer-

ica), Bland married Elizabeth Randolph, daughter of William Randolph I of Turkey Island.

To them was born on May 6, 1710, the second Richard
Bland, the subject of this chapter. His father a Bland, his
mother a Randolph, his birthplace a large and successful
plantation on the James, young Richard Bland was marked
from birth for social and political leadership. His goodly
inheritance, the estate at Jordan's, came to him earlier than
he might have expected. Elizabeth Bland died in January
1720, her husband less than three months later. Young
Richard, an orphan at nine and now master of Jordan's,
was placed by his father's will in the guardianship of his
eminent uncles, William and Richard Randolph.

We know next to nothing of the quality of Bland's
training and education, although the character and learning of the end-product are evidence enough that it was
the best Virginia had to offer. From his father and uncles
he learned to manage his affairs and serve his community;
from his mother and the rector of Martin's Brandon he
learned the rudiments; from a succession of roving tutors,
or perhaps like his father at a small private school, he got
a good enough classical education to gain admission to
William and Mary; and from the president and six professors of the college he acquired the training in rhetoric,
science, mathematics, and classical studies that launched
him on his career as one of the most learned men in colonial
Virginia. It has been asserted that Bland's course at William
and Mary was topped off by residence at the University of
Edinburgh, but there is no evidence in the records to support this belief.

Self-education must have been a particularly important
ingredient in Bland's training, as indeed it was in that of
any man of his time who was eager for knowledge and

alert to the deficiencies in the bare-bones system of formal education. He taught himself enough law to qualify for admittance to practice in 1746 and enough history to become a notable collector of old Virginia documents. John Adams of Massachusetts, a man who knew what he was talking about in such matters, described Bland in his diary as "a learned, bookish man," and at the end of his own life Washington remembered him as "a man of erudition and intelligence." Bland could learn from experience as well as from his library: He acquired much more advanced views than did many of his fellow planters on the questions of paper currency and slavery. We have Jefferson's testimony on the latter issue:

In the first or second session of the Legislature after I became a member, I drew to this subject the attention of Col. Bland, one of the oldest, ablest, & most respected members, and he undertook to move for certain moderate extensions of the protection of the laws to these people. I seconded his motion, and, as a younger member, was more spared in the debate; but he was denounced as an enemy of his country, & was treated with the grossest indecorum.

While eighteenth-century Virginia was a land of status and stratification, it was also one of opportunity, adventure, and increasing mobility. A man, if his skin was white, could rise in his lifetime from the lowest to the highest class; conversely, he could enter the world at the top and leave it a financial wreck and social cipher. Though birth, inheritance, and training were all in Bland's favor, they by no means guaranteed him a permanent grip on the top rung of the ladder. That he died as well as he was born—leaving rich lands, thirty Negroes, large herds of livestock, a fine library, and an unrivaled reputation—was a reasonably stiff measure of his character, ability, and intelligence.

Again we must acknowledge that we know a good deal less of Bland than we should like to know. If this chapter had set out to portray a representative Virginian in the role of planter or family man or soldier, it would have passed over Bland and seized upon any one of a dozen men about whose private lives and characters we have considerable documentary information. Since our concern is with the political beliefs and attitudes of the Virginian, and since Bland was the most articulate political thinker active in the years before Jefferson, the Lees, and Mason, we must give what substance we can to his shadowy figure. The extant records, never especially satisfactory for the Southern colonies, are in this instance distressingly spare. The total number of private and public letters we can assign to Bland is exactly ten. The colonial records of his parish, Martin's Brandon, have vanished completely. Most of his library and collection of old documents, which were purchased after his death by Jefferson, went up in the fire that gutted the Library of Congress in 1851. The surviving records of his county, Prince George, consist of one order book (1714-1720), one minute book (1737-1740), one book of deeds (1713-1729), and one of land entries. And every scholar in colonial history is sadly aware of the huge gaps in the files of the *Virginia Gazette* for the years when it must have carried news and letters of Bland. Even his portrait has been lost to posterity, slashed by British soldiers in 1781 and quite possibly carried off by one of Ben Butler's boys in 1864.

From scattered sources comes our knowledge of Bland's character. He was honorable, capable, dependable, public-spirited. He seems to have been more eloquent with pen than in debate, and indeed was often so intent upon the business at hand as to have experienced difficulty speaking out. On occasion he could show himself to be thoroughly human, for example, as a behind-the-scenes politician and a careless borrower of books. He was not overly ambitious and cared not in the least for show. A Virginia historian writes, "In personality Bland was of that type of Virginian which is best illustrated by the figure of George Mason, that type considered characteristically Virginian,—half practical farmer, half classical scholar and lawyer; genial, well-mannered, personally somewhat untidy and careless of clothes."

Certainly he was a man whom no one could afford to treat lightly, for the pages of the only surviving minute book of Prince George County Court are full of litigations involving "Richard Bland, Gent." And in a letter to a friend in England he could give a vinegary account of the rise and character of one of his godly adversaries. Although spare of build he must have enjoyed good health and have had energy to burn. The records of the House of Burgesses show him to have been a faithful attendant and a horse for work. Moreover, he had three wives and twelve children, which is better than average for learned, bookish men. His wives were Anne Poythress, the mother of all twelve children; Martha Macon, widow of William Massie; and Elizabeth Blair, daughter of John Blair and widow of John Bolling.

Bland's learning was apparently matched by his sense of fair play and clarity of mind. In a letter of Jerman Baker to Duncan Rose, dated February 16, 1764, appears this neat compliment to his intelligence:

Indeed you may remember that in Virginia I was constantly amongst the Enemies to a paper Currency, and expressed my-self often so warmly on that subject as to bring upon myself some warm altercation with many Blockheads, & some men of Senses among the latter I recon Col°. R. Bland.

Roger Atkinson wrote of Bland in 1774 that he was

a very old experienced veteran at ye Senate or ye Bar—staunch
& tough as Whitleather—has something of ye look of musty old
Parchen'ts w'ch he handleth & studieth much.

Taken all in all, Bland seems to have been an admirable
representative of the Virginia aristocracy. Messrs. Dixon
and Hunter of the *Virginia Gazette* were probably not
far from the truth when they saluted his death with this
terse but warm accolade:

In short, he possessed all the inestimable qualifications that
could render him dear to society—all that could form the
virtuous upright man.

II

Bland's performance as public figure was equaled by few
and surpassed by no Virginians of the mid-eighteenth century. The dazzling exploits of Washington, Henry, Jefferson, R. H. Lee, Mason, and other great Virginians of the
Revolution have all but wiped out the memory of Bland
and his contemporaries, the men who came to power two or
three decades before the Stamp Act and who, in their own
way and time, did their share to prepare the colonies for
ultimate freedom. A brief review of Bland's public life
will therefore serve us doubly: It will provide a solid background against which to project and study his political
ideas, and it will remind us that there were brave men
before Washington, freedom-loving men before Jefferson,
and irritating men before Henry.

The business of governing men occupied Bland's energies
from his coming of age until his sudden death in Williamsburg October 26, 1776. At each of the three levels of
Virginia government he filled the office that was his both

as matter of right and as reward of ability: vestryman of his parish, Martin's Brandon; justice of the peace of his county, Prince George; and for more than thirty years (1742-1775) one of the two burgesses representing Prince George in the lower house of the Virginia Assembly. His hold on the reins of Prince George politics must have been especially tight. In 1745 Bland accepted an unidentified "Place of Profit," whereupon the Assembly asked the governor, as was routine in such cases, to issue a writ of election for a burgess to serve in his stead. The electors of Prince George promptly re-elected Richard Bland. And for one five-year period, 1761-1765, the delegation from Prince George was Richard Bland and Richard Bland, jr.

He was commissioned in the county militia in 1739 and in due season gained the expected rank of colonel. In the events leading to the Revolution he served, as we shall see, in a dozen or more positions of trust and honor. For years he was, like his father before him, a visitor of William and Mary. And through all these decades he devoted a good part of his time to the private pursuits of the landed aristocrat: keeping his plantation a going concern; speculating, like all men of his rank and age, in western lands; and engaging in small enterprises (such as contracting to make improvements in the church of a neighboring parish) to help reduce the debts that even a levelheaded planter could run up with his London agents.

Bland was one of the busiest and most important members of the House of Burgesses. He was especially in demand as historian, parliamentarian, and draftsman. Hugh Blair Grigsby had this to say of him:

His great learning lay in the field of British history in its largest sense; and especially in that of Virginia. With all her ancient charters, and with her acts of Assembly in passing which for nearly the third of a century he had a voice, he was familiar;

and in this department he may be said to have stood supreme. What John Selden was in the beginning of the troubles in the reign of Charles the first to the House of Commons, was Richard Bland to the House of Burgesses for thirty years during which he was a member. During that time on all questions touching the rights and privileges of the Colony he was the undoubted and truthful oracle.

In all colonies, nowhere more purposefully than in Virginia, the assembly tried to place the execution of as many laws as possible in the hands of its own members, acting as individuals or in groups. The reasons for this common practice should be easy to understand: Government was simple and had little use for the specialist; the doctrine of the separation of powers had not yet become an article of blind faith; and this was a splendid device for keeping power out of the hands of the royal governor and his lieutenants. A random listing of some of Bland's varied services indicates the extent of this practice as well as the nature and scope of governmental activity in a world far simpler than any we could possibly imagine. It indicates, too, the confidence placed in Bland by his fellow burgesses.

These were some of the executive tasks for which Bland was singled out: to act as commissioner for Virginia's Indian trade; to serve on a delegation to meet with envoys of other colonies to discuss the Indian trade; to settle the accounts of claimants suffering losses of tobacco in the burning of a public warehouse; to value a glebe; to act as trustee of "docked" lands; to direct the spending of £10,000 "for the encouragement and protection of the settlers upon the waters of the Mississippi"; to contract for the deportation of undesirable aliens (neutral French!); to spend a sizable sum for "the improving of arts and manufactures" in Virginia; to manage an official lottery to raise funds for improving navigation on the Potomac; and to perform a number of tasks vital to the prosecution of the French and Indian War.

Bland was for years the man whose constant attendance was most necessary to keep the legislative machinery of Virginia's government in motion. The records of the House of Burgesses are full of Richard Bland. From his first days as burgess he was drafting and reporting bills that dealt with such important subjects as taxation, proceedings of the county courts, distribution of estates of persons dying insolvent, currency adjustment, and revision of the laws; acting as one of the managers of the lower house in conference with the Council; and generally serving as the workhorse of a body not always given to hard and painstaking work. Later, at the height of his career, he was chairman and reporter of each of the chief committees through which the house did its business: Privileges and Elections, Propositions and Grievances, and Public Claims. In several sessions he sat—the only man to do so—on all three committees, as chairman of one and senior member of the other two.

The house piled other work on him, apparently without compunction. It called on him again and again to help draw up an address to the Governor or the King (or to that soldier of the King, Jeffrey Amherst), sent him to act as its go-between in dealings with Council and Governor, rarely if ever left him off the important special committees to examine enrolled bills and inspect the Treasurer's accounts, set him to testing the claims of several "quacks," and for years entrusted him alone with the delicate business of drafting the bill "for paying the Burgesses Wages in Money, for this present Session." No job was too big or little for Bland to tackle. In his last years he held the vital post of chairman of the committee of the whole house, yet he also found time to draft and present "a Bill,

To prevent Hogs running at Large in the Town of Port Royal" and "a Bill for destroying Crows and Squirrels in the County of Accomack." Finally, he served almost as a matter of course on *ad hoc* committees of the House of Burgesses set up to meet such crises in the life of the colony as the posthumously discovered defalcation of Treasurer John Robinson, the prosecution of a member of the Council for offending the honor of the House of Burgesses, and the battles over the Two-Penny Act and the Stamp Act.

Bland's record as burgess has been spread upon these pages for two good reasons: first, because it was a microcosm of political life in eighteenth-century America; and second, because there could be no more convincing evidence of his integrity, learning, sense of duty, assiduity, and prominence. If he was the model of a colonial legislator, it was the very finest model.

III

Bland was a thoroughly committed participant in at least six incidents or controversies in the course of his career: the affair of the Pistole Fee (1753-1755), the French and Indian War, the storm over the Two-Penny Act (1758-1764), the fight against the establishment of an American episcopate (1771), the Stamp Act crisis (1764-1766), and the series of events that led Virginia to rebellion and independence. In each of these episodes his pen was active, expressing a body of principles and prejudices that was in outline and detail the guiding political faith of the men who ruled eighteenth-century Virginia.

The affair of the Pistole Fee was a minor incident in the course of colonial politics, yet it was just this sort of "minor incident" that spurred the growth of an independent American spirit. Shortly after his arrival in Virginia, Governor Dinwiddie decided to put a stop to the loose methods of granting lands which had been allowed to develop over the years. To this end he issued orders that no land was to be granted except by patent, the fee for which was set at one pistole (about $3.60 in Virginia). In this action, which came at the end of a session and took the House of Burgesses completely by surprise, Dinwiddie had the consent of the Council. Since more than a thousand patents were ready for issue, and since several thousand more would now have to be sought for lands already held under warrant of survey, the Governor was set to reap a bountiful harvest. So, too, was the Crown, for Dinwiddie was determined to collect back quit-rents on lands obtained by warrant of survey and not subsequently patented.

When the Assembly reconvened for its next session several months later, a storm of protest broke on Dinwiddie's viceregal head. From six frontier counties, one of them just named Dinwiddie in the new Governor's honor, came petitions against the fee, whereupon the lower house, in an unusual display of the new colonial temperament, asked the Governor "to acquaint us with the Authority that impowers you to demand" this "extraordinary Fee." The Governor's reply, which in effect informed the burgesses that it was none of their business, was met by this Whiggish rejoinder:

We do humbly, but in the strongest Terms, represent to your Honour, that it is the undoubted Right of the Burgesses to enquire into the Grievances of the People: They have constantly exercised this Right, and we presume to affirm, that the drawing it into Question, in any Manner, cannot but be of dangerous Consequence to the Liberties of his Majesty's faithful Subjects, and to the Constitution of this Government.

The Rights of the Subject are so secured by Law, that they cannot be deprived of the least Part of their Property, but by their own Consent: Upon this excellent Principle is our Constitution founded, and ever since this Colony has had the Happiness of being under the immediate Protection of the Crown, the Royal Declarations have been, "That no Man's Life, Member, Freehold or Goods, be taken away or harmed, but by established and known Laws."

But the Demand of a Pistole, as a Fee for the Use of the Public Seal, being not warranted by any known and established Law, is, we humbly conceive, an Infringement of the Rights of the People, and a Greivance highly to be complained of.

Again the Governor stuck to the letter of the law as read in England—that grants of land were "a Matter of Favour from the Crown, and not a Matter relative to the Administration of Government"—and again the house used phrases that smacked of Pym and Hampden:

Resolved, That the said Demand is illegal and arbitrary, contrary to the Charters of this Colony, to his Majesty's, and his Royal Predecessors Instructions to the several Governors, and the Express Order of his Majesty King *William* of Glorious Memory, in his Privy-Council, and manifestly tends to the subverting the Laws and Constitution of this Government.

Resolved, That whoever shall hereafter pay a Pistole, as a Fee to the Governor, for the Use of the Seal to Patent for Lands, shall be deemed a Betrayer of the Rights and Privileges of the People.

The unexpected vigor of these resolutions led Dinwiddie to make sour comments to his private correspondents about "republican Principles." He could hardly have realized how good a seer he was, for this whole affair—with its confusion of rights and wrongs and its cast of overbearing royal agents and oversensitive colonials—was a prophetic miniature of things to come.

The House of Burgesses sent Attorney General Peyton Randolph to London with authority to prosecute an appeal to the Crown, as well as to hire a permanent agent to represent the colony's interests (as understood by the colonists). The end result of the usual complicated maneuvering in the Privy Council and Board of Trade was a compromise that sustained Dinwiddie in principle but set important limits to the use of the fee. Since the burgesses, if not the petitioning settlers, were primarily concerned with the principle rather than with the amount of the fee—which they insisted on regarding as a tax—the real issue was left for the future to resolve.

Bland was a key participant in this squabble, thanks to his pen, his knowledge of land tenures and charters, and his concern for Virginia's liberties. He sat on each of the committees created to study the problem and draw up resolves and addresses; he acted as one of the managers of the proceedings in the house; and he composed a piece, *A Modest and True State of the Case,* a fragment of which is the only surviving example of public comment on this issue. A comparison of the official addresses and resolutions with Bland's arguments leaves little doubt of the identity of the chief penman for the burgesses. His arguments for the inseparability of taxation and representation and for the peculiar competence of the legislative power were Whiggish to the core.

Bland was a strong supporter of Virginia's exertions in the great war with the French for North America. In a political-military situation marked by extravagant contrasts of conduct—heroism and cowardice, highmindedness and pettifogging, selfless patriotism and feckless provincialism —Bland proved himself one of the most resolute, generous-spirited members of the House of Burgesses. He was chosen along with such stalwarts as John Robinson, Charles Carter, George Wythe, and Peyton Randolph to serve on a series of extraordinary committees to spend the sums appropriated for the defense of the colony. He acted as commissioner

for Indian trade in a broadly conceived scheme to lure untrustworthy tribes into friendship or at least benevolent
neutrality. When ticklish occasions arose, such as the necessity to appoint committees to settle the accounts of the
militia, his known integrity made him a certain choice.
And when more pleasant duties beckoned, such as waiting
upon a hero like Captain Robert Stobo with the thanks of
the House of Burgesses, Bland joined George Washington,
Richard Henry Lee, and Robert Carter Nicholas in a
delegation that must have flavored gratitude with the salt
of manly charm.

He acted as chief draftsman of statutes like "the Act
for the better Regulating of the Militia," various levies of
money "for the Protection of his Majesty's Subjects in this
Colony, against the Insults and Encroachments of the
French," and "an Act for the Defense of the Frontiers of
this Colony." When the lower house stopped battling
Dinwiddie long enough to call his attention to a need upon
which all could for once agree (a guard for the magazine
at Williamsburg), Bland seemed just the right man to
wait upon the governor—which he did with success.

Finally, Bland had a good deal of active contact with
the forces in the field. He was one of a five-man committee appointed "to enquire into the Conduct of the Officers
and Men lately sent out upon an Expedition" that had
turned out a miserable failure. Never too busy to see a
small task left undone, he headed another committee to
determine whether an Indian fighter was entitled to a reward for having "killed and scalped four *Shawnese Indians
in Augusta.*" As "Lieutenant of the County of Prince
George" he armed "the Men draughted out of that County,
at his own Expence," later being repaid to the penny. And
on the occasion of the notorious newspaper attack launched
in 1756 against Washington and the Virginia regiment

("The Virginia Centinel, No. X"), Bland stood forth as an eloquent defender of the unhappy young colonel and his sorely taxed officers and men. He had foreseen such an attack and had previously written Washington:

As I have some tho'ts of writing an account of our transactions which I desire to communicate to public view in order to wipe off all reflections from my country and the several persons concerned in the conduct of our military enterprizes so far as they can be justified, I shall take it as a particular mark of friendship if at your leisure hours, if you have any, you would send me short heads of such things relative to the French invasion with the dates when they happened as you judge most interesting and proper for such a work. I will speak the truth with boldness, and I hope with approbation from every honest and good man, amongst whom I assure you without flattery, I place you in the first rank.

Bland apparently made good his promise, for in Washington's papers there is a hard-hitting rejoinder to the "Virginia Centinel," endorsed in Washington's hand as "written, it is supposed, by Col⁰ Richd Bland, 1756." Internal evidence leaves small room for doubt that Bland was the author of this piece and that it appeared in one of the lost issues of the *Virginia Gazette*. In this writing, as in all his actions during this trying period, Bland showed himself an advocate of vigorous measures at home and on the frontier.

IV

Historical interest in the Two-Penny Act centers today in the "Parsons' Cause," the occasion for Patrick Henry's first bold appearance in colonial politics. Yet this affair had more significance than as the debut of any one man, even Patrick Henry, and it had other participants than the fiery Hanoverian. The facts of the episode make clear that it was, as William Wirt Henry wrote, yet another strain upon "the bond between the King and the colonists, and was the prelude to the great contest which snapped that bond asunder."

In 1758, because of a sharp rise in the price of tobacco, the Assembly passed and the Governor approved a law, to be in force one year, permitting debts, contracts, levies, rents, and fees due in tobacco to be paid either in that staple or "in money, at the rate of sixteen shillings and eight pence for every hundred pounds of nett tobacco." The price of tobacco was on the way up to six pence per pound, and the Assembly, in reducing its value as a circulating medium to the normal two pence per pound, was making a reasonably sincere attempt to prevent creditors and salaried persons "from taking advantage of the necessities of the people." Although the law was general in provision, the ministers of the established church were the only colonial claimants to raise an outcry. For generations their yearly pay had been sixteen thousand pounds of tobacco. This sum had been fixed by law as recently as 1748, and they liked not at all to be deprived of the pleasure of having their salaries tripled by the circumstances of war, speculation, and a bad crop.

Royal instructions insisted categorically that no law approved by the King could be repealed by a colonial assembly unless the repealing law contained a suspending clause. The purpose of such a clause was to delay the execution of the repealing law until the King's pleasure could be made known. Seizing upon the notorious fact that the Two-Penny Act had incorporated no suspending clause, the clergy attacked it as not only unjust but unconstitutional. Rev. John Camm of York-Hampton Parish went to England in behalf of the clergy in 1759 and there obtained an order of the Privy Council disallowing the Two-Penny

Act. Neither Camm nor any other minister ever got much satisfaction from his vestry. Camm's suit to recover the full market-value of his salary was kicked about for years by the stubborn Virginia courts and was finally dismissed on a technicality in 1767 by a calculating Privy Council. The suits of other ministers were being given much the same treatment in Virginia when Henry's eloquence and the jury's award of one penny to Rev. James Maury in Hanover County (December 1762) ended the contest in a rout of the clergy.

There is no question that the heat of this controversy quickened the self-governing urges of the ruling Virginians. By no means were the members of the clergy entirely in the wrong, for they, too, had been hit hard by inflation. Moreover, the Assembly seemed to recognize no limits to its capacity to tamper with these salaries. The Assembly had begun to appear in exactly the same unfavorable light as the vestry: Each in its own way was claiming supremacy for the state over the church. Yet the shortsighted manner in which the clergy cut themselves loose completely from all other groups in Virginia and appealed for relief to the royal prerogative did much to weaken the control of the mother country in political as well as ecclesiastical affairs. In any event, we can agree with a Virginia historian, H. J. Eckenrode, that "the conflict was probably inevitable on account of the incongruousness of a church establishment dependent, in a final sense, upon a foreign and monarchical power, in a state every day growing more republican and more self-conscious."

Henry's burst of eloquence has deprived Bland of the recognition due him as champion of the popular cause. In fact, the records would seem to show that Bland was the chief instigator of the whole affair. A petition of the in-

habitants of Prince George County first called attention to
the need for action, and Bland was what later and less
polite generations would have labeled the Ed Flynn of
Prince George County. He then acted as a committee of
one in preparing a bill to meet "the Prayer of the said
Petition" and saw it to successful enactment by Assembly
and Governor. A committee of correspondence was set up
by the two houses in February 1759. The business of this
committee, of which Bland was a faithful member from
its beginning in 1759 to its decline in 1770, was to correspond generally with an agent chosen to "represent the
affairs of this colony" in London, but the clergy's appeal
to the Privy Council to void the Two-Penny Act was the
prime cause of its creation. The committee served the
colony faithfully as an instrument of Virginia autonomy
and reminded all Englishmen (who had eyes to see) that
the people of Virginia had interests peculiarly their own.

When members of the clergy, taking heart from a letter
of the Bishop of London to the Board of Trade recom-
mending that the Two-Penny Act be voided, attacked the
act in public print, Bland became the chief pamphleteer
for the popular cause. Three of his writings, *A Letter to
the Clergy of Virginia* (1760), a letter printed in the
Virginia Gazette, October 28, 1763, and *The Colonel Dismounted* (1764), state all the arguments—factual, historical, political, ecclesiastical, and constitutional—for the Assembly's point of view. *The Colonel Dismounted* was a
first-rate performance, combining as it did a satirical attack
on Camm under pretense of defending him and a line of
argument for colonial self-rule unprecedented for the time
and place of publication.

The strength and unanimity of popular reaction to the
tactics of the clergy in the Two-Penny affair convinced
most Virginia ministers that they would do well to swim

with the tide of colonial autonomy. As a result, the campaign of the Anglican clergy in the Northern colonies for an American episcopate found surprisingly little clerical support in Virginia. The one direct attempt was made in 1771 by a splinter group led by Commissary James Horrocks and the irrepressible John Camm, which met in Williamsburg in June and resolved somewhat lamely to petition the King for an episcopate. Bland, who had been accused by spokesmen for the clergy of bringing all Virginia to a high "pitch of insolence" with his tracts on the Two-Penny Act, was ready once again to help the popular cause. Two Anglican ministers from the faculty at William and Mary, Samuel Henley and Thomas Gwatkin, wrote so convincingly against any such scheme that Bland and other veterans of battles with the clergy could afford to stand at ease. It is altogether possible that Bland did write a pamphlet on this issue that has since been lost. The evidence of his standing among the opponents of the episcopate is to be found in a modest but firm letter to Thomas Adams in London (August 1, 1771), some bitter remarks by Camm during the debate in Dixon and Hunter's *Virginia Gazette,* and the unanimous resolution of the House of Burgesses (July 12, 1771), which called on Bland and R. H. Lee to thank the anti-episcopal clergymen for their "wise and well-timed Opposition" to a project "by which much Disturbance, great Anxiety and Apprehension, would certainly take Place among his Majesty's faithful American Subjects."

In the letter to Adams appears a statement by Bland that captures almost perfectly the blend of secularism, independence, dislike of old-world pomp, and yet simple faith that marked the attitude toward religion of the Virginia gentleman, of the dutiful squire who had led many services in the absence of the parish minister.

I profess my self a sincere Son of the Established Church; but I can embrace her Doctrines without approving of her Hierarchy, which I know to be a Relick of the Papal Incroachments upon the Common Law.

The plan for an American episcopate could not possibly have succeeded in these troubled times. The self-governing Virginians had got in the habit of controlling their church, and, as Bland made plain in his letter to Adams, the imposition of a bishop would have abrogated most of the statutes regulating ecclesiastical affairs. In his opposition to any sort of hierarchy, Bland, an Anglican to the bone, was acting out of political rather than religious principle.

V

The Stamp Act roused Bland to his best literary effort, *An Inquiry into the Rights of the British Colonies*. Once again his urge to pamphleteer came at the end of a train of public events in which he was an active participant. From the arrival of the shocking news of Parliament's mind to tax the colonies until the last drunken huzzah for the repeal of the Stamp Act, Bland was at the storm center of Virginia politics. For the first time in his career he was associated with men who were more willing than he to break a lance with champions of prerogative and imperial power. A new breed, personified by that "Pillar of Fire" Patrick Henry, was coming to prominence in Virginia, and Bland was to be known in his last ten years as a warm but conservative friend to liberty.

In June 1764, immediately upon receiving news of Parliament's intentions, the committee of correspondence drafted a letter to their agent in London calling upon him to lobby against any sort of stamp tax. The first reaction of the House of Burgesses, which came together October

30, was to appoint a committee of eight to draw up an
address to the King and memorials to Lords and Commons. The committee was established November 14; six
days later, as if to get it moving, Bland was added; and
on December 18, after considerable give-and-take between
the two houses, the General Assembly adopted an address
and two memorials politely but manfully informing King
and Parliament that they had no right to lay taxes upon a
people unrepresented in the taxing legislature. The authorship of these protests has never been conclusively fixed.
Bland, R. H. Lee, Wythe, Carter, Edmund Pendleton, and
Peyton Randolph have all received primary credit for one
or more of them.

An obstinate King, ministry, and Parliament were only
hardened in their purpose by colonial lectures on the British
Constitution. The news that the Stamp Act had become a
reality was the call to arms for Patrick Henry and the
rising radical party. Bland's position in the session of May
1765 was that of the prudent conservative. Jefferson was
later to write of the passage of the Stamp Act resolutions:

The famous stamp act was, however, past in Jan., 1765 and
in the session of the Virgi assembly of May following, mr.
Henry introduced the celebrated resolns of that date. These
were drawn by George Johnson, a lawyer of the Northern
neck, a very able, logical and correct speaker. Mr. Henry moved
and Johnston seconded these resolns successively. They were opposed by Randolph, Bland, Pendleton, Nicholas, Wythe & all the
old members whose influence in the house had till then been un-
broken. They did it, not from any question of our rights, but
on the ground that the same sentiments had been at their preceding session expressed in a more conciliatory form to which
the answers were not yet received. But torrents of sublime
eloquence from mr Henry, backed up by the solid reasoning
of Johnston prevailed. The last however, & strongest resoln was
carried but by a single vote. The debate on it was most bloody.

This would seem a fair representation of Bland's motives for opposing this sudden salvo. He could agree whole-heartedly with Henry's resolves, even those which were rejected, for he had said no less about the rights of the colonists in his attack on the Pistole Fee and defense of the Two-Penny Act. But he was getting older, and Henry was a man he could not quite understand; and so he could take the position that these were very poor tactics. We know nothing of Bland's part in Virginia's out-of-doors protest against the arrival of the stamps, although we can be sure he had no intention of ever using stamped paper.

In March 1766, two months before the colony would know of the repeal of the Stamp Act, Bland's *Inquiry* was published by Alexander Purdie in Williamsburg. It was reprinted twice in London in 1769, in the *Political Register* and in a separate edition by John Almon, and seems to have won a wide and thoughtful audience. Purdie and Dixon's *Gazette* printed a letter from London dated April 25, 1769, which said:

I assure you no argument or pains have been omitted by the Agents for the colonies; they have taken their instructions from the best writers: If the Parliament will not hear BLAND and DICKENSON, neither will they be persuaded if one rose from the dead.

This comment attests the importance attached by Virginians to Bland's pamphlet and at the same time explains why it has never since received much attention. Dickinson's "Letters from a Farmer in Pennsylvania," which appeared in all but three or four American newspapers in late 1767 and early 1768, were from the moment of their publication the scripture of the colonists. Bland was not the only political author forgotten by the colonists in their wild scramble to offer devotion to Dickinson and his fine-

spun legalities. In this regard it is interesting to hear what
Jefferson had to say to William Wirt fifty years later:

Your characters are inimitably and justly drawn. I am not
certain if more might not be said of Colonel Richard Bland. He
was the most learned and logical man of those who took
prominent lead in public affairs, profound in constitutional lore,
a most ungraceful speaker, (as were Peyton Randolph and
Robinson, in a remarkable degree.) He wrote the first pamphlet
on the nature of the connection with Great Britain which had
any pretension to accuracy of view on that subject, but it was
a singular one. He would set out on sound principles, pursue
them logically till he found them leading to the precipice which
he had to leap, start back alarmed, then resume his ground, go
over it in another direction, be led again by the correctness of
his reasoning to the same place, and again back about, and try
other processes to reconcile right and wrong, but finally left his
reader and himself bewildered between the steady index of
the compass in their hand, and the phantasm to which it seemed
to point. Still there was more sound matter in his pamphlet than
in the celebrated Farmers' letters, which were really but an
ignis fatuus, misleading us from true principles.

Jefferson's criticism had a good deal of truth in it but
was not altogether fair to Bland. If Jefferson meant, as he
probably did mean, that the analysis of the power of Parliament in his own *Summary View of the Rights of British
America* was more precise and bold than that worked out
by Bland, he was unquestionably correct. But when we
remember that Jefferson wrote his tract in 1774 with earlier
efforts like the *Inquiry* to steer by, and in a time of far
less concern for English sensibilities, we may excuse Bland
for some of the backing and filling that dismayed Jefferson.
In any case, in 1766 Bland's pamphlet was acclaimed by the
popular party as the finest piece of political writing to have
come out of Virginia. Nor were local partiots unaware that

Bland was occupying high ground. Said the Sons of Liberty in Norfolk in a resolution of thanks to Bland:

When the LIBERTY of a State is in Danger, the Man surely deserves well of his Country, who is instrumental in removing the impending Evil; but as the Means are various, we believe none preferable to reasonable Conviction.

Bland in return saluted the Sons of Liberty for having championed "the glorious Cause of LIBERTY" against "the detestable Stamp-Act," and spoke eloquently of the "lasting Monuments of their patriotic Spirit and Love of Country."

Bland's part in the events leading to independence was of a piece with his actions in the Stamp Act crisis. He was handed a dozen difficult jobs and did all of them well; he remained a constant friend to the patriotic cause; but he showed his age and his inability to keep pace with the radicals by counseling conservatism at several critical junctures.

With the repeal of the Stamp Act Virginia politics settled back into the usual routine. The next step toward ultimate independence was taken in 1768 upon arrival of news of the Townshend Acts. Again the bolder counties petitioned the House of Burgesses, and again the lower house decided to speak directly to the sovereign authorities at home. Bland was the key figure at every step of this new protest against arbitrary power. He chaired the committee of eleven set up to address King and Parliament; he wrote all three messages, reshaping in his own words the arguments of the past decade; and he succeeded in persuading the Council to go along with the memorials as reported to the lower house.

These protests, of course, were given exactly the same ice-cold reception in England as those of 1764. When the newly arrived Governor, Lord Botetourt, dissolved the Assembly May 17, 1769, only eleven days after he had called

it together, the time had come for something more com-
municative than words. The result was the unprecedented,
extra-constitutional meeting of the burgesses at the house
of Anthony Hay on the afternoon of the dissolution. On
May 18 this group, which included all important members
of the popular party, adopted some profoundly anti-British
resolutions, the cutting edge of which was a mutual pledge
to refrain from purchasing a long list of imported goods.
Third in the list of 108 signers of the Williamsburg Association of 1769 was Richard Bland. The non-importation
resolutions of 1769 were in practice pretty much a failure,
and a new Association was organized June 22, 1770, each
signer pledging himself to have nothing to do socially with
any individual who refused to join or live up to the articles
of agreement. Again Bland's name was at the top of the
list.

VI

For three years Virginia simmered without major incident,
while events in the other colonies moved toward inevitable
bloodshed. On March 12, 1773 the House of Burgesses took
a fateful step when it appointed "a standing Committee of
Correspondence and inquiry,"

whose business it shall be to obtain the most early and Authentic
intelligence of all such Acts and *Resolutions* of the *British
Parliament,* or proceedings of Administration, as may relate to
or affect the British Colonies in America, and to keep up and
maintain a Correspondence and Communication with our Sister
Colonies, respecting these important Considerations; and the
result of such their proceedings, from Time to Time, to lay
before this House.

Bland was an active member of the Virginia Committee
of Correspondence from this first establishment to its de-

cline in 1775. Although the kind of daring leadership he had offered in 1753 and 1758 was now exhibited by the Lees, Henry, Jefferson, Washington, and others, Bland was still a useful man for the radicals to have at their side, especially since he seemed willing in the end to go along with their every step. The record of his service in the critical years is a virtually inclusive listing of those committees, conventions, and delegations which guided Virginia to final independence: member of the Committee of Correspondence (1773-1775); signer of the Association of 1774; a leader of the patriot party in the last House of Burgesses; deputy from Prince George County to the five Virginia Conventions of 1774-1776, which gradually supplanted the General Assembly as the colony's legislature and finally took on the duties of a constitutional convention; member of the Virginia Committee of Safety (1775-1776), which was the executive arm of the colony in the period between the departure of Lord Dunmore and establishment of state government; delegate with Randolph, Washington, Henry, R. H. Lee, Pendleton, and Benjamin Harrison to the first Continental Congress in 1774; and delegate with the same immortal band to the second in May 1775. John Adams wrote of the Virginians and Bland at Philadelphia in 1774:

These gentlemen from Virginia appear to be the most spirited and consistent of any. Harrison said he would have come on foot rather than not come. Bland said he would have gone, upon this occasion, if it had been to Jericho.

Purdie's *Gazette* of June 16, 1775 carried news that Bland had returned from Congress "charged with some important business from that august body to be laid before the Assembly of this colony." Actually, Bland was beginning to show his age and had left Philadelphia because of ill health. He was elected to Congress a third time August

11, 1775, but the next day declined in an exchange that the Journal of the Convention describes in these words:

RICHARD BLAND, Esq. returned the Convention his most grateful acknowledgements for the great honour they had pleased a third time to confer on him, by appointing him one of the deputies to represent this colony in General Congress, and said this fresh instance of their approbation was sufficient for an old man, almost deprived of sight, whose greatest ambition had ever been to receive the plaudit of his country, whenever he should retire from the public stage of life; that the honorable testimony he lately received of this approbation, joined with his present appointment, should ever animate him, as far as he was able, to support the glorious cause in which America was now engaged; but that his advanced age rendered him incapable of taking an active part in these weighty and important concerns, which must necessarily be agitated in the great council of the United Colonies, and therefore begging leave to decline the honor they had been pleased to confer on him, and desiring that some person more fit and able might supply his place.

Resolved unanimously, That the thanks of this Convention are justly due to the said *Richard Bland,* Esq. one of the worthy deputies who represented this Colony in the late Continental Congress, for his faithful discharge of that important trust; and this body are only induced to dispense with his future services, of the like nature, on account of his advanced age.

The President accordingly delivered the thanks of the Convention to the said *Richard Bland,* Esq. in his place, who expressed the great pleasure he received from this distinguished testimony of his country's approbation of his services.

Bland's refusal was greeted by Henry and the others with mixed feelings of regret and relief—regret because he was one of the last of the old colonial fighters for Virginia's rights and privileges, relief because the policy of no compromise would now go forward more smoothly. True to his desire for peaceful settlement of this imperial dispute, Bland had opposed Henry's resolution to arm the colony passed by the convention of March 1775.

There was life in Bland yet, it would seem, for he remained active in Virginia's temporary legislature, discharged faithfully his duties with the Committee of Safety, served on a committee to encourage domestic manufactures, and performed a number of the small executive tasks he had learned to do so well in the French and Indian War. He seems to have put up some of his own money to encourage manufacture of saltpeter for gunpowder, practicing what he had preached to a relative, "I fear supineness possesseth all ranks among us; why do we talk, and not act?" In the Convention of 1776 he served on the committee that drew up the Declaration of Rights and the first constitution of the State of Virginia. And as if all these duties were not enough for "an old man, almost deprived of sight," he kept his grip on the home county by heading its Committee of Intelligence.

In July 1775 Bland was given a dose of the same bitter medicine that America has somehow managed to reserve for some of its most honorable public servants: He was accused of disloyalty and secret correspondence with the enemy. Bland, unlike some of those so recklessly denounced in 1951 and 1952, was able to face his accuser publicly and spit the medicine right back in his face. On his return from ordination in England in 1775, Rev. Samuel Sheild undertook to repay Bland for his anticlerical activities by spreading a cock-and-bull story that Bland had promised to support the colonial policies of the Crown in return for an appointment as collector of duties on tea. After Bland had demanded proof and Sheild had offered it, the tough old patriot went straight before his peers. The Journal of the Convention carries these entries:

For July 22, 1775,

RICHARD BLAND, Esq. a member of this Convention, and one of the deputies appointed to represent this colony in General Congress, informed the Convention, that certain false and scandalous reports, highly reflecting on him in his publick character, had been propagated; to wit, that he had made application to the earl of *Dartmouth*, or some of the ministry, for an appointment to collect the taxes imposed on *America* by parliament; and that, as an inducement to them to grant the same, had promised to promote the designs of the ministry against this country; and also, that his conduct in General Congress had been such that he was obliged suddenly to decamp from the city of *Philadelphia*:

That he had served as a member of the General Assembly for upwards of 30 years, and hoped the part he had always publickly taken would have secured him, in his age, from an imputation so injurious to his character: That he earnestly requested a full and publick inquiry should be made into the truth of the said reports, and that the Rev. *Samuel Shield* [*sic*], the Rev. *John Hurt*, and *Samuel Overton*, and *Joseph Smith* who, he understood, had propagated the said reports, should be summoned to attend the said inquiry; and that every other person who had heard anything of the said reports would also attend, that the fullest examination might be made into the truth thereof.

Resolved, That this Convention will, on *Friday* next, examine into the truth of the reports mentioned in the said information.

For July 28,

The Convention, according to the order of the day, went into an examination of the reports said to have been propagated to the prejudice of *Richard Bland*, Esq. a member of this Convention, and one of the deputies appointed to represent this Colony in General Congress; and, after examination of the Rev. *Samuel Shield*, and the Rev. *John Hurt*, and many other witnesses, and a full inquiry into the same, do find the said reports to be utterly false and groundless, and tending not only to injure the said *Richard Bland* in his publick character, but to prejudice the glorious cause in which *America* is now embarked.

Resolved unanimously, That this Convention do consider it as their duty to bear to the world their testimony that the said *Richard Bland* hath manifested himself the friend of his country, and uniformly stood forth an able asserter of her rights and liberties.

A week later Bland read a full report of his triumph in the newspapers and two weeks later was re-elected to Congress. Having been thus dramatically vindicated, he resigned his seat.

How important was Bland in the movement toward independence? H. J. Eckenrode once insisted that he "more than any other man was the author of the Revolution in Virginia," adding on another occasion: "The role enacted by western Virginia was not the creation of a movement but the precipitation of it. Patrick Henry was not the father of the Revolution but the heir of Richard Bland and his political executor." If Eckenrode's salute was to Bland the man, it was plainly a case of overenthusiasm. But if, as seems more likely, it was a tribute to the historical primacy of the tidewater region and to Bland as its representative political figure, there can be little argument with the historian or his rhetorical device. The Revolution, like the earlier struggles for self-government, was largely the handiwork of the planter aristocracy, aided to be sure by the awakening democracy of the western counties. For Bland, the veteran of a half-dozen tussles with the Crown and several score with the Crown's agents, the Revolution was the climax to a life spent defending Virginia. All honor to the men of the west, who had their own troubles with the tidewater aristocracy, but all honor, too, to an aristocracy that was willing to hazard its fortunes in an authentic rebellion. Bland was not "more than any other man . . . the author of the Revolution," but he was a leader of the class of men in whose keeping the destiny of

Virginia rested. He journeyed to Philadelphia with Washington, Henry, and Lee, and that should be glory enough for any one man.

VII

Bland's writings are an accurate representation of the dominant political and constitutional thought of eighteenth-century Virginia. His ideas about civil liberty, the right of resistance, the royal prerogative, and the competence of the Assembly were the ideas not only of Robinson, Randolph, Wythe, and the entire House of Burgesses, but of planters and yeomen everywhere, even in the newly settled regions. Eighteenth-century Virginia, indeed eighteenth-century America, was dedicated with astounding unanimity to a "party line." Virginia planter, Boston merchant, Jersey farmer, and Pennsylvania printer might have different notions about the location of hell or purpose of an aristocracy, but as children of England they spoke the same political language. The principles of Whiggery, altered to American requirements, claimed the allegiance of all but a reactionary or radical handful of the colonists. These pages present the political faith of Richard Bland, but it is essential to recall that all Virginia agreed with Bland and most of America with Virginia.

Bland probably wrote at least seven pamphlets, a literary output altogether unique in the political history of the Southern colonies. Each of these efforts, or at least each that has survived, was an occasional contribution to a political controversy in which he was an active combatant. His arguments were therefore largely immediate in appeal, and the political thought supporting them was tossed off casually rather than worked out carefully. Bland's political, social, economic, and religious ideas were, like those of the other gentlemen with whom he governed Virginia, matters of faith rather than of reasoned conviction. They were all the more authoritative for being self-evident truths.

Bland's surviving works are *A Modest and True State of the Case* (1753), of which only a fragment remains, *A Letter to the Clergy of Virginia* (1760), *The Colonel Dismounted* (1764), and *An Inquiry into the Rights of the British Colonies* (1766). The lost works included a study of land tenure in Virginia, a treatise on water baptism written to refute the Quakers, and probably, although the evidence is less convincing, a tract on the subject of an American episcopate. In addition, we learn something of Bland's ideas from his letters to the *Gazette* and to friends, from the protests of 1768 against the Townshend Acts, and from the laws, resolves, and addresses he penned for the House of Burgesses. If all this seems a skimpy production, especially when contrasted with the flood of political tracts in old and New England, we must remember that we have almost nothing else political from a Virginia pen in this period. If the style seems rough and the logic circuitous, we must remember that, when words are few, content rather than artistry has first claim to the listener's attention.

A word should be said about the sources of Bland's political and historical learning. For the most part, they were the writings with which any Virginia gentleman would become acquainted if he paid attention to his parents, the tutor and rector, the professors at the college, and the first page of the *Gazette*. Bland gives evidence of familiarity with Locke, Vattel, Domat, and William Wollaston; Coke, Holt, and Sir William Temple; Bacon, Shaftesbury, Cervantes, Milton, Swift, and Pope; Hakluyt, Salmon, and Brady; and such classical writers as Thucydides, Lactantius, and Cicero. He was also conversant with contemporaneous political writing, a good deal of which he found reprinted in the various *Gazettes*, especially after the political awakening of the colonial press in 1765. And since he was the recognized oracle of Virginia history, he must have had a rare knowledge of the original sources, of the charters and documents that granted Virginia her liberties.

What did Bland, the archetype of the American Whig, believe to be rock-bottom political truth? His creed—and it was more a creed than a philosophy—had four principal articles of faith: the eternal validity of the natural-law doctrines most cogently stated by John Locke; the superiority over all other forms of government of the English Constitution, of which an uncorrupted model or extension was the peculiar property of the Virginians; the like superiority of those unique rights and liberties which were the heritage of the freeborn Englishman; and the conviction that the good state rests on the devotion of men of virtue, wisdom, integrity, and justice. Let us examine Bland's testimony to each of these beliefs.

The magnificent principles of natural law and natural rights were the common property of the American colonies. This doctrine was made to order for a proud colonial people on the way to independence through various stages of self-government. Bland, like his fellow colonists of every section, accepted these principles at face value; there is no indication at any place in his writings that he considered them even a little inconsistent, unhistorical, or illogical. A representative passage from Bland's *Inquiry into the Rights of the British Colonies* shows him a faithful adherent of the natural-law philosophy:

Men in a State of Nature are absolutely free and independent of one another as to sovereign Jurisdiction, but when they enter into a Society, and by their own Consent become Members of it, they must submit to the Laws of the Society according to which they agree to be governed; for it is evident, by the very Act of Association, that each Member subjects himself to the Authority of that Body in whom, by common Consent, the legislative Power of the State is placed: But though they must submit to the Laws, so long as they remain Members of the Society, yet they retain so much of their natural Freedom as to have a Right to retire from the Society, to renounce the Benefits of it, to enter into another Society, and to settle in another Country; for their Engagements to the Society, and their Submission to the publick Authority of the State, do not oblige them to continue in it longer than they find it will conduce to their Happiness, which they have a natural Right to promote. This natural Right remains with every Man, and he cannot justly be deprived of it by any civil Authority.

Here in a narrow compass are most of the ancient ideas that Locke had refined so persuasively in his famous treatise: the historical and logical state of nature, in which men are possessed of absolute freedom; the impulse to enter society in search of protection; the act of voluntary consent or compact, in which some freedom is renounced so that the remainder may be sure; the contingent retention of enough natural freedom to withdraw from the compact for sufficient cause; and the promotion of men's happiness as the chief end of society and government. If Bland did not expand on any of these concepts, it was probably because he thought it completely unnecessary. He might as well have expanded on the Sixth Commandment.

The core of this philosophy was, of course, the contract or compact, the notion that political obligation originates in the freely given consent of the individual. For Bland and his contemporaries the compact was no idle abstraction but a reality visible in the form of their ancient charters. However the Stuarts and early Virginians had looked upon the charters and confirmations, the descendants of the early Virginians, for whom Bland was the oracle, considered them voluntary compacts between a king in search of subjects and subjects in search of a king. But it was not so much the compact that interested Bland and his fellow colonials as the manner in which it might be abrogated by those who had, for more than trivial reasons, become dissatisfied with its terms. Bland put forward two solutions to this problem: the right of resistance and the right of migration, each a necessary theoretical support to the practical arguments of the colonial apologists. The free individual could oppose and refuse obedience to unlawful acts of the sovereign power, or he could choose "to retire from the Society, to renounce the Benefits of it . . . and to settle in another Country."

Bland had little of a positive nature to say about the right of resistance. He was not, like Jonathan Mayhew or Patrick Henry, the sort of man to go around shouting about rebellion before it was plainly necessary to rebel. Yet he did say enough in the *Inquiry* and *The Colonel Dismounted* to make clear his Whiggish disdain for the principles of passive obedience and his Whiggish belief in the natural right to resist unlawful statutes and exertions of prerogative. An example of arbitrary action that would justify resistance is presented in the *Inquiry*:

The Colonies are subordinate to the Authority of Parliament; subordinate I mean in Degree, but not absolutely so: For if by a Vote of the *British* Senate the Colonists were to be delivered up to the Rule of a *French* or *Turkish* Tyranny, they may refuse Obedience to such a Vote, and may oppose the Execution of it by Force.

If a Man invades my Property, he becomes an Aggressor, and puts himself into a State of War with me: I have a Right to oppose this Invader; If I have not Strength to repel him, I must submit, but he acquires no Right to my Estate which he has usurped. Whenever I recover Strength I may renew my Claim, and attempt to regain my Possession; if I am never strong enough, my Son, or his Son, may, when able, recover the natural Right of his Ancestor which has been unjustly taken from him.

And much closer to home, in *The Colonel Dismounted*:

I have, replied the Colonel, a high Reverence for the Majesty of the King's Authority, and shall upon every Occasion yield a due Obedience to all its just Powers and Prerogatives; but Submission, even to the supreme Magistrate, is not the whole Duty of a Citizen, especially such a Submission as he himself does not require: Something is likewise due to the Rights of our Country, and to the Liberties of Mankind. . . .

I do not deny but that the Parliament, as the stronger Power, can force any Laws it shall think fit upon us; but the Inquiry is not what it can do, but what Constitutional Right it has to do so: And if it has not any Constitutional Right, then any Tax respecting our INTERNAL Polity, which may hereafter be imposed on us by Act of Parliament, is arbitrary, as depriving us of our Rights, and may be opposed. But we have nothing of this Sort to fear from those Guardians of the Rights and Liberties of Mankind.

As conciliatory as the last sentence may have sounded— and we must remember that it was written in 1763— there should have been no doubt in the minds of Bland's readers that he and his fellow burgesses claimed an ultimate right to resist the commands of an arbitrary sovereign or Parliament. Bland never did make clear just how far the British ministry would have to go in oppressing the colonies before armed resistance would be justified, but like all subscribers to Lockean principles he believed that the amount of resistance would be determined by the extent of oppression. The passage of one oppressive law would justify opposition to that law alone. The passage of a number of such laws would justify general resistance. Absolute oppression would justify absolute rebellion, but in 1763 and 1765 no colonist was talking in these terms.

The natural right of migration was a handy colonial doctrine. It permitted Americans to argue that their ancestors had left England as free agents, that they had therefore been in a position to bargain for a new compact with the sovereign they were leaving behind, that each generation of colonists consented anew to this compact, and that any attempt to violate it could be openly resisted. The right of migration, the compact, and the right of resistance were closely associated in colonial argument. "I have observed before," writes Bland,

that when Subjects are deprived of their civil Rights, or are dissatisfied with the Place they hold in the Community, they have a natural Right to quit the Society of which they are Members, and to retire into another Country. Now when Men exercise this Right, and withdraw themselves from their Country, they recover their natural Freedom and Independence: The Jurisdiction and Sovereignty of the State they have quitted ceases; and if they unite, and by common Consent take Possession of a new Country, and form themselves into a political Society, they become a sovereign State, independent of the State from which they separated. If then the subjects of *England* have a natural Right to relinquish their Country, and by retiring from it, and associating together, to form a new political Society and independent State, they must have a Right, by Compact with the Sovereign of the Nation, to remove into a new Country, and to form a civil Establishment upon the Terms of the Compact. In such a Case, the Terms of the Compact must be obligatory and binding upon the Parties; they must be the Magna Charta, the fundamental Principles of Government, to this new Society; and every Infringement of them must be wrong, and may be opposed.

A passage like this should be evidence enough of the American Whig's unquestioning dedication "to the Law of Nature, and those Rights of Mankind which flow from it," to a set of fundamental principles "applicable to every

Sort of Government, and not contrary to the common Understandings of Mankind." Bland's faith in the teachings of Locke and Wollaston was like his faith in the teachings of Jesus. They were "true, certain, and universal," not to be improved upon and certainly not to be fretted over. They were the pikes and cutlasses in a gentleman's intellectual armory, to be stored away when things were going well and to be dragged out and brandished when things went wrong.

VIII

Throughout the colonial period and right down to the last months before the Declaration of Independence, politically conscious Americans looked upon the British Constitution rather than natural law as the bulwark of their cherished liberties. Practical political thinking in eighteenth-century America was dominated by two assumptions: that the British Constitution was the best and happiest of all possible forms of government, and that the colonists, descendants of freeborn Englishmen, enjoyed the blessings of this constitution to the fullest extent consistent with a wilderness environment.

The British Constitution, we learn from Bland's writings, had at least four honorable claims to superiority over all other charters or systems of government: First, "the Laws of the Kingdom," the working rules of the Constitution, were "founded upon the Principles of the Law of Nature." The Constitution was as pure a distillation of those "true, certain, and universal" principles "applicable to every Sort of Government" as mortal men could be expected to enjoy. Newton's laws of attraction were no more valid than the common law of England. Second, the British Constitution was founded, unlike many constitutions, in "the common consent of the People." Third, this consent had been given repeatedly "from time immemorial;" it went back at least as far as the coming of the Saxons. The antiquity of the British Constitution was as important a quality as its conformity to nature. And finally, it was peculiarly designed to promote liberty and justice, by protecting the subject from that old bugaboo "arbitrary power" and by governing him through techniques of "mildness and equity." Bland put his faith in the Constitution in these guileless words:

Under an *English* Government all Men are born free, are only subject to Laws made with their own Consent, and cannot be deprived of the Benefit of these Laws without a transgression of them. To assert this is sufficient, to demonstrate it to an *Englishman* is useless: He not only KNOWS, but, if I may use the Expression, FEELS it as a vital Principle in the Constitution, which places him in a Situation without the reach of the highest EXECUTIVE Power in the State, if he lives in an Obedience to its laws.

The content of this best of constitutions was apparently so well known as to require no particular exposition. It included the common law, Magna Charta and other hard-won documents of the past, and the nexus of customs and understandings which brought balance to government and protection to the people. The most notable of these was, of course, the still-inchoate doctrine of the separation of powers. Although Bland was apparently unaware of Montesquieu's magnificent misinterpretation, he was nevertheless committed in a general way to the concept of three great branches of government, each with powers and a life of its own.

The key institution of government in this good Whig's philosophy was the legislative assembly. Government should be balanced and the powers separated, but Bland, following in the inconsistent steps of Locke and the other heroes of the Whig tradition, had a special affection for the legislature, "the natural Guardians of [the] Liberties" of the people. The early American disposition to look to the legislature rather than to the executive or judiciary for care and protection, a disposition deriving from experience as well as tradition, is plain in the writings of this model burgess.

If then the People of this Colony are free born, and have a Right to the Liberties and Privileges of *English* Subjects, they must necessarily have a legal Constitution, that is, a Legislature, composed, in Part, of the Representatives of the People, who may enact Laws for the INTERNAL Government of the Colony, and suitable to its various Circumstances and Occasions; and without such a Representative, I am bold enough to say, no law can be Made.

The meridian of Bland's dedication to the legislative way of life is reached in *The Colonel Dismounted*. Throughout his argument runs a feeling of loyal enthusiasm for the competence and dignity of the Virginia Assembly.

Bland had little to say about the importance of an independent judiciary, principally because he was a writer on immediate topics, which in his time were the powers of King and Parliament or of Governor and Assembly. Though he used the sacred word "unconstitutional" and asserted that "the Constitution cannot be destroyed . . . by any Act of the General Assembly" or of Parliament, he did not go on to place the final guardianship of the Constitution in the courts. The doctrine of judicial review was unknown to Bland and his colleagues. Yet the independent judiciary and the great popular institution associated with it—the jury of peers—were certainly regarded as essentials of the Constitution.

The existence of a monarch—pledged to protect the people under the terms of the compact, yet wielding a prerogative of whose limits he was the only short-range

judge—was a basic assumption of Whig constitutionalism.
Again and again Bland acknowledged the necessity of a
king, not because he was anxious to play the dutiful subject but because he believed sincerely that a visible sovereign
governing through the consent of the governed brought
stability, dignity, effectiveness, and legitimacy to the best
of all possible constitutions. Bland must have regarded as
utter nonsense the charges of "republicanism" hurled at
the Virginians by frustrated royal agents, for he meant
what he said when he composed addresses that spoke of
"the best of Kings" and of "our Loyalty and Attachment
to his [Majesty's] Royal and Illustrious Person and Family."
A special committee headed by Bland said this to the
Governor at the opening of the critical session of May 1755:

We His Majesty's most dutiful and loyal Subjects, the Burgesses of *Virginia*, now met in General Assembly, return your
Honor our sincere Thanks for your Speech at the Opening of
this Session.

The many Instances we have received of His Majesty's pa-
ternal and tender Concern for the Protection and Happiness of
this Colony, do justly demand from us, the strongest Testimo-
nies of the most inviolable Fidelity to his sacred Person and
Government; and it would argue the highest Ingratitude, if
we did not acknowledge ourselves truly affected with the
Benefits which must arise to us by his Royal Care and Munifi-
cence, in sending to our Assistance, at the Expence of the Crown
of *Great-Britain*, a Body of regular Forces, with a large Train of
Artillery, under the Command of an able and experienced
General.

We beg Leave to assure your Honor, that we will take the
important Matters, recommended to us by your Honor, under
our most serious Consideration, and that His Majesty's Interest,
and the public Good of our Country, which are inseparably
united, shall govern us in all our Resolutions.

Here was the essence of the Whig doctrine of a constitutional king: the inseparability of the interest of the monarch, the welfare of the country, and "the Rights of the Subjects." The Glorious Revolution had once again reminded Englishmen and their kings that, while the rights of the people were sheltered by the throne, the throne rested on the rights of the people. Bland rejected categorically Robert Filmer's theories of royal authority, especially when these theories were dredged up by the ministers in their defense of the prerogative in the Two-Penny crisis. The point at issue, it will be remembered, was the right of the Assembly to ignore the royal instruction concerning suspending clauses. Said Bland in explaining the absence of such a clause in the act of 1758:

To say that a royal Instruction to a Governour, for his own particular Conduct, is to have the Force and Validity of a Law, and must be obeyed without Reserve, is, at once, to strip us of all the Rights and Privileges of British Subjects, and to put us under the despotic Power of a *French* or *Turkish* Government; for what is the real Difference between a *French* Edict and an *English* Instruction if they are both equally absolute? The royal Instructions are nothing more than Rules and Orders laid down as Guides and Directions for the Conduct of Governours. These may, and certainly ought to be, Laws to them; but never can be thought, consistently with the Principles of the *British* Constitution, to have the Force or Power of Laws upon the People.

The Royal Prerogative is, without Doubt, of great Weight and Power in a dependent and subordinate Government: Like the King of *Babylon's* Decree, it may, for aught I know, almost force the People of the Plantations to fall down and worship any Image it shall please to set up; but, great and powerful as it is, it can only be exerted while in the Hands of the best and most benign Sovereign, for the Good of his People, and not for their Destruction.

The King, acting through the person of the royal governor, was an indispensable element of the British Constitution as extended to the colonies. He was, however, an agent of popular consent, deserving of "the deepest Loyalty" only so long as he acted as "the Father of his People." It was in this sense that the Virginians appealed to him in 1764, out of "a Confidence that the Royal Benignity would never suffer them to be deprived of their Freedom (that sacred Birthright and inestimable Blessing)." Not until the monarchy had been stripped of the aura of benignity by Thomas Paine and the course of events did Americans reluctantly turn republican. Few colonists—certainly not Bland—believed they could do without the divinity that doth hedge a king.

Toward the end of the colonial period, Americans became more and more convinced that they, not the English, were the trustees and beneficiaries of the British Constitution. The English people, it was asserted, had fallen on evil days, and their manifest lapse in morality had infected the best of all possible constitutions. As Bland wrote in the *Inquiry*:

> If what you say is a real Fact, that nine Tenths of the People of *Britain* are deprived of the high Privilege of being Electors, it shows a great Defect in the present Constitution, which has departed so much from its original Purity; but never can prove that those People are even *virtually* represented in Parliament. And here give me Leave to observe that it would be a Work worthy of the best patriotick Spirits in the Nation to effectuate an Alteration in this putrid Part of the Constitution; and, by restoring it to its pristine Perfection, prevent any "Order or Rank of the Subjects from imposing upon or binding the rest without their Consent." But, I fear, the Gangrene has taken too deep Hold to be eradicated in these Days of Venality.

Although there was little hope that the English could restore the Constitution to its original purity, this did not mean that the Constitution had no home. In an address to the Governor in 1756, Bland and Peyton Randolph, a committee of two, spoke of the Virginians as men "who enjoy the Blessings of a *British* Constitution, reduced to its original Purity, and breathing nothing but Freedom and Justice." The colonists believed that the ancient, pure, uncorrupted Constitution was their peculiar possession and trust.

IX

The distinctive "Blessings of a *British* Constitution" were the celebrated rights and privileges flowing from it, and to these the Americans, "the Heirs and Descendants of free born *Britons*," laid positive claim. The time had not yet come for them to talk of "natural" rights. The rights for which they contended were "constitutional," "civil," "ancient," and "British." These were, to be sure, especially precious because they, like the Constitution, were uniquely conformable to nature, the most perfect conceivable earthly reproductions of the rights that belonged to all men everywhere. Yet their particular attraction for pre-Revolutionary Americans like Bland was their British pedigree. The fact that these rights were ancient and had been bought with the blood of secular martyrs recommended them especially to colonial minds. The Saxons had brought them, the Angles had absorbed them, the first Virginians had transported them, Hampden ("that Great Man") had defended them, King William "of Glorious Memory" had confirmed them—and now they were safe in the keeping of the colonists, a people as uncorrupted as the early Britons and therefore worthy of this noble heritage. Bland never doubted that the colonists were "in full Possession of the Rights and Privileges of *Englishmen*."

Like most other Whigs, Bland placed the defense of

British rights in the legislative assembly. Although all branches of government existed primarily to protect the rights of the subject—King, courts, and House of Lords— the lower house of the legislature, the House of Commons (or House of Burgesses), had the chief responsibility for transmitting them unspoiled to future generations. Unless we recall the peculiar feeling of trusteeship that guided Bland and many of his colleagues, they often appear like so many posers, hypocrites, and babblers. It was hard for a good Whig to be anything but a member of the popular house; once called to membership, his first duty was clear.

Bland wrote at one time or another in explanation or defense of all the well-known rights to which Virginians laid claim: representation, "a Right without which, by the ancient Constitution of the State, all other Liberties were but a Species of Bondage"; taxation only by elected representatives, "an essential Part of *British* Freedom"; and property, perhaps the best example of a right both natural and British. The intimate association of these three freedoms in the mind of the good Whig is clear in Bland's writings. In the memorial of 1768 to the House of Lords he said of the Virginians:

They presume not to claim any other than the natural Rights of *British* Subjects; the fundamental and vital Principles of their happy Government, so universally admired, is known to consist in this: that no Power on Earth has a Right to impose Taxes upon the People or to take the smallest Portion of their Property without their Consent, given by their Representatives in Parliament; this has ever been esteemed the chief pillar of their Constitution, the very Palladium of their Liberties. If this Principle is suffered to decay, the Constitution must expire with it, as no Man can enjoy even the shadow of Freedom; if his property, acquired by his own Industry and the sweat of his brow, may be wrested from him at the Will of another without his own Consent.

This Truth is so well established that it is unnecessary to attempt a Demonstration of it to *Englishmen,* who feel the Principle firmly implanted in them diffusing through their whole frame Complacency and Chearfulness.

And in his argument against the Pistole Fee he wrote:

The Rights of the Subjects are so secured by Law that they cannot be deprived of the least part of their property without their own consent. Upon this Principle of Law, the Liberty and Property of every Person who has the felicity to live under a British Government is founded. The Question then ought not to be about the smallness of the demand but the Lawfulness of it. For if it is against Law, the same Power which imposes one Pistole may impose an Hundred, and this not in one instance only but in every case in which this Leviathan of Power shall think fit to exercise its authority.

LIBERTY & PROPERTY are like those precious Vessels whose soundness is destroyed by the least flaw and whose use is lost by the smallest hole. Impositions destroy their Beauty nor are they to be soldered by patch-work which will always discover and frequently widen the original Flaw.

This shews the Iniquity of every measure which has the least tendency to break through the legal Forms of government and the expediency, nay the necessity of opposing in a legal way every attempt of this sort which like a small spark if not extinguished in the beginning will soon gain ground and at last blaze out into an irresistable Flame.

The purpose of this vigilance was to guarantee to all men "the Fruits of their own Labour, with a Security which Liberty only can impart."

Bland also mentioned a half-dozen other liberties that he found essential to a Whig society. Of freedom of speech and press he wrote to Washington:

If what I may say should give Offence to any, for I give you free Liberty to communicate it, tell them, that I have the

Honour to be a British Subject, and, under that glorious Character, enjoy the Privileges of an Englishman, one of which is to
examine with Freedom, our public Measures, without being
liable to the Punishments of French Tyranny; and, if I think
proper, to expose those public Errors which have had to[o]
long a Course, and which have been blindly embraced by many,
as the most true Opinions.

Bland was only one of many Virginians who used the
columns of the *Gazette* to expand on all manner of controversial topics. Although he several times mentioned the
necessity of speaking and writing "with a proper Deference
to Persons in High Office," he could be tart and testy in
his comments on certain public men. Yet he never forgot
that the responsibility to argue "with Candour and Integrity" went along with the freedom to argue at all.

Freedom of petition, trial by jury ("fair, open and
publick"), and freedom of religion were other privileges
Bland found imbedded in the Constitution. The first was
essential because it permitted men to advertise their grievances and forced government to redress them. Trial by jury
was hardly less important than representation itself, although Virginians did not get wrought up over it until
the ministry proposed to remove certain American offenders
to England for trial. Freedom of religion was, of course,
the kind of freedom guaranteed by the Act of Toleration,
which Bland considered to have been extended to Virginia.
At other times he seemed to define freedom of religion as
the power of the vestry to ignore the Bishop of London or
the happy fact that Virginia harbored no "Papists." In any
case, Bland held a firm belief in the practical necessity of a
live-and-let-live attitude toward religious doctrines. "For
let me tell you," he wrote in 1771, "a Religious Dispute is
the most Fierce and destructive of all others, to the peace
and Happiness of Government."

X

No people since the Romans have done more talking about virtue than the Whigs of eighteenth-century England and their immediate ancestors. The Americans, Whigs to the core, filled their papers and pamphlets with salutes to the noble virtues: wisdom, justice, temperance, courage, honesty, frugality, sincerity, modesty, integrity, benevolence, sobriety, piety, simplicity, and a dozen other admirable qualities. At the same time, they made clear their belief that men who displayed these virtues would be free and that men who did not would be slaves. The free state and all its accessories—constitutional monarchy, the legislature, representation, trial by jury, freedom of religion, freedom of expression, security of property—depended for existence on men of wisdom and integrity. This had been true of republican Rome, the most glorious state in all recorded history; this was true of England, the Rome of the modern world; this was especially true of America, the Rome of the future, to which Virtue was even now moving her seat.

Bland did not express this interesting refinement of Whig political thought as clearly as he might have, principally because he had no immediate use for that sort of argument. Yet through all his writings there runs a strain of high morality. He assumed, as did a thousand writers to the English and American press, that a certain proportion of men (never precisely fixed) with a sincere belief in "the Roman virtues" was the first requisite for the existence of free government, and he acknowledged the intimate association of public virtue and private morality. Truth, wisdom, candor, integrity, decency, industry, honesty, frugality, and "good manners" were the particular virtues to which Bland paid tribute.

On the statue of Lord Botetourt at the entrance to the College of William and Mary are carved these words, which Bland composed at the request of the Assembly:

LET WISDOM AND JUSTICE PRESIDE IN ANY COUNTRY THE PEOPLE WILL REJOICE AND MUST BE HAPPY.

Public virtue and private morality, carefully learned in youth and actively cultivated in maturity, were far more essential to the preservation and advancement of human liberty than was any law or institution or constitutional technique. Indeed, the great Constitution itself could not be worked except in an atmosphere of integrity and morality, one in which the Whiggish distinction between *power* and *right* would be known to all men and violated by none.

Two aspects of Bland's thought remain to be examined briefly: his reliance on facts and history for support of his major arguments, and the nature and originality of the theory of the British empire worked out in his writings on the Two-Penny and Stamp acts.

Bland the oracle used history rather than logic to confute the defenders of parliamentary supremacy, while Bland the country lawyer used facts rather than dogmas to harry the minions of ecclesiastical aristocracy. Although he never found time to carry through a projected history of Virginia, he was generally acknowledged to be the colony's chief intellectual link with its past. Jefferson saluted Bland as "a great antiquarian," and there is little doubt that his own interest in documentary materials was stimulated by friendship with this wise old man. Bland's career as collector of the basic documents of Virginia history would have been enough in itself to establish him as a leading figure of the colonial period. If Bland was a descendant of Englishmen in his devotion to history and its uses, he was a forerunner of later Americans in his blunt assertion that "opinion shall never influence my Judgment; I will examine Facts, and from them discover Truths." Bland, like later Americans, could never free himself completely from the sway of opinion, but certainly his writings are loaded with enough hard facts to give them a decidedly modern flavor. Two examples of his practical approach to political problems will be sufficient to illustrate this truth. To those burgesses obsessed with doctrinaire Whig notions about the menace of a standing army Bland wrote:

In a British Government, where the Laws controul even the Sovereign's Power, it is impossible that military Enterprizes can be carried on with Advantage without a proper Assistance from those who are intrusted with the Disposition of the People's Money. If the Supplies, necessary to give Life and Vigour to our Arms, are refused or granted with too much Frugality, we must never expect to succeed against an Enemy subject to a despotic Prince, who can dispose of the Lives and Fortunes of his Subjects as he pleases.

And to those ministers who proclaimed the inviolability of the royal instructions:

When, therefore, the Governour and Council . . . find, from the Uncertainty and Variableness of human Affairs, that any Accident happens which general Instructions can by no Means provide for; or which, by a rigid Observation of them, would destroy a People so far distant from the Royal Presence, before they can apply to the Throne for Relief; it is their Duty as good Magistrates, to exercise this Power as the Exigency of the State requires; and, though they should deviate from the strict Letter of an Instruction, or perhaps, in a small Degree, from the fixed Rule of the Constitution, yet such a Deviation cannot possibly be *Treason*, when it is intended to produce the most salutary End, the Preservation of the People: In such a Case it deserves Commendation and Reward.

The Royal Instructions ought certainly to be obeyed, and nothing but the most pressing Necessity can justify any Person for infringing them; but, as *salus populi est suprema lex*, where this Necessity prevails, every Consideration must give Place to it, and even these Instructions may be deviated from with Impunity: This is so evident to Reason, and so clear and fundamental a Rule in the *English* Constitution, that it would be losing of Time to produce Instances of it.

This justification of an admittedly questionable action on the plea of "the most pressing Necessity" has few counterparts in early American political writing. Bland, who was fond of pointing to such ineluctable facts as the distance of the colonies from England, was an interesting example of the growing American tendency to argue politics in practical terms. When he wrote that "Facts can be known and Truth discovered," he put his finger on one of the vital assumptions of the American tradition. When he paid a high tribute to common sense, he sounded almost like a Southern Franklin.

The whole trend of colonial argument after 1763 on the crucial constitutional issue of the nature of the British empire was away from loyal confusion and toward radical precision. In 1764-1768 men talked of difficult distinctions between internal and external taxation, internal and external legislation, taxation for revenue and taxation for regulation of trade. In 1775-1776 they were content to deny the power of Parliament completely and to point to the Crown as the tie that bound. While Franklin, John Adams, James Wilson, and Jefferson now get most of the credit for this embryonic dominion theory, the crude spadework of men like Bland raised a foundation on which they could build their polished dialectical structures.

Bland's ideas on this subject were never entirely coherent, for he wrote his most important tracts at a time when even the keenest colonial minds were floundering about in the swamps of "loyal confusion." If in his theory of parlia-

mentary power there are inconsistencies between one time
and another, or even between pages 25 and 26 of the same
pamphlet, we must remember that his was a pioneer attempt to grapple with a problem never before examined
carefully by colonial minds, a problem whose only practical
solutions were the slavish alternative of total submission or
the visionary alternative of dominion status. Bland the
Whig would have none of the former; Bland the loyal
colonial would take time to digest the latter. Hence we
discover that Virginia was and was not dependent on England, that the colonies were both sisters and daughters of
the home country, and that Parliament could and could
not regulate intercolonial affairs.

Yet these points should be noted in support of a Virginia
Tyler's claim that Bland wrote "the great initial paper of
the American Revolution," and a Yankee Tyler's acknowl-
edgement that he was the first expounder of a "prodigious
innovation in constitutional doctrine": his sharp denial,
first stated in 1764 and stated again in 1766, that Parliament had the right to lay "any Tax respecting our IN-
TERNAL Polity"; his more timid denial (for here he walked
on eggs) that Parliament could even *legislate* on internal
concerns of the colonies; his historical argument, so necessary to the American case, that the first colonists had exercised the natural right of migration, had expended their
own treasure in settling the colonies, and had thereupon
made a voluntary compact with the King of England; his
blunt insistence in the *Inquiry* that the Navigation Acts,
however venerable, "deprived the Colonies . . . of the
Privileges of English Subjects, and constituted an unnatural
Difference between Men under the same Allegiance, born
equally free, and entitled to the same civil Rights"; his
absolute rejection of the sophistry of virtual representation; and his interesting observation, which he did not

carry through to its logical conclusion, that Charles II "was King in *Virginia* some Time before he had any certain Assurance of being restored to his Throne in *England*."

Bland expounded ideas that were in every thinking colonist's mind, and the course of thought on this constitutional problem would have wandered in the same direction had he never lived at all. Yet his gropings of 1764 and 1766 came early enough in the battle to give him a reasonable claim to primacy among the hundreds of defenders of colonial self-government. *The Colonel Dismounted*, in which Bland first set down his ideas, was written in 1763 as the climax to the Two-Penny crisis. Bland denied Parliament's authority to lay internal taxes months before the Stamp Act was even proposed. He first among Americans stated clearly and boldly:

Any Tax respecting our INTERNAL Polity, which may hereafter be imposed on us by Act of Parliament, is arbitrary, as depriving us of our Rights, and may be opposed.

XI

Bland died as he probably wanted to die: suddenly, painlessly, and on active political service. In the fall of 1776 he had come down the river to Williamsburg as one of Prince George's delegates to the first state legislature. There, in a gathering of men only four of whom had been in the old House of Burgesses when he had attacked the Pistole Fee, he plied his trade with the same skill and learning he had shown for thirty-five years. He was still the oracle, still the cautious progressive. He was chairman of the special committee that reported Jefferson's bill "to enable tenants in taille to convey their lands in fee simple" and a member of the small committee set up to revise the laws. While walking the streets of Williamsburg October 26, probably on his way to the first session of the week, he collapsed and was taken to the house of his friend, John Tazewell. In a few hours he was dead.

Bland's name passed quickly from the memories of a people who were even then surfeited with heroes. His was not a life to excite or a personality to intrigue. He had fought no battles, cleared no forests, suffered no tortures; he had swamped no assemblies with torrents of eloquence. And Americans then as now liked their heroes to go off half-cocked. Yet in his own quiet and persevering manner he was more representative of a memorable way of life than any of the great Virginians who come so readily to mind. His career is a case study in the development of representative government. His writings are an accurate indication of the political values of the governing class in colonial America. His service in each of Virginia's three legislatures reminds us that in one colony at least the transition from subordination to independence was marked by precious little social upheaval. And his whole performance, in 1775 as in 1753, proves that we owe something to our aristocrats as well as to our democrats.

The tradition for which Bland was the penman and politician came to flower in Jefferson, Mason, and Madison. What finer tribute could we pay this American Whig than to acknowledge him the elder brother of such men as these?

6

BENJAMIN FRANKLIN
The First American

CAN any new thing be written of Benjamin Franklin? Is there a corner of his far-ranging mind or an aspect of his towering influence that is not the most familiar public property? He has had a dozen or more notable biographers and a legion of faithful investigators of one or another of his activities and interests. In his own writings, public as well as private, he examined himself with discrimination and revealed himself with candor.

Yet much remains to be hypothesized and verified in "the Franklin science." We need (and at last are getting) a new and revised edition of his complete writings, an expanded bibliography, a scientific biography, additional calendars of his papers, and a Franklin dictionary. We need a fuller biography than Carl Van Doren's, as Van Doren himself once wrote, something "half again as long"; we need a fuller one even than that, something with the sweep and detail of the Freeman *Washington*. And while all this work proceeds, every writer who looks anew at a topic that Franklin touched with his kaleidoscopic genius must interpret the great man for himself and fit him into his own pattern.

The subject of this little book is a case in point. Although an essay on Franklin as political thinker must go over ground that has been worn to ruts, it may also bring new insight to his thought and career. It is in the character of influential and representative colonial democrat that we shall observe Dr. Benjamin Franklin. I shall try to confine him rigidly—as if he could be confined at all—to his years as colonial (1706-1765) and his significance as political thinker. If the narrative runs over into 1770 or 1775 or even 1787, it is because the Revolution was for Franklin the dramatic climax to his colonial career. If the talk of politics runs over into economics, science, religion, social problems, and a dozen other fields, it is because we deal with no ordinary man, but, in Van Doren's famous phrase, "a harmonious human multitude." And since thought and action, the idea and the fact, were tied closely together in Franklin's scheme of life, we must say a few words about his public career before we can probe his public mind.

I

Puritan Boston bred Benjamin Franklin. Dr. Holmes was only exaggerating when he poked fun at other people's civic pride by endorsing Franklin as a "citizen of Boston who dwelt for a little while in Philadelphia." He was born in Milk Street January 17, 1706, the tenth son and seventeenth child of Josiah Franklin, tallow chandler and soap boiler. His father had come from Northamptonshire, Eng-

land, some time around 1683. His mother Abiah, Josiah's
second wife, was a Folger from Nantucket. The Franklins
were plain people—poor, pious, hardworking—but apparently well respected in the town of ten thousand that
looked upon Joseph Dudley, Increase and Cotton Mather,
and Samuel Sewall as its leading citizens. In 1694 Josiah
had been stamped with the seal of righteousness that but
one man in five could carry: church membership. The day
Benjamin was born he was whisked across the street to be
baptized in Old South Church—a likely beginning for a
noted skeptic.

Even in infancy Benjamin displayed extraordinary apti-
tude. As an old man he told his son, "I do not remember
when I could not read." Josiah intended him, "as the tithe
of his sons, to the service of the Church," but after less
than two years of schooling he was set to work making
soap and candles. Apprenticed to his brother James, a
printer, at the age of twelve, he began that notable regimen
of labor at desk and press that made him the most skilled
producer and printer of the written word in colonial
America.

Franklin's life is colonial America's most gratifying and
widely known success story. The early exercises in reading
and writing, the frustrated yearning for the sea, the difficulties with brother James, the escape by land and water to
distant Philadelphia, the charming encounter with the
"three great puffy rolls" and his future wife, the misguided but edifying trip to England to buy printing equip-
ment, the return to his trade in Philadelphia—these are
tales of his youth that millions of Americans know as well
as their own lives. Rather than retrace his steps to prosperity and fame, let me discuss briefly the various careers he
pursued, five or six at a time, between 1730 and 1765. From
each of his major activities he drew important elements

of his working philosophy. In each he exhibited one or more of those qualities of mind and habit that made him "the Father of all the Yankees," "the first American," "the essence of eighteenth-century America"—in short, the most important figure in the colonial experience. Let us consider Franklin as printer-businessman, scientist-inventor, author-moralist, community organizer, and politician-diplomat.

Franklin's will, dated 1788, began with the words, "I, Benjamin Franklin, of Philadelphia, printer, late Minister Plenipotentiary from the United States of America to the Court of France, now President of the State of Pennsylvania." It was not false humility that led one of the most famous men in the world to style himself "printer," but solid pride in seventy years of skill and success in every line of an honorable trade. "He that hath a Trade," said Poor Richard, "hath an Estate." It was not caprice that led him to set up his private press at Passy in 1777, but the need of a sea-anchor for a storm-tossed old shell. "He that hath a Calling, hath an Office of Profit and Honour."

Franklin the printer was more than an adept artisan. He was a successful businessman—the most remarkable self-made man in colonial America, the ancestor and patron saint of millions of other hardworking, clear-thinking, risk-calculating Americans. He did not gamble or speculate wildly, yet was willing to take a chance on something less than a sure bet. He cut no illegal corners, yet played the competitive game with some show of toughness. And while he pursued an accepted trade with skill, imagination, and hard work, he owed much of his success to the fact that in business as in diplomacy he was always alert to the main chance and willing to seize it.

The course of Franklin's career moved steadily onward: self-education in the printing trade in Boston, Philadelphia, and London; experience in a Quaker merchant's shop, where "I attended the business diligently, studied accounts, and grew, in a little time, expert at selling"; his first partnership in 1728; sole ownership of the business at twenty-four; and then eighteen years of increasing fame and fortune, to which the *Pennsylvania Gazette,* the almanac, public printing contracts, a stationer's shop, bookselling, partnerships with journeymen printers, and a dozen other ventures contributed handsomely. His own talents as author fitted neatly into his scheme for prosperity. In 1729,

I wrote and printed an anonymous pamphlet . . . entitled *The Nature and Necessity of a Paper Currency.* It was well received by the common people in general; but the rich men disliked it, for it increased and strengthened the clamour for more money; and they happening to have no writers among them that were able to answer it, their opposition slackened, and the point was carried by a majority in the House. My friends there, who considered I had been of some service, thought fit to reward me by employing me in printing the money—a very profitable job and a great help to me. This was another advantage gained by my being able to write.

Another element in Franklin's success was his shrewd understanding of the profits that come from a good reputation. In one of the most celebrated passages of the *Autobiography* he confesses:

In order to secure my credit and character as a tradesman, I took care not only to be in *reality* industrious and frugal, but to avoid all *appearances* of the contrary. I dressed plain and was seen at no places of idle diversion. I never went out a fishing or shooting; a book, indeed, sometimes debauched me from my work, but that was seldom, snug, and gave no scandal; and to show that I was not above my business, I sometimes brought home the paper I purchased at the stores, thro' the streets on a wheelbarrow. Thus being esteemed an industrious, thriving, young man, and paying duly for what I bought . . . I went on swimmingly.

So swimmingly indeed that by 1748 he had had enough of active business, whereupon with a characteristic display of well-ordered values and business acumen he entered into partnership with his foreman, David Hall, and retired to other and more interesting careers. Under the terms of this bargain he was relieved "of all care of the printing office" and assured an income of quite livable proportions. In this partial break with his calling Franklin showed himself a good deal wiser than most of the millions of Americans who were to follow his every step but the last. Few men have been able to withdraw so gracefully, seasonably, and profitably from a business in which they have wearied of everything but the money it brings.

Franklin's real purpose in retiring from active business was to devote his best energies to science, to what his age called "natural philosophy." "I flattered myself that, by the sufficient tho' moderate fortune I had acquired, I had secured leisure during the rest of my life for philosophical studies and amusements." Unfortunately for science, but fortunately for the future Republic, this period of "leisure" was to last only six years, until the Albany Congress of 1754 drew him off into a career of diplomacy. Nevertheless, in this short time Franklin pushed so far into unknown territory that he achieved lasting fame as one of America's great men of science.

Just why a colonial tradesman in his early forties, with practically no formal education or contact with the learned world, should suddenly have presented mankind with experiment-tested explanations of ancient mysteries is itself a mystery that no Franklin scholar will ever answer to our complete satisfaction. We must be content with the partial answers that his mind was vast and curious, that he could master thoroughly or perform adroitly anything to which he would devote even a fraction of his attention, and that from the day he met "natural philosophy" as a young printer in England he never ceased to tinker and ruminate, no matter how exhausting the press of business or diplomacy.

His reputation as scientist rests largely on his experiments in electricity, and no one should be misled by their apparent simplicity. Working with kite, pump handle, salt cellar, vinegar cruet, lightning rod, "electric tube," and "Muschenbroek's wonderful bottle" (the Leyden jar), he converted electricity from a curiosity to a science. A measure of his influence may be found in these electrical terms he first used in print in English: armature, battery, brush, charge, condense, conductor, discharge, electrician, electrify, minus and plus, and shock. The "single fluid" theory, a description of the essential phenomena of the condenser, and the legend-making identification of electricity and lightning were his principal legacies to this field of science.

In other fields his mind was hardly less active. Any instance of natural phenomena was sure to claim his attention and produce an idea to be tested by experiment. Oceanography (his pioneer work in locating the Gulf Stream), meteorology (his discovery that northeast storms come from the southwest), heat physics (his measurements of heat absorption with regard to color), and medicine (his invention of a flexible metal catheter and musings on the cause of colds) are a few of the sciences in which his influence was felt. And he has at least an arguable claim as America's pioneer social scientist. His *Observations concerning the Increase of Mankind* (1751) and *The Interest of Great Britain Considered* (1760) made brilliant use of vital statistics in the scientific study of problems of population.

The sudden and surprising fame that Franklin's "philosophical studies and amusements" brought him in Europe and America—fame that was attested by unnumbered memberships in royal societies, honorary degrees, popular accolades, friendly epigrams, and malicious attacks—tried him exhaustively and found him sound in mind and heart. Forty years of honors were to flatter but not corrupt, and the most eminent American of his day remained always the humane and democratic person that the world came to identify with America itself. Because Franklin was an eminent scientist he could "stand before kings" and get a hearing for the colonies; and because he stood before each king without forgetting that he was "Benjamin Franklin, of Philadelphia, printer," he got a much wider and more sympathetic hearing among the king's subjects. He played the part of the honest colonial with unswerving fidelity and introduced a new nationality to the courts and people of curious Europe. American independence and American democracy owe a vast debt to the manner in which Franklin handled his glories as scientist.

If Franklin had any major limitation in his character as scientist, it was the overly practical, utilitarian, unspeculative mood in which he approached his experiments, which is another way of saying that he was a notable representative of the developing American mind. His character was limned most sharply by Sir Humphry Davy:

The experiments adduced by Dr. Franklin . . . were most ingeniously contrived and happily executed. A singular felicity of induction guided all his researches, and by very small means he established very grand truths. The style and manner of his publication on electricity are almost as worthy of admiration as the doctrine it contains. He has endeavoured to remove all mystery and obscurity from the subject; he has written equally for the uninitiated and for the philosopher; and he has rendered his details amusing as well as perspicuous, elegant as well as simple. Science appears in his language in a dress wonderfully decorous, the best adapted to display her native loveliness. He has in no case exhibited that false dignity, by which philosophy is kept aloof from common applications, and he has sought rather to make her a useful inmate and servant in the common habitations of man, than to preserve her merely as an object of admiration in temples and palaces.

Franklin is remembered as tinkering inventor—of stove, lightning rod, bifocals, and clock—more often than as conscious scientist. He should also be remembered as an inventor who, out of regard for the human race, refused to seek patents for his own devices.

Finally, Franklin was one of the first Americans to recognize that the elements of scientific method are more than coincidentally similar to basic democratic procedures. His approach to natural science had a profound influence upon his approach to political and social science. In the one as in the other he could see the necessity of free inquiry, free exchange of information, optimism, pragmatism, and humility. For him it was a logical step from the free republic of science to the free Republic of the United States.

II

Franklin pursued devotedly the calling of author-moralist from the age of seven (a poem to his uncle in London) to eighty-four (a satire on the slave trade). In all these years his pen was rarely at rest, as he examined, recorded, or publicized his every interest in a style that is generally regarded to have been the most forceful in colonial America.

He wrote influentially in several dozen fields, as a few titles will bear witness: *Dissertation on Liberty and Necessity, Pleasure and Pain; A Modest Enquiry into the Nature and Necessity of a Paper Currency; Proposals Relative to the Education of Youth in Pensilvania; On the Causes and Cure of Smoky Chimneys;* and *Information to Those Who would Remove to America.*

We run into all manner of difficulties in seeking to assess Franklin as a man of letters, principally because his life was so much more memorable than anything he could possibly have written about it. Were his writings flat and dreary they would none the less be read widely, for they were the ponderings of the great man of a great age on some of its most basic problems. The happy fact is, of course, that they were nothing of the sort. Franklin was an author of unusual clarity, force, discipline, and charm; he was uniquely skilled in fitting style to subject. Whether he wrote satire for the press, sweet nonsense to a lady, bagatelles for his circle, propaganda for the populace, messages of state to a high-toned foreign minister, advice to the poor and humble, or descriptions of his experiments to be read before the Royal Society, he rarely missed the goal for which the rest of us strive in vain: perfect communication. Although he never wrote a full-sized book (and projected only one, the stillborn *Art of Virtue*), his letters and pamphlets are proof that he could easily have written half a hundred. It is remarkable that his style should have been so consistently artistic and exciting in its own right, for he was one of the most "occasional" authors in American literature.

Franklin the author is best remembered for his moral tracts. Although they form only a fraction of his public writings and present only a sliver of his fabulous character, the *Autobiography*, the prefaces to *Poor Richard*, and *The Way to Wealth* were the first American contributions to universal literature. These lessons in bourgeois morality, the written record of his rage for self-improvement and for transmitting his experience to those who might profit from it, have worked a far-reaching influence on the character of American democracy. The legendary Franklin—frugal, industrious, shrewd, practical, ingenious, self-sustaining and self-reliant—is still praised or damned as the specimen American. The fact that his thirteen "virtues" were listed merely for instruction, and were a catalogue of commandments—chastity, for example—that he himself had trouble enough obeying, has long since been swallowed up in the uses to which Americans have put his advice. In the teachings of Poor Richard "the American, this new man" was to find at least half his character. That he often found the whole of it and saw no reason to inquire about or imitate the other Franklin—the cultured, traveled diplomat retired from his trade—is the measure of Franklin's genius as preceptor to "the middling people."

Had eighteenth-century Philadelphia been moved to commemorate Civic Virtue, the statue would surely have been one of Benjamin Franklin. His adopted city remembers him most warmly for his achievements as community organizer and supporter of good causes. He could always be counted on to help his fellow citizens—and to organize his fellow citizens to help themselves. Among the results of Franklin's civic energy were the city police; clean, paved, and lighted streets; the first organized militia in Pennsylvania; and the famous volunteer fire companies that made Philadelphia heaven for thousands of small boys. He was then a leading instigator, and is now a hallowed founder, of the American Philosophical Society, the Pennsylvania Hospital, and the University of Pennsylvania. Skeptic and deist, he nevertheless gave support to all the churches "for building their new Places of Worship." As early as 1731 he conceived and organized the first circulating library in America, later to be known as the Library Company. His press, too, was always in public service—sometimes for pay, sometimes not. The *Pennsylvania Gazette* was an institution in itself, and it must be regretted that so promising a journalist should have devoted so little time and pains to this public service. Franklin's activities as journalist were clearly subsidiary to his careers as printer, author, and community organizer. Even the unsuccessful *Philadelphische Zeitung* (the first German-American newspaper) and *General Magazine* were civic undertakings set in motion by the outward-turning of his inner drive toward self-improvement. Franklin was also an early and enthusiastic Mason, a fact of considerable importance for his intercolonial and European reputations.

Franklin's performance as community organizer is a significant chapter in the rise of American liberty. Voluntary action, the fruit of what we too often mock as "public spirit," has been one of the glories of free society, important alike in the material benefits and mental stimulation it has brought to thousands of American communities. Even today, when men turn ever more confidently toward government for solutions to community needs, the area for voluntary action is practically boundless. In Franklin's day civic improvements came from the people or came not at all. The war against civic indolence may seem endless and futile, but the day it ceases will mark the end of free society. Present-day "good citizens" can take heart and lessons from Benjamin Franklin, who knew how to use tact, imagination, perseverance, and democratic sympathy to help his friends make their city "a good place to live."

III

Franklin's key career was that of politician-diplomat. Entering provincial politics in 1736 as clerk to the Assembly, intercolonial politics in 1753 as deputy Postmaster-General for North America, and imperial affairs in 1757 as special agent of the Assembly in London, he became a wise and able practitioner at every level of public life. He knew what it was to stump for office, palaver with Indians, correspond with governors, wheedle appointments, administer important enterprises, convert popular sentiment, dicker with lords and gentlemen, write laws and constitutions and, finally, to stand before kings as a master diplomat. In all this, being Franklin, he was constantly engaged in self-education, putting principles to the test and finding new principles in the testing. We cannot estimate the vigor of his political faith unless we recall the variety of experience on which it drew.

In Pennsylvania he was clerk of the Assembly (1736-1751), deputy postmaster at Philadelphia (1737-1753), printer to the province, common soldier and colonel of the Pennsylvania militia, representative in the Assembly (1751-1764), and Speaker (1764)—and in addition filled a half dozen other offices from alderman to Indian commissioner. In a muddled political situation that found the Assembly appealing to the Crown for conversion from a proprietary to a royal colony, Franklin was a shrewd leader of the popular party. The struggle between Governor and Assembly in Pennsylvania was little different in character from the legislative-executive battles in other capitals of North America. The fact that the Governor represented Penns rather than Hanovers only sharpened popular resentment against privilege and legalized inequality. Lingering feudal-

ism was the issue in Pennsylvania, and against it Franklin
was a shrewd and relentless warrior. The chief proprietor
paid him an unwitting compliment in his private correspondence:

He broaches a Doctrine . . . that Obedience to Governors
is no more due than protection to the People. . . . It is not
fit to be always in the heads of the unthinking Multitude. . . .
He is a dangerous Man and I should be glad he inhabited any
other Country, as I believe him of a very uneasy spirit, however as he is a Sort of Tribune of the People, he must be treated
with regard.

As North American Franklin filled two important posts.
Although he shared the postmaster-generalship with William Hunter of Virginia, his own energy and Hunter's ill
health combined to lodge in Franklin the chief responsibility. His success in improving this long-neglected service
and in making it pay revenues to the mother country was
one of his most satisfying achievements. He introduced
uniform accounting-methods, selected new routes, speeded
deliveries, instituted the penny post and dead-letter office,
and generally astounded the post office in London with his
efficiency and zeal. More important, he helped draw the
colonies more closely together and in his tours of inspec-
tion won a unique comprehension of their common problems. His knowledge of the population, geography, products, and sentiments of North America was unsurpassed.
Franklin's second service to all the colonies was his performance as commissioner from Pennsylvania to the Albany
Congress of 1754. His farsighted but rejected "Plan of
Union" shows how his mind was running on before those
of his fellow Americans. Had colonists or Crown heeded
his prophetic voice, the course of British-American relations
might have run in stiller channels.

Franklin's progression from politician to statesman and

from colonial administrator to imperial diplomat was effected during his first mission to England. Dispatched in 1757 to plead the popular cause against the proprietors, particularly to persuade the Privy Council to permit the proprietary estates to be taxed like other lands, Franklin achieved the purpose of his mission, reaped the first rich harvest of his fame, and after five happy years returned home a citizen of the world. By the time of his next two adventures abroad—in England (1764-1775) as a sort of ambassador extraordinary from the colonies, and in France (1776-1785) on the most famous of all American diplomatic missions—Franklin's and America's colonial phase had drawn to an abrupt close.

Through all these years, colonial and Revolutionary, Franklin never wandered from the libertarian faith that he had first proclaimed publicly in 1722: "I am . . . a mortal Enemy to arbitrary Government and unlimited Power. I am naturally very jealous for the Rights and Liberties of my Country." Even when assailed by bitter enemies and misguided friends, he clung to a belief in the capacity of plain people to govern themselves. In fame as in obscurity Franklin showed himself a convinced democrat. It was America's good fortune to be represented at the points of decisive diplomacy by a man not only wise, famous, and infinitely able, but also benevolent, good-humored, and thoroughly democratic. The tune of Franklin's diplomacy was pitched almost scientifically to the aspirations and attitudes of the rising American multitude.

IV

Franklin's political thought is as perplexing as it is intriguing, as elusive as it is important. He was an able and productive political pamphleteer. He reflected with peculiar accuracy the changing political moods of eighteenth-century America, and was looked upon as the representative colonist by the keenest observers of his time. He helped introduce to the American mind four or five fundamental assumptions about government and society. Yet he was never in the ordinary sense a theorist or philosopher in the field of political science.

The proof of this observation lies in Franklin's own writings: The sum total of his strictly philosophical musings about government and politics would fill, quite literally, about two printed pages. He wrote authoritatively about scores of events and problems that had persuaded other men to philosophize at length about the nature and purpose of government, but his own arguments were descriptive, statistical, propagandistic, and totally lacking in any appeal to fundamentals. He was the one American patriot to write influentially about the events of 1763-1776 without calling upon natural law, the rights of man, and the social contract.

If ever Franklin expressed a clear and conscious thought on such matters as the origin of government or the nature of authority, the research for this chapter, which has led through a half-dozen libraries and several hundred letters, pamphlets, and rough scribblings, has been unable to find it. He seems to have been constitutionally incapable of the kind of writing done by Williams, Wise, Mayhew, Otis, and almost every other political figure in colonial or Revolutionary America. If one small trickle of theory had leaked through somewhere out of the vast structure of his political writings, we might rejoice to have found the sure source of his ideas. The amazing fact that he never once permitted this to happen leaves us wondering if this refusal to philosophize was not the result of a calculated, rigidly observed rule of political argument.

His early and unhappy venture into speculation about the cosmos could well have conditioned his subsequent thinking about politics. "The great uncertainty I found in metaphysical reasonings disgusted me, and I quitted that kind of reading and study for others more satisfactory." The nature of his task should also be remembered: Most of his mature political arguments were letters to the English press, not speeches to the American assemblies. He could hardly have rung the changes on natural rights and revolution in the *London Chronicle* or *Public Advertiser*. And certainly one piece like his *Rules by which a Great Empire may be reduced to a Small One* was worth a hundred passionate appeals to God and nature in the attempt to sway British opinion. In any case, there is no acceptable explanation why Benjamin Franklin, of all people, should have been one of the least philosophical statesmen in American history.

Were the person under analysis anyone but Franklin, this chapter would end here. Yet we are dealing with the great democrat of colonial America, and we must somehow wring from his practical arguments the political faith that he doggedly refused to make articulate. One method of accomplishing this task is to describe Franklin's beliefs as other men saw them. This technique is not ordinarily to be trusted, but in a case like this it is the only alternative to no technique at all. And we have reasonable evidence, drawn particularly from Franklin's consistent actions in support of the popular cause, that he did espouse the principles ascribed to him by friend and foe. These principles may be reduced to two major headings: natural law and radical Whiggery.

It is impossible to evaluate the extent of Franklin's dedication to natural law and natural rights. As scientist, skeptic, and unprejudiced student of universal history, he could not have missed the inconsistencies and historical distortions in Locke's political writings. On the other hand, his pragmatic mind, which was always more concerned with the effects of a political philosophy than with its logic or symmetry, would have been the first to recognize the usefulness to the popular cause of a system that was based on the notion of government by the consent of the governed. Among the bits of evidence proving that Franklin accepted the dominant theory of his time and class are these: He studied and admired "the great Mr. Locke's" philosophical writings and was hardly less devoted to Algernon Sidney; as a member of the Committee of Five he read over and endorsed Jefferson's rough draft of the Declaration of Independence; and he was widely credited, especially in England, with the authorship of *Common Sense,* which Paine had published anonymously in Philadelphia. It was even rumored that the Queen had caught the Prince of Wales redhanded with "Dr. Franklin's pamphlet Common Sense."

Scattered through Franklin's pamphlets, letters, and notes are other witnesses to his tacit conformity to the "party line," phrases and sentences that glimmer here and there in the great mass of his practical arguments. To quote these out of context would be unfair to Franklin, and indeed quite misleading. It must therefore suffice to state the impression they leave: that Franklin endorsed as useful doctrines the state of nature (in which all men are free and equal), the social contract, natural law, natural rights (including "life, liberty, and property," as well as freedom of inquiry, expression, petition, religion, and migration), and the happiness and security of the people as the purpose of government. As the most conspicuous Revolutionary of

1776, Franklin could hardly have doubted the right of resistance and revolution, but we may search his writings in vain for any clear statement of this doctrine.

The only elements in the natural rights-natural law theory that Franklin seems to have enlarged upon were property and equality. Although he shared generally the popular view of the sanctity of property—"Does not *every Man's Feelings* Declare that his Property is not to be taken from him without his Consent?"—he seems to have entertained a somewhat more radical, socially minded view of the relation of any one man's possessions to the common weal. The Franklin touch is manifest in this passage:

All Property, indeed, except the Savage's temporary Cabin, his Bow, his Matchcoat, and other little Acquisitions, absolutely necessary for his Subsistence, seems to me to be the Creature of public Convention. Hence the Public has the Right of Regulating Descents, and all other Conveyances of Property, and even of limiting the Quantity and the Uses of it. All the Property that is necessary to a Man, for the Conservation of the Individual and the Propagation of the Species, is his natural Right, which none can justly deprive him of: But all Property superfluous to such purposes is the Property of the Publick, who, by their Laws, have created it, and who may therefore by other Laws dispose of it, whenever the Welfare of the Publick shall demand such Disposition. He that does not like civil Society on these Terms, let him retire and live among Savages. He can have no right to the benefits of Society, who will not pay his Club towards the Support of it.

Franklin's belief in equality was the obverse of his well-known impatience with "places, pensions, and peerages," with the stupidity and injustice of legalized inequalities of any description. He came to this belief gradually, for in his earlier years he flirted with the doctrine of the stake-in-society. In the end, his naturally democratic sympathies triumphed resoundingly. Near the close of his life, in argu-

ing against property as a qualification for the suffrage, he
had this to say to the proponents of aristocracy:

The Combinations of Civil Society are not like those of a
Set of Merchants, who club their Property in different Proportions for Building and Freighting a Ship, and may therefore
have some Right to vote in the Disposition of the Voyage in
a greater or less Degree according to their respective Contributions; but the important ends of Civil Society, and the personal Securities of Life and Liberty, these remain the same in
every Member of the society; and the poorest continues to have
an equal Claim to them with the most opulent, whatever Difference Time, Chance, or Industry may occasion in their Circumstances.

Franklin believed in natural rights and natural law as
much as he could believe in any body of doctrine, and he
subscribed with extra fervor to the basic Lockean belief in
"a Society in which the Ruling Power is circumscribed by
previous Laws or Agreements." Like all men of his time he
put his faith in limited government, government in which
the rulers were the servants of the people.

In considering Franklin a radical Whig the men about
him were recognizing his kinship with scores of other representatives of the popular party in the colonial assemblies.
With Pitt and King William as their heroes, the Glorious
Revolution as their golden age, and the uncorrupted
British Constitution as their idea of a perfect governmental
system, the colonial Whigs were preparing the ground in
which American democracy was to grow. The battle cry of
the good Whig, in the colonies as in England, was "Liberty!"—by which he meant constitutionalism, representation, government by "the people" (those who had some
property), "the rights of Englishmen," and a system of
balanced government in which the legislature was actually
dominant. Through most of his life, indeed through all of

it as colonial, Franklin was in the van of the liberty-loving Whigs, hoping always to settle his colony's constitution "firmly on the Foundations of Equity and English Liberty." Not all colonial Whigs—Franklin's friend Joseph Gallo-way, for example—were able to make the transition to independence, fewer still from there to democracy. Frank-lin seems to have had no trouble. He was a notable speci-men of that uncommon species, the man who grows more democratic with age, fame, respectability, and the gout.

Among Franklin's literary remains was a printed paper, endorsed in his hand with the statement, "Some Good Whig Principles." In point of fact, these principles pushed well beyond sound Whiggery into radical country, which ex-plains why he found them especially "good." These could easily have been his own words as he arrived in the mother country in 1764:

It is declared,

First, That the government of this realm, and the making of laws for the same, ought to be lodged in the hands of King, Lords of Parliament, and Representatives of *the whole body* of the freemen of this realm.

Secondly, That *every man* of the commonalty (excepting infants, insane persons, and criminals) is, of common right, and by the laws of God, *a freeman,* and entitled to the free enjoy-ment of *liberty.*

Thirdly, That liberty, or freedom, consists in having *an actual share* in the appointment of those who frame the laws, and who are to be the guardians of every man's life, property, and peace; for the *all* of one man is as dear to him as the *all* of another; and the poor man has an *equal* right, but *more* need, to have representatives in the legislature than the rich one.

Fourthly, That they who have *no* voice nor vote in the elect-ing of representatives, *do not enjoy* liberty; but are absolutely *enslaved* to those who have votes. . . .

And, sixthly and lastly . . . that it is *the right* of the commonalty of this realm to elect a *new* House of Commons once in *every year,* according to the ancient and sacred laws of the land. . . .

Two more preliminary observations, and we shall be ready to outline Franklin's special contributions to the American tradition. The first touches upon his habits of thought. The methods Franklin employed in weighing political issues were hardly less significant than the decisions he reached. We will have a good deal less trouble with his political mind if we will remember that he was pragmatist, insisting that all ideas be judged by their effects; scientist, distrusting dogma and prizing free inquiry; skeptic, doubting all certainty and never "wholly committed" to any cause or truth; and generalist, ranging through all disciplines and integrating them masterfully into one grand comprehension of human knowledge.

The second point concerns the location of his recorded ideas. For the most part, they are the same as for the other great figures of his time, who wrote copiously, influentially, and with absolutely no system. Pamphlets on current issues, letters to the press, private correspondence, and formal papers are the categories of authorship in which his contributions are to be sought. Hardly less important are the so-called "marginalia," notes made by Franklin in the margins of his copies of other men's pamphlets. Some of these notes are testimony to a universal human urge, the urge to scribble "This Wiseacre," "No!", "Childish," "All mere Quibbling," and "A Falsity!" alongside the brash paragraphs of enemy pamphleteers. Most of them, however, were written in a serious, searching vein, for they were one of his favorite methods of preparing retorts to the press. Although Albert H. Smyth considered these scribblings "crude and fragmentary," "never intended for publication," and therefore not worth printing, other scholars have valued them highly. These precious indications, in Franklin's own hand, of his innermost thoughts on the great issues of the 1760's are preserved in the Library of Congress, the New York Public Library, the Yale Library, the Philadelphia Athenaeum, and the Historical Society of Pennsylvania. They are a unique source of his political ideas.

Franklin's specific contributions to the aggregate of libertarian principles inherited by the Revolutionary generation were a patchwork of utility, reason, and warm human sympathy. Some of his offerings were directly and consciously bestowed on his fellow citizens. Some were working principles of method and attitude that he was content to practice and to let other men spin out into theories of liberty. All were essential supports of the new way of life and thought that he represented so magnificently before the rulers and people of Europe. Political pragmatism, conciliation and compromise, freedom of speech and press, economic individualism, and federalism were the elements of American democracy to which Franklin devoted special attention.

V

Pragmatism as a rule of conscious political action has never had a more eminent exponent than Benjamin Franklin. There were great pragmatists before this greatest of pragmatists. Indeed, much of the political history of colonial America was written by men who had "the attitude of looking away from first things, principles, 'categories,' supposed necessities; and of looking towards last things, fruits, consequences, facts." But in Franklin's life and political arguments this method became an acknowledged if yet nameless American fundamental. William James, in his lectures on pragmatism in 1906 and 1907, described this philosophy as "a new name for some old ways of thinking." While Franklin might have been perplexed by the label, he would certainly have recognized his own ways of thinking. No man could have been less concerned with origins and first principles or more concerned with consequences and facts. The character of his natural science left its mark on his political science. He was perhaps the most thorough-going utilitarian America has produced.

Franklin's political pragmatism was simply one influential expression of his general attitude toward life and its problems. He was not a political philosopher; he was not a philosopher at all. He was prepared to investigate every principle and institution known to the human race, but only through practical and unspeculative methods. He limited his own thought-process to the one devastating question: *Does it work?*, or more exactly, *Does it work well?* Most men who call themselves pragmatists, especially in politics, examine the evidence of consequences and facts from a predetermined observation-post constructed out of strongly held articles of faith. They are pragmatists within limits, within a context that itself may not be put to the test and may well be an irrational inheritance or a rationalized faith. Not so Franklin, who seemed willing to subject even his most basic beliefs, if they could be called that, to the test of experience. He was democrat, Whig, and friend of liberty because democracy, Whiggery, and liberty had demonstrated themselves to his uncommitted mind to be the best practical solutions to the problems facing men in society. He had proved and found solid the very context of his pragmatism.

An example of Franklin's consistent devotion to political pragmatism was his well-known attitude on the social usefulness of organized religion. Himself a pagan skeptic with

no need for pastoral intervention, he nevertheless had pronounced and favorable views of the value of religion to a
free and stable society. He had decided, after much observation in Boston and Philadelphia, that one of the essentials of self-government was a high level of public morality.
He had decided further that such a condition of public
morality was largely the product of organized religion. The
churches and sects of New England and the middle colonies had helped create a collective state of mind conducive
to habits of self-reliance and self-government. It had
nourished the way of life that his other observations had
already pointed out as the most blessed for the average
man. Organized religion had worked, and worked well, in
the colonies. It must therefore be supported, even by the
skeptic. Franklin went to church, when he went to church,
because it was "decent and proper," not because he was a
believer. In his proposals that led to the founding of the
Academy, he advocated the teaching of history because it
would "also afford frequent Opportunities of showing the
Necessity of a *Publick Religion,* from its Usefulness to the
Publick; the Advantage of a Religious Character among
private Persons; the Mischiefs of Superstition, etc., and the
Excellency of the CHRISTIAN RELIGION above all others
antient or modern." He abandoned logical deism because
"this doctrine, though it might be true, was not very useful." He turned back to give support to Christianity because this doctrine, though it might be untrue, was highly
indispensable to his kind of society.

Education, too, was important because useful. Franklin's
faith in education had a dozen outlets. The American
Philosophical Society, the Library Company, the University
of Pennsylvania, and the Franklin Funds of Boston and
Philadelphia are present-day reminders of his high regard
for formal and informal education of all classes, ages, and

conditions of men. The famous *Proposals Relating to the Education of Youth in Pensilvania* (1749) are utilitarian to the core. The modern reader cannot suppress the pleasant suspicion that Franklin's ideal academy would be geared to turn out the maximum number of young Franklins.

The proprietary government of Pennsylvania, target of his early popularism, was likewise put to the test, but found wanting. Franklin could easily have based his mistrust of this system on principle alone; he preferred to condemn it for its harmful effects. In a characteristic passage from the aptly titled *Cool Thoughts on the Present Situation* (1764), he launched this pragmatic attack on the proprietary system:

Considering all Circumstances, I am at length inclin'd to think, that the Cause of these miserable Contentions is not to be sought for merely in the Depravity and Selfishness of human Minds. . . . I suspect therefore, that the Cause is radical, interwoven in the Constitution, and so become of the very Nature, of Proprietary Governments; and will therefore produce its Effects, as long as such Governments continue. And, as some Physicians say, every Animal Body brings into the World among its original Stamina the Seeds of that Disease that shall finally produce its Dissolution; so the Political Body of a Proprietary Government, contains those convulsive Principles that will at length destroy it.

I may not be Philosopher enough to develop those Principles, nor would this Letter afford me Room, if I had Abilities, for such a Discussion. The *Fact* seems sufficient for our Purpose, and the *Fact* is notorious, that such Contentions have been in all Proprietary Governments, and have brought, or are now bringing, them all to a Conclusion.

A final example of Franklin's political pragmatism was his oft-repeated warning against laws that outrage a people's fundamental opinions. This was the sort of argument—calling attention to consequences rather than constitutional rights—with which he attempted to dissuade the advocates of harsh measures for the colonies. He even printed small cards describing "The Result of England's Persistence in Her Policy Towards the Colonies."

History affords us many instances of the ruin of states, by the prosecution of measures ill suited to the temper and genius of their people. The ordaining of laws in favour of *one* part of the nation, to the prejudice and oppression of *another,* is certainly the most erroneous and mistaken policy. An *equal* dispensation of protection, rights, privileges, and advantages, is what every part is entitled to, and ought to enjoy; it being a matter of no moment to the state, whether a subject grows rich and flourishing on the Thames or the Ohio, in Edinburgh or Dublin. These measures never fail to create great and violent jealousies and animosities between the people favoured and the people oppressed; whence a total separation of affections, interests, political obligations, and all manner of connexions, necessarily ensue, by which the whole state is weakened, and perhaps ruined for ever!

Franklin's supremely practical observation, "the *Fact* seems sufficient for our Purpose, and the *Fact* is notorious," has become a major working principle of this race of pragmatists, and to him and his popular writings must go at least some of the credit.

VI

Franklin placed extraordinary value on the spirit and techniques of conciliation and compromise. By nature and experience he was disposed to seek peace and harmony in whatever controversy he might have wandered into by design or accident. His nature was skeptical and undogmatic; he could even doubt his own opinions. The benign and artful speech that James Wilson delivered for him on

the last day of the Convention of 1787 was characteristic
of a lifetime of active political argument.

I confess that I do not entirely approve of this Constitution
at present, but Sir, I am not sure I shall never approve it: For
having lived long, I have experienced many instances of being
obliged, by better information or fuller consideration, to change
opinions even on important subjects, which I once thought right,
but found to be otherwise. It is therefore that the older I grow
the more apt I am to doubt my own judgment, and to pay
more respect to the judgment of others. Most men indeed as
well as most sects in religion, think themselves in possession of
all truth, and that wherever others differ from them it is so
far error. Steele, a Protestant, in a dedication tells the Pope,
that the only difference between our two churches in their
opinions of the certainty of their doctrine, is, the Romish
Church is infallible, and the Church of England is never in
the wrong. But tho' many private persons think almost as highly
of their own infallibility as of that of their Sect, few express
it so naturally as a certain French lady, who in a little dispute
with her sister, said, I don't know how it happens, Sister, but
I meet with nobody but myself that's *always* in the right. *Il
n'y a que moi qui a toujours raison.*

In these sentiments, Sir, I agree to this Constitution, with all
its faults, if they are such; because I think a general Government necessary for us . . . I consent, Sir, to this Constitution,
because I expect no better, and because I am not sure that it
is not the best. The opinions I have had of its errors I sacrifice
to the public good. I have never whisper'd a syllable of them
abroad. Within these walls they were born, and here they
shall die. . . .

On the whole, Sir, I cannot help expressing a wish, that
every member of the Convention who may still have objections
to it, would with me on this occasion doubt a little of his own
infallibility, and to make *manifest* our *unanimity*, put his name
to this Instrument.

Experience confirmed his natural faith in conciliation. He was a shrewd observer of proceedings in the Junto, the Assembly, and a thousand public meetings. He noted the differing consequences of the differing ways in which men might hold and express the same opinions. Having decided that the spirit of compromise was an essential of political success and the basis of stable, peaceful, effective self-government, he acted in character by laying down rules that would improve himself and others in this important respect.

I made it a rule to forbear all direct contradiction to the sentiments of others and all positive assertion of my own. I even forbade myself . . . the use of every word or expression in the language that imported a fixed opinion, such as "certainly," "undoubtedly," etc.; and I adopted instead of them, "I conceive," "I apprehend," or "I imagine" a thing to be so or so, or "It so appears to me at present." When another asserted something that I thought an error, I denied myself the pleasure of contradicting him abruptly and of showing immediately some absurdity in his proposition; and in answering I began by observing that in certain cases or circumstances his opinion would be right, but that in the present case there "appeared" or "seemed to me" some difference, etc. I soon found the advantage of this change in my manners: The conversations I engaged in went on more pleasantly; the modest way in which I proposed my opinions procured them a readier reception and less contradiction; I had less mortification when I was found to be in the wrong, and I more easily prevailed with others to give up their mistakes and join with me when I happened to be in the right.

The Junto conducted its discussions deliberately in this spirit.

Our debates were to be under the direction of a president, and to be conducted in the sincere spirit of enquiry after truth,

without fondness for dispute or desire of victory; and to prevent
warmth, all expressions of positiveness in opinion or of direct
contradiction were after some time made contraband and pro-
hibited under small pecuniary penalties.

Franklin never made the mistake of identifying conciliation and compromise with democracy, of regarding
this spirit as an end in itself. In the Assembly and before
the House of Commons his "desire of victory" was keen
and apparent, but he was certain that victory would be
easier to gain if "fondness for dispute" were erased from
his nature or at least not betrayed in debate. He could take
a firm stand—even commit himself to an advanced position, as he did with few qualms in subscribing to the
Declaration of Independence—but he was satisfied that
first he had explored all possible alternatives and had done
his best to avoid the final break.

The significance of conciliation and compromise for successful democracy has never been examined satisfactorily
in philosophical terms. It is to be deeply regretted that
Franklin could never bring himself to theorize in letter
or pamphlet about this fundamental principle of his personal code and public faith. It "worked well," and that was
enough for him. Yet any political scientist who attempts
to fix with finality the place of conciliation and compromise in the American tradition will be well advised to
study Franklin's political conduct. His life argues power-
fully that democracy depends on men with a nice feeling
for the proper balance between faith and skepticism,
principle and compromise, tenacity and conciliation. Franklin was boasting, not complaining, when he wrote from
London to his American posterity:

Hence it has often happened to me, that while I have been

thought here too much of an American, I have in America been deem'd too much of an Englishman.

He could hardly have given himself a finer compliment.

VII

Franklin was an influential defender of the twin freedoms of speech and press. As the leading printer and journalist of the middle colonies, as scientist dedicated to free inquiry and international exchange of information, and as politician convinced that discussion and compromise were the essence of self-government, he had intense personal reasons for championing freedom of expression.

Through seventy years he never wavered in his belief in the social usefulness of freedom of speech, nor ever shrank from active conflict with those who would suppress it. In 1722, when Benjamin was only sixteen years old, his brother James was "taken up, censured, and imprisoned for a month" for printing in his *New-England Courant* a political piece that "gave offence to the Assembly."

During my brother's confinement, which I resented a good deal notwithstanding our private differences, I had the management of the paper, and I made bold to give our rulers some rubs in it, which my brother took very kindly, while others began to consider me in an unfavourable light as a young genius that had a turn for libelling and satire. My brother's discharge was accompanied with an order from the House (a very odd one) that "James Franklin should no longer print the paper called the *New England Courant*." There was a consultation held in our printing house amongst his friends in this conjuncture. Some proposed to elude the order by changing the the name of the paper; but my brother seeing inconveniences in that, it was finally concluded on as a better way to let it be printed for the future under the name of "Benjamin Franklin."

The piece in which the apprentice "made bold to give our rulers some rubs" was the eighth of his communications to the *Courant* from "Silence Dogood." In this letter he quoted at length the most famous of *Cato's Letters*, which he presented as an "Abstract from the London Journal." Even over a pseudonym it was a bold swipe at authority, and the wonder is that Benjamin did not follow James to jail.

WITHOUT Freedom of Thought, there can be no such Thing as Wisdom; and no such Thing as publick Liberty, without Freedom of Speech; which is the Right of every Man, as far as by it, he does not hurt or controul the Right of another: And this is the only Check it ought to suffer, and the only Bounds it ought to Know.

This sacred Privilege is so essential to free Governments, that the Security of Property, and the Freedom of Speech always go together; and in those wretched Countries where a Man cannot call his Tongue his own, he can scarce call any Thing else his own. Whoever would overthrow the Liberty of a Nation, must begin by subduing the Freeness of Speech; a *Thing* terrible to Publick Traytors. . . .

The Administration of Government is nothing else but the Attendance of the *Trustees of the People* upon the Interest and Affairs of the People: And as it is the Part and Business of the People, for whose Sake alone all publick Matters are, or ought to be transacted, to see whether they be well or ill transacted; so it is the Interest, and ought to be the Ambition, of all honest Magistrates, to have their Deeds openly examined, and publickly scan'd. . . .

Misrepresentation of publick Measures is easily overthrown, by representing publick Measures truly; when they are honest, they ought to be publickly known, that they may be publickly commended; but if they are knavish or pernicious, they ought to be publickly detested.

Franklin carried these youthful beliefs through seventy

years of political storms. To freedom of speech, as it was known and cherished in the Whig tradition, he was "wholly committed."

The publisher of the *Pennsylvania Gazette* had considerable influence upon the development of a free and responsible press. Like the best papers in London, the *Gazette* adopted a policy of neutrality in public controversies. Franklin refused to make his paper the organ of the antiproprietary party, but threw its columns open to opinions from all sides. At the same time, he kept constant watch on the political winds that blew and weathered several storms by discreetly reefing his sails. As long as freedom of the press was uncertain in Pennsylvania, he was careful merely to antagonize, not enrage, the proprietary party. Meanwhile he did his best to cement this freedom by printing a responsible journal, by calling attention to the value of differing opinions, and by publishing an account of the trial of John Peter Zenger.

By 1750, the press in England and the colonies had achieved a remarkable measure of freedom. Franklin, who wrote to the *Public Advertiser* that "Free Government depends on Opinion, not on the brutal Force of a Standing Army," made full use in England of what he had helped create in America: an unlicensed, uncensored press in which the public could find all important issues thoroughly, even controversially debated.

Franklin's most influential statement on freedom of press was "An Apology for Printers," which appeared in the *Gazette* June 10, 1731. This "apology" is worth quoting at length, for it is an accurate representation of the principles of a free press which governed popular thinking, if not the law, in eighteenth-century America.

BEING frequently censur'd and condemn'd by different Persons for printing Things which they say ought not to be printed, I have sometimes thought it might be necessary to make a standing Apology for my self, and publish it once a Year, to be read upon all Occasions of that Nature. . . .

I request all who are angry with me on the Account of printing things they don't like, calmly to consider these following Particulars.

1. That the Opinions of Men are almost as various as their Faces; an Observation general enough to become a common Proverb, *So many Men so many Minds*.

2. That the Business of Printing has chiefly to do with Mens Opinions; most things that are printed tending to promote some, or oppose others.

3. That hence arises the peculiar Unhappiness of that Business, which other Callings are no way liable to; they who follow Printing being scarce able to do any thing in their way of getting a Living, which shall not probably give Offence to some, and perhaps to many; . . .

5. Printers are educated in the Belief, that when Men differ in Opinion, both Sides ought equally to have the Advantage of being heard by the Publick; and that when Truth and Error have fair Play, the former is always an overmatch for the latter: Hence they chearfully serve all contending Writers that pay them well, without regarding on which side they are of the Question in Dispute. . . .

10. That notwithstanding what might be urg'd in behalf of a Man's being allow'd to do in the Way of his Business whatever he is paid for, yet Printers do continually discourage the Printing of great Numbers of bad things, and stifle them in the Birth. I my self have constantly refused to print anything that might countenance Vice, or promote Immorality; tho' by complying in such Cases with the corrupt Taste of the Majority I might have got much Money.

To this shrewd and useful set of working principles should be added a reflection penned by Franklin in a private letter more than a half century later.

It is a pleasing reflection, arising from the contemplation of our successful struggle . . . that liberty, which some years since appeared in danger of extinction, is now regaining the ground she had lost, that arbitrary governments are likely to become more mild and reasonable, and to expire by degrees, giving place to more equitable forms; one of the effects this of the art of printing, which diffuses so general a light, augmenting with the growing day, and of so penetrating a nature, that all the window-shutters despotism and priestcraft can oppose to keep it out, prove insufficient.

The old man at Passy was not so lucid as he had been in London or Philadelphia, yet his faith in the power of truth and in the influence of the printed word was as strong as ever. Franklin went to his republican grave secure in the knowledge that he had done as much as any other man to advertise freedom of expression to the American political consciousness.

VIII

Many Americans would argue that Franklin's reputation as herald of democracy should rest in the first instance upon his contributions to economic individualism. Certainly no one, whether friend or foe of the American system, would deny that our political democracy is underpinned and shaped by a well-defined set of economic principles and institutions. Our economic and political systems, like our economic and political traditions, have always been inseparable, mutually nourishing elements of "the American way of life." American democracy has been, in the best and truest sense of the terms, middle-class, bourgeois, free-enterprise democracy. The twentieth-century trend toward government regulation and the welfare state has, if anything, sharpened our comprehension of this historical truth.

In the light of this truth, Franklin's significance is

unmistakable. As self-made business success he represented to the world the rise to prominence of the American bourgeoisie; as author and moralist he preached to "the middling people" the personal virtues that a nation of businessmen was to practice and cherish; as the best-known economist in colonial America he was a respected foe of mercantilism and advocate of the liberating principles of laissez-faire.

The first and second of these points may be considered together, for Franklin's moralizing was an unsolicited testimonial to his own "way to wealth." Father Abraham's formula for worldly success—*"Industry and Frugality"*—paired virtues that Franklin had not come by naturally. He had cultivated these qualities consciously in order to win financial independence, and he saw no reason why they could not be cultivated by other men in business. The unique features of the American democratic culture owe a good deal to these memorable words from *The Way to Wealth:*

It would be thought a hard Government that should tax its People one-tenth Part of their *Time*, to be employed in its Service. But *Idleness* taxes many of us much more, if we reckon all that is spent in absolute *Sloth*, or doing of nothing, with that which is spent in idle Employment or Amusements, that amount to nothing. *Sloth*, by bringing on Diseases, absolutely shortens Life. *Sloth, like Rust, consumes faster than Labour wears; while the used Key is always bright,* as Poor Richard says. *But dost thou love Life, then do not squander Time, for that's the stuff Life is made of,* as Poor Richard says. How much more than is necessary do we spend in sleep, forgetting that *The sleeping Fox catches no Poultry,* and that *There will be sleeping enough in the Grave,* as Poor Richard says.

If Time be of all Things the most precious, wasting Time must be, as Poor Richard says, *the greatest Prodigality;* since, as he elsewhere tells us, *Lost Time is never found again; and what we call Time enough, always proves little enough:* Let us then up and be doing, and doing to the Purpose; so by Diligence shall we do more with less Perplexity. *Sloth makes all Things difficult, but Industry all easy,* as *Poor Richard* says; and *He that riseth late must trot all Day, and shall scarce overtake his Business at Night;* while *Laziness travels so slowly, that Poverty soon overtakes him,* as we read in *Poor Richard,* who adds, *Drive thy Business, let not that drive thee;* and *Early to Bed, and early to rise, makes a Man healthy, wealthy, and wise.*

So what signifies *wishing* and *hoping* for better Times. We may make these Times better, if we bestir ourselves. *Industry need not wish,* as *Poor Richard* says, *and he that lives upon Hope will die fasting. There are no Gains without Pains; then Help Hands, for I have no Lands,* or if I have, they are smartly taxed. And, as *Poor Richard* likewise observes, *He that hath a Trade hath an Estate; and he that hath a Calling, hath an Office of Profit and Honour;* but then the *Trade* must be worked at, and the Calling well followed, or neither the *Estate* nor the *Office* will enable us to pay our Taxes. If we are industrious, we shall never starve; for as *Poor Richard* says, *At the working Man's House Hunger looks in, but dares not enter.* Nor will the Bailiff or the Constable enter, for *Industry pays Debts, while Despair encreaseth them,* says *Poor Richard.* What though you have found no Treasure, nor has any rich Relation left you a Legacy, *Diligence is the Mother of Goodluck* as *Poor Richard* says *and God gives all Things to Industry. Then plough deep, while Sluggards sleep, and you shall have Corn to sell and to keep, says Poor Dick. . . .* 'Tis true there is much to be done, and perhaps you are weak-handed, but stick to it steadily; and you will see great Effects, for *Constant Dropping wears away Stones,* and by *Diligence and Patience the Mouse ate in two the Cable;* and *Little Strokes fell great Oaks,* as *Poor Richard* says in his Almanack, the Year I cannot just now remember. . . .

So much for Industry, my Friends, and Attention to one's own Business; but to these we must add *Frugality,* if we would make our *Industry* more certainly successful. A Man may, if he knows not how to save as he gets, *keep his Nose all his Life to the Grindstone,* and die not worth a *Groat* at last. *A fat Kitchen makes a lean Will,* as *Poor Richard* says. . . . *If you would be wealthy,* says he, in another Almanack, *think of Saving as well as of Getting: The Indies have not made Spain rich, because her Outgoes are greater than her Incomes.*

Away then with your expensive Follies, and you will not then have so much Cause to complain of hard Times, heavy Taxes, and chargeable Families; for, as *Poor Dick* says,

> Women and Wine, Game and Deceit,
> Make the Wealth small and the Wants great.

And farther, *What maintains one Vice, would bring up two Children.* You may think perhaps, that a *little* Tea, or a *little* Punch now and then, Diet a *little* more costly, Clothes a *little* finer, and a *little* Entertainment now and then, can be no *great* Matter; but remember what *Poor Richard* says, *Many a Little makes a Mickle;* and farther, Beware of little *Expences; A small Leak will sink a great Ship;* and again, *Who Dainties love, shall Beggars prove;* and moreover, *Fools make Feasts, and wise Men eat them.*

Whether industry and frugality were qualities of Puritain origin—whether Franklin was, as many scholars have insisted, an ideological middleman between Cotton Mather and John D. Rockefeller—is a question of scant meaning for his status as prophet of American capitalism. The young Franklin could easily have read about the pleasant consequences of industry and frugality in several non-Calvinistic writers, or could have learned them from the Quaker merchants of Philadelphia. It is highly probable that this lesson, too, was learned pragmatically, out of his own experience. In any case, his unsophisticated, straightforward writings on the elements of business success—the prefaces to *Poor Richard, The Way to Wealth,* and after his death the priceless *Autobiography*—were translated and retranslated into a dozen languages, printed and reprinted in hundreds of editions, read and reread by millions of people, especially by young and impressionable Americans. The influence of these few hundred pages has been matched by that of no other American book.

Industry and frugality can hardly be called political principles. Yet as the central elements in the American creed of economic individualism their influence upon our politics has been pronounced and lasting. The character of a nation cannot be other than the aggregate of the characters of its citizens, and American democracy surely owes a healthy portion of its past and present character to the efforts of many of its citizens to imitate the Franklin of the *Autobiography*. The frugal, industrious, self-reliant, community-minded businessman and farmer—the typical American—lives even today in the image of "Benjamin Franklin, printer." Carlyle was not too far from the truth when he looked at Franklin's portrait and exclaimed, "There is the father of all the Yankees."

The Puritan virtues, if we may call them that, do not add up to an especially pleasant and well-rounded personality. Franklin, however, never intended that they should stand alone, and such persons as D. H. Lawrence have done the great bourgeois no honor in confusing his full-bodied character with that of the mythical Poor Richard. All that Franklin was trying to tell his fellow Americans was that first things must be attended to first: When a man had worked and saved his way to success and independence, he could then begin to live a fuller or even quite different life. This is what Franklin had in mind when he had Father Abraham declare, "Be *industrious* and *free*; be *frugal* and *free*." The expansion of America is evidence enough that as elements of a larger tradition, as facets of a whole personality, industry and frugality have given fiber alike to nation and individuals. The American tradition stands fast in the belief that these virtues are indispensable props of freedom and independence, for as Father Abraham observed, "A Ploughman on his Legs is higher than a Gentleman on his Knees."

IX

We must be extremely cautious in presenting Franklin as an early advocate of laissez-faire. Like Jefferson and Lincoln he has been rudely appropriated and glibly quoted as the patron saint of some of our most reactionary movements and organizations. And like Jefferson and Lincoln he was a good deal more benevolent, progressive, and community-minded than those who now call him to judgment against all social legislation.

Franklin's most imposing service to the triumph of laissez-faire was his attack on the restrictive doctrines of mercantilism. He was a colonial tradesman who resented the assignment of America to an inferior economic position. He was a friend of liberty who disliked the efforts of any exploiting group—whether proprietors, princes, priests, or English manufacturers—to prevent the mass of men from realizing their full capabilities and impulses toward freedom. Small wonder that he had no use for mercantilist policies. His central position in the controversy over Parliament's power to legislate for the colonies and his cordial relations with the French Physiocrats strengthened his earlier, provincial convictions that free trade among all nations and colonies was the way to peace and economic prosperity, and that mercantilism, like all unnecessary tampering with "the order of God and Nature," was unwise, unjust, unprofitable, and ultimately unworkable. It is amusing and instructive to notice the very different thought-processes by which Franklin and the Physiocrats arrived at identical conclusions about the unwisdom of government regulation of the economy and the beauties of free trade. The Physiocrats regarded free trade as part of their "natural order"—in the words of Gide and Rist, "that order which seemed obviously the best, not to any individual whomsoever, but to rational, cultured, liberal-minded men like the Physiocrats. It was not the product of the observation of external facts; it was the revelation of a principle within." Nothing could have been further removed from Franklin's pragmatic method of fixing his gaze upon effects and consequences.

Perhaps the clearest evidence of Franklin's devotion to a free economy is to be found in a copy of George Whatley's *The Principles of Trade* in the Library of Congress. This anti-mercantilist tract was published in 1765 and was republished in 1774 with many new notes. The Library of Congress copy, a second edition, bears this inscription on the flyleaf: "The gift of Doctr. B. Franklin to Th. Jefferson," and this note on page 2: "Notes marked B. F. are Doctr. Franklin's." Some of the most important notes in the book are marked "B. F." in Jefferson's hand, and there is little doubt that these were Franklin's contributions to Whatley's new edition. Whatley spoke in his preface of "some very respectable Friends" who had indulged him "with their Ideas and Opinions." The most significant of "B. F.'s" ideas was the note on pages 33-34, a hard-packed essay containing at least four phrases found elsewhere in Franklin's writings. The spelling is Whatley's, but the words are Franklin's:

Perhaps, in general, it wou'd be better if Government medled no farther wide Trade, than to protect it, and let it take its Cours. Most of the Statutes, or Acts, Edicts, Arets and Placaarts of Parliaments, Princes, and States, for regulating, directing, or restraining of Trade; have, we think, been either political Blunders, or Jobbs obtain'd by artful Men, for private Advantage, under Pretence of public Good. When Colbert assembled some wise old Merchants of France; and desir'd their Advice and Opinion, how he cou'd best serve and promote Comerce; their Answer, after Consultation, was, in three words only, *Laissez nous faire.* Let us alone. It is said, by a very solid Writer of the same Nation, that he is wel advanc'd in the Science of Politics, who knows the ful Force of that Maxim *Pas trop gouverner:* Not to govern too strictly, which, perhaps, wou'd be of more Use when aply'd to Trade, than in any other public Concern. It were therefore to be wish'd that Comerce were as fre between al the Nations of the World, as it is between the several Countrys of England.

In his own writings, too, Franklin was outspoken in his praise of the new principles of laissez-faire that were shortly to be more scientifically demonstrated by Adam Smith and others. He did as much as any American to dig the grave of mercantilism. In an age when radical thought was strongly and naturally opposed to government regulation of the economy, a passage such as this was a hard blow for freedom:

It seems contrary to the Nature of Commerce, for Government to interfere in the Prices of Commodities. Trade is a voluntary Thing between Buyer and Seller, in every Article of which each exercises his own Judgment, and is to please himself. . . . Where there are a number of different Traders, the separate desire of each to get more Custom will operate in bringing their goods down to a reasonable Price. It therefore seems to me, that Trade will best find and make its own Rates; and that Government cannot well interfere, unless it would take the whole Trade into its own hands . . . and manage it by its own Servants, at its own Risque.

Franklin's limitations as laissez-faire economist should be clearly understood. In addition to the obvious and characteristic fact that he refused to draw together his scattered arguments against mercantilism into a balanced economic philosophy, several points should be considered by economic individualists who insist upon invoking his illustrious shade: the strong, quite Jeffersonian agrarian bias ("Agriculture is the great Source of Wealth and Plenty"); his community-minded views on the nature of private property; his perception of the social evils of emergent industrialism ("Manufactures are founded in poverty"); his vigorous opposition to government by plutocracy; his consistent hostility to the erection of tariff barriers; and his refusal to pursue the pound after 1748. Franklin was an economic individualist, not because he had any mystic faith in the utility of the profit motive or benefits of an industrial society, but because economic individualism led to personal independence, which in turn enabled a man to live virtuously and usefully. Franklin could hardly have foreseen the great concentrations of wealth and economic power that were to signal the successes of American free enterprise, but we may rest assured that he would have found them poisonous to the simple, friendly, free, communal way of life he hoped his countrymen would cultivate and cherish. In any case, he did much to shape the economy that in turn has helped shape the American governmental system.

X

In most political theories or popular traditions federalism has been at best a convenient technique of constitutional organization; more often than not it has been passed over completely. In the United States of America it has been an article of faith. The Republic was founded upon the concept of limited government, and the existence of the states, semisovereign entities with lives and powers of their own, has always been considered the one trustworthy limit upon all urges toward centralized absolutism. The federal principle is something more fundamental and emotion-provoking than one more check in a system of checks and balances.

Franklin made rich contributions to the theory and practice of American federalism. Almost alone among Americans of the mid-eighteenth century he saw, as usual from a wholly practical point of view, the solid advantages that each colony would derive from a solemn union for well-defined purposes. He was far ahead of the men about him in abandoning provincialism for an intercolonial attitude—too far, it would seem, for his efforts to speed up the slow development of American federalism ended in a magnificent failure.

Franklin tells the story of his adventure in intercolonial diplomacy so frugally and honestly that it would be absurd to hear it from anyone but him:

In 1754 war with France being again apprehended, a congress of commissioners from the different Colonies was by an order of the Lords of Trade to be assembled at Albany, there to confer with the chiefs of the six nations concerning the means of defending both their country and ours. Governor Hamilton having received this order, acquainted the House with it . . . naming the Speaker (Mr. Norris) and myself to join Mr. Thomas Penn and Mr. Secretary Peters as commissioners to act for Pennsylvania . . . we met the other commissioners at Albany about the middle of June. In our way thither, I projected and drew up a plan for the union of all the Colonies under one government, so far as might be necessary for defence and other important general purposes. . . . I ventured to lay it before the Congress. It then appeared that several of the commissioners had formed plans of the same kind. A previous question was first taken whether a union should be established, which passed in the affirmative unanimously. A committee was then appointed, one member from each colony, to consider the several plans and report. Mine happened to be preferred, and with a few amendments was accordingly reported. By this plan the general government was to be administered by a president-general appointed and supported by the Crown and a grand council to be chosen by the representatives of the people of the several Colonies met in their respective Assemblies. The debates upon it in Congress went on daily hand in hand with the Indian business. Many objections and difficulties were started, but at length they were all overcome, and the plan was unanimously agreed to, and copies ordered to be transmitted to the Board of Trade and to the Assemblies of the several provinces. Its fate was singular. The Assemblies did not adopt it, as they all thought there was too much *prerogative* in it; and in England it was judged to have too much of the *democratic*. The Board of Trade therefore did not approve of it; nor recommend it for the approbation of His Majesty.

The powers of the president-general and grand council in Franklin's plan were sharply limited by the purpose of the proposed union—defense of the frontier. They were directed to four specific problems: Indian treaties "in which the general interest of the colonies may be concerned"; war and peace with the Indians; purchases and settlement of western lands; and regulation of Indian trade. To these ends the union was authorized to "raise and pay soldiers," "build forts," and "equip vessels," as well as to "make laws, and lay and levy such general duties, imposts, or taxes, as to them shall appear most equal and just." Representation on the council was to be proportioned to each colony's contributions to the common treasury, and the council was protected against dissolution or prorogation by the president-general. Finally, the interests of the mother country were secured by subjecting all laws to the scrutiny and possible veto of the King-in-Council.

The Albany Plan was not so much the creation of one

man's lively genius as the product of several fine minds
working toward a long-contemplated goal, all arrangements being conditioned sharply by the fear of offending
shortsighted Crown and stubborn colonies. Yet Franklin's
plan was preferred to all others and was adopted by the
commissioners with few changes. Although he did not yet
have a well-developed understanding of the federal principle, he did recognize the advantages and delicacies of confederation for defense. The Albany Plan is a landmark on
the rough road of union that leads through the first Continental Congresses and the Articles of Confederation to
the Constitution of 1787. It was a notable expression of
Franklin's faith in co-operative effort in a common cause.
He never ceased to believe that in this matter at least he
was right and other men wrong.

I am still of opinion it would have been happy for both sides
the water if it had been adopted. The Colonies so united would
have been sufficiently strong to have defended themselves; there
would then have been no need of troops from England; of
course the subsequent pretence for taxing America and the
bloody contest it occasioned would have been avoided. But such
mistakes are not new; history is full of the errors of states and
princes.

In June 1775, as delegate to the second Continental
Congress, Franklin proposed a plan, "Articles of Confederation and Perpetual Union" for the "United Colonies of
North America," which was based on his Albany Plan and
several other instances of colonial federation. Although the
Congress was not ready for any such radical step, Franklin
had once again pointed the way for other men to follow.
In the crucial matter of representation Franklin, a "large-
state" man with no shred of provincial prejudice, was
strongly opposed to the Articles of Confederation eventually adopted. Representation in his proposed Congress was

to be proportioned to population. He was not entirely satisfied with the solution adopted by the Convention of 1787, but he was strong in his final faith in federal union.

Franklin's opinions on imperial federation and the power of Parliament to tax and govern the colonies deserve brief mention. He, too, took part in the process of backing and filling through which leading colonists moved toward the dominion theory finally implied in the Declaration of Independence. Having passed and repassed through the intermediate stages—acknowledgment of Parliament's power to legislate for the colonies, advocacy of colonial representation in Parliament (an old favorite of Franklin's), assertion of the finespun distinction between internal and external taxation, simultaneous and confusing assertion of the distinction between taxation for revenue and taxation for regulation of commerce—Franklin took final refuge in the useful conclusion that the colonies, as equals of the mother country, were united to her only "by having one common sovereign, the King." Under this interpretation of the colonial system, the achievement of independence, at least on paper, involved nothing more than renouncing allegiance to a tyrannical king.

XI

One final observation must be made and supported before we can close the circle of Franklin's political philosophy: In thought, action, and argument he was a warmhearted democrat, in the best and fullest sense of the word. Origin, temperament, environment, and experience all helped produce the leading democrat of the age. The last of these, experience, was especially instrumental. The delightful fact that Franklin, as he saw more and more of the way the world did its business, grew more and more sour on the supposed merits of monarchy and aristocracy leads us to believe that his democracy, too, was of pragmatic origin. Whatever the explanation, there is ample proof of his ever-growing respect for the right and capacity of ordinary men to govern themselves. While his faith in the judgment of the people was not completely uncritical, it was a faith on which he was willing to act.

One example was the manner in which Franklin refused to abandon the tenets of radical Whiggery, but rather refined and republicanized them into a profoundly democratic system of constitutional principles. Franklin was one of the few old Revolutionaries at the Convention of 1787 who did not embrace the new faith in the separation of powers. He signed the Constitution willingly, believing that it was the best obtainable under the circumstances, and hoping that it would not frustrate the natural course of democratic progress. Yet he would have preferred a constitution with these radically different arrangements: a plural executive, unsalaried and probably elected by the legislature; a unicameral legislature, with representation proportioned to population; annual elections for all holders of public office, including officers of the militia; universal manhood suffrage, with no bow to property; a straightforward, unqualified bill of rights; and an easy method of formal amendment.

Since he practiced what he preached and "doubted a little of his own infallibility," he did not find it necessary to withdraw from the Convention. Yet it is clear that he was much in sympathy with the opposition of the radicals to the Constitution. The one point at which he departed from their doctrine may well have been decisive: Having abandoned the provincial attitude before most of the anti-Federalists were born, Franklin had little sympathy for their anti-national point of view. The old imperialist had

great faith in the advantages of a "general government."
He hoped out loud that each member of the proposed Congress would "consider himself rather as a Representative
of the whole, than as an agent for the Interests of a particular State." And he supported a motion that "the national
legislature ought to be empowered to negative all laws,
passed by the several States, contravening, in the opinion
of the national legislature, the articles of union . . . or
any Treaties subsisting under the authority of the union."
Franklin's final political faith was as "national" as it was
"democratical." He was one of the few men in America
unafraid to use both of these adjectives in public.

Another example of Franklin's progress toward an ever
purer democratic faith was his change in attitude on the
question of Negro slavery. Although the Junto had taken
an early stand against slavery, the organizer of the Junto
was not above dealing in "likely young Negroes" as a sideline. In time he came to see the monstrous injustice of the
thing and gave full backing to several organizations devoted to freeing and educating the Negro slave. His last
public act was performed as President of the Pennsylvania
Society for Promoting the Abolition of Slavery, when he
signed a memorial to the House of Representatives calling
for measures to discourage the slave trade. His last public
writing was a letter to the *Federal Gazette* satirizing the
arguments of a Georgia congressman in defense of this
traffic. By the time of his death he had expressed all the
fundamental economic and ethical arguments against slavery, asserting in particular that it was unjust, unnatural,
and inhuman, and a corrupting menace to free institutions
and the love of liberty.

Finally, Franklin was firmly in the popular ranks in his
sanguine opinion of political parties (as, of course, they
existed and were understood in his time). He did not con

sider them "factions" but natural products of free government, ventilators of public issues, and effective instruments
of the popular will. In *The Internal State of America,* an
undated but late sociological musing, Franklin had these
characteristic words to say on a problem that gave some
Framers sleepless nights:

It is true that in some of our States there are Parties and
Discords; but let us look back, and ask if we were ever without
them? Such will exist wherever there is Liberty; and perhaps
they help to preserve it. By the Collision of different Sentiments,
Sparks of Truth are struck out, and political Light is obtained.
The different Factions, which at present divide us, aim all at
the Publick Good; the Differences are only about the various
Modes of promoting it. Things, Actions, Measures and Objects
of all kinds, present themselves to the Minds of Men in such a
Variety of Lights, that it is not possible we should all think
alike at the same time on every Subject, when hardly the same
Man retains at all times the same Ideas of it. Parties are therefore the common Lot of Humanity; and ours are by no means
more mischievous or less beneficial than those of other Countries,
Nations and Ages, enjoying in the same Degree the great Blessing
of Political Liberty.

These are the thoughts of a wise, kindly, democratic
old man who looked upon co-operation through organization as the motive power of free society.

XII

Conclusions are dangerous, especially when they deal with
great men, even more so when the great man in question
has already been rounded off by Van Doren and Carl
Becker. This conclusion will therefore be narrow and ap-
posite. Skirting any evaluation of Franklin's complete character and accomplishments, omitting any further mention

of his influence on the American tradition, it will confine itself rigidly to one date and place—February 13, 1766, in the British House of Commons—and one question: What political faith did Franklin express and represent as he stood before the members and answered their questions about British North America?

First, he represented a pattern of popular political thought ancient in origin but new in sweep. The more perceptive gentlemen, among them Franklin's well-wishers, could look behind his spare phrases and see the mind of a whole continent in political ferment. Whiggery, under several names and guises, had swept America, and the ultimate Whig was now at the bar. It must have been an unsettling experience for some members to hear the blessed words "unjust," "unconstitutional," "liberties," "privileges," and "common consent" drop from the lips of this middling person. Here before them was walking evidence that the people of the colonies were beginning to think in terms, not only of the constitutional rights of Englishmen, but of the natural rights of all men.

Second, Franklin represented new habits of thinking about political and social problems. However legalistic were most arguments out of Boston and Philadelphia, his brand of persuasion was more expressive of the average colonial mind. Franklin's method was an informed, hardheaded appeal to facts. "The *Fact* seems sufficient for our Purpose, and the *Fact* is notorious." His case for repeal of the Stamp Act could be compressed in the warning, "It doesn't work; it never will." America's favorite argument was seeing its first heavy duty.

He likewise represented the incipient fact of American federalism. Himself a uniquely *American* official— "I am Deputy Postmaster-General of North-America"—he breathed the continental spirit that was to power the final drive toward independence and nationhood. He could tell the House that "every assembly on the continent, and every member in every assembly" had denied Parliament's authority to pass the Stamp Act. From this day forward, throughout the next nine years, Franklin was unofficial ambassador for all the colonies. The American union was hastening to be born, and the sign of union was Dr. Franklin.

Next, Franklin represented the growing American conviction that the colonies were marked for a future state of "glory and honor" that would dwarf that of the mother country. As early as 1752 Poor Richard had echoed the widespread belief that America was a God-ordained haven for the oppressed of every land:

> Where the sick Stranger joys to find a Home,
> Where casual Ill, maim'd Labour, freely come;
> Those worn with Age, Infirmity or Care,
> Find Rest, Relief, and Health returning fair.
> There too the Walls of rising Schools ascend,
> For Publick Spirit still is Learning's Friend,
> Where Science, Virtue, sown with liberal Hand,
> In future Patriots shall inspire the Land.

God's plans for America were even more challenging than that:

> I have long been of opinion, that *the foundations of the future grandeur and stability of the British empire lie in America;* and though, like other foundations, they are low and little now, they are, nevertheless, broad and strong enough to support the greatest political structure that human wisdom ever yet erected.

A different sort of empire, cast loose from the mother country, was to rise on this foundation and satisfy the prophecies of destiny that Franklin had pronounced.

Finally, and most important, Franklin stood before Commons and the world as the representative colonial. This person who knew so much more about America than anyone else, who talked of rights and resistance so confidently, this was no Belcher or Hutchinson, no placeman or royal governor, but a new breed of man to be heard in high places. Although Franklin was actually the most extraordinary man of the century, on that memorable day he was the true colonist and thus, in an important sense, the first American—self-contained, plain-spoken, neither arrogant nor humble, the visible expression of the new way of life and liberty that was to occupy the continent. And as men looked in wonder at him and America, so he and America looked in disbelief at England. The eyes of the colonists seemed open for the first time to the corruption and self-interest that cankered and degraded all British politics. The new world was at last face to face with the old and about to reject it for something more wholesome. The old world would realize too late that Franklin spoke for a multitude even then turning away to a faith of its own when he said of the British nation, "It knows and feels itself so universally corrupt and rotten from Head to Foot, that it has little Confidence in any publick Men or publick Measures."

Now that these things have been written, now that Franklin has surrendered his identity to colonial America, perhaps it would be proper to rescue him and to end with our attention fixed on him alone. He was, after all, Dr. Benjamin Franklin, the most amazing man America has produced, as untypical in the whole as he was typical in his parts. And in fixing our attention we must recall the one conviction that brought harmony to this human multitude: the love of liberty—in every land, in every time, and for every man.

God grant, that not only the Love of Liberty, but a thorough Knowledge of the Rights of Man, may pervade all the Nations of the Earth, so that a Philosopher may set his Foot anywhere on its Surface, and say, "This is my Country."

INDEX